A SELECT BIBLIOGRAPHY OF ADULT EDUCATION
IN GREAT BRITAIN

A SELECT BIBLIOGRAPHY OF ADULT EDUCATION IN GREAT BRITAIN

including works published
to the end of the year

1961

Edited by
THOMAS KELLY
M.A., Ph.D., F.R.Hist.S.

*Director of Extra-Mural Studies
in the University of Liverpool*

Published by the
NATIONAL INSTITUTE OF ADULT EDUCATION
on behalf of the Institute and the
UNIVERSITIES COUNCIL FOR ADULT EDUCATION
LONDON 1962

First published 1952
Second edition 1962

Printed in Great Britain by
TINLINGS of LIVERPOOL

CONTRIBUTORS

* *Contributor to first edition only*
† *Contributor to second edition only*

†A. J. ALLAWAY, M.A., J.P., Professor of Adult Education, Leicester University.

*Miss R. C. BANDY, Handicrafts Organiser, National Federation of Women's Institutes.

†P. T. BARFORD, M.A., B.Mus., Extra-Mural Staff Tutor in Music, Liverpool University.

†F. J. BAYLISS, M.A., Ph.D., Extra-Mural Staff Tutor in Economics and Industrial Relations, Nottingham University.

J. BURR, M.A., Deputy Director of Extra-Mural Studies, Liverpool University.

F. W. CHANDLER, M.A., Extra-Mural Librarian and Staff Tutor, Manchester University.

*M. H. CLIFFORD, M.A., Ph.D., Extra-Mural Staff Tutor in Science, Cambridge University.

G. CUNLIFFE, B.Sc., Extra-Mural Staff Tutor in Natural Science, Bristol University.

Miss M. P. DOWNIE, M.A., F.L.A., Librarian, Ministry of Education.

D. R. DUDLEY, M.A., F.S.A., Professor of Latin, Birmingham University.

*E. C. EAGLE, B.Sc.Econ., formerly Extra-Mural Staff Tutor in Economics, Nottingham University.

†W. A. HALL, B.A., B.D., General Secretary, National Adult School Union.

†N. V. L. HILL, M.A., Ph.D., Extra-Mural Staff Tutor for West Cheshire, Liverpool University.

A. JOHNSON, B.Sc., Lecturer in the Departments of Economics and Extra-Mural Studies, Leeds University.

A. JONES, B.A., Extra-Mural Librarian and Staff Tutor, Liverpool University.

*H. A. JONES, M.A., Principal, City Literary Institute, London.

Mrs. E. KELLY, B.A., Visiting Lecturer, Liverpool College of Commerce.

†T. E. M. LANDSBOROUGH, M.A., Honorary Secretary, Scottish Institute of Education.

C. D. LEGGE, B.A., Senior Lecturer in Adult Education, Manchester University.

*H. E. S. MARKS, M.A., H.M. Inspector of Schools.

v

†R. L. Marshall, O.B.E., M.A., Principal, Co-operative College.

†Miss E. F. May, B.A., Ph.D., Extra-Mural Staff Tutor in Psychology, Liverpool University.

*W. H. Mellers, M.A., B.Mus., Extra-Mural Staff Tutor in Music, Birmingham University.

*J. E. Nesbitt, M.A., Lecturer in Education, Manchester University.

P. P. Newmark, B.A., Lecturer, Holborn College of Law, Languages and Commerce.

†J. B. Newton, M.A., Warden, Burton Manor Residential College.

†A. M. Parker, M.A., Director of Extra-Mural Studies, Birmingham University.

†B. W. Pashley, B.A., Research Assistant in Adult Education, Liverpool University.

*S. G. Raybould, B.Sc., Ph.D., Professor of Adult Education and Director of Extra-Mural Studies, Leeds University.

*E. C. Read, M.A., B.Sc.Econ., Secretary, Central Committee for Adult Education in H.M. Forces.

C. Russell, D.A.Edin., Extra-Mural Staff Tutor in Fine Arts, Birmingham University.

†C. Sayer, M.A., Head of the Department of Physical Education, Loughborough Training College.

*R. Shaw, B.A., Extra-Mural Lecturer in Philosophy, Leeds University.

H. P. Smith, M.A., Tutorial Secretary, Oxford University Extra-Mural Delegacy.

*L. Speak, M.A., Extra-Mural Staff Tutor, London University.

W. E. Styler, M.A., Director of Extra-Mural Studies, Hull University.

*Miss M. C. Tayler, Technical Adviser, Central Council of Physical Recreation.

R. R. Wright, M.A., Ph.D., Extra-Mural Staff Tutor in Literature, Liverpool University.

*B. A. Yeaxlee, O.B.E., M.A., B.Litt., Ph.D., Research Secretary, Institute of Christian Education.

PREFACE

THE first edition of this *Bibliography* appeared in 1952, and included works published up to the end of 1950. It has since been supplemented by annual lists compiled first by Professor Waller and Mr. C. D. Legge and afterwards by Mr. Legge alone. The present edition has been expanded to include not only the major items from these annual supplements but also a great deal of other new material; and the plan on which it is arranged has been substantially modified. Space has been found for general works dealing with the religious, social and economic background of adult education; the somewhat arbitrary division between History of Adult Education and Recent and Contemporary Developments has been abolished; and new sections dealing with the mass media have brought together much material formerly scattered under a variety of headings. A brief subject index has also been added, and it is hoped that this, together with the author index, will greatly facilitate the use of the work.

As in the first edition, we have sought to include all books of substantial merit, together with a selection of pamphlets and articles presenting information or points of view not adequately represented in book form. Articles still account for a considerable proportion of the entries, but it is encouraging to note the increase in the number of major works in this field, especially on the historical side. We have again included relevant works published abroad and we have drawn rather more extensively than hitherto upon the vast adult educational literature of North America. Further guidance in this field may be had from the Center for the Study of Liberal Education for Adults, 4819 South Greenwood Avenue, Chicago 15, and the Canadian Association for Adult Education, 113 St. George Street, Toronto 5.

In general we have excluded works published after the close of 1961, but an exception has been made in favour of a few publications of major importance which appeared during the early months of 1962. These will be repeated in the first of the annual supplements, which henceforth will appear in September of each year in the *Year Book* of the National Institute of Adult Education.

As Editor I have taken personal responsibility for Sections I and II of the Bibliography and for much of the historical material in

Section III, but for most of Section III and the whole of Section IV I have been indebted to the contributors whose names appear on another page. Unfortunately the re-arrangement that has taken place makes it no longer possible to attach the names of individual contributions to particular sections or sub-sections, and I must therefore be content with this general but very sincere acknowledgment of their generous and willing help.

I would like to thank, too, all those others who have assisted in so many ways. Librarians, officials of government departments, secretaries of educational organisations, and extra-mural colleagues have all been most helpful in supplying me with information and material, and most patient in answering queries. I am particularly grateful to my own University Library in Liverpool, and to the National Institute of Adult Education. Mr. Edward Hutchinson, the Secretary of the Institute, has given the project his constant support and encouragement, and as in the first edition he and his staff have actively collaborated in the task of selection and assessment.

The arrangement of individual entries remains much as it was in the first edition, and is explained in the notes that follow this Preface. There are two minor changes. One is that for the convenience of the reader, and also to economise space, we have made rather more extensive use of the device of grouping items of cognate interest under a leading entry. The other is that in response to requests from users abroad we have added the names of publishers in the case of works published after 1900.

The final responsibility for inclusion, exclusion, and comment has rested with the Editor, to whom alone therefore must attach the blame for any errors or omissions.

It remains only to add that of the works listed herein nearly all those published during the present century, and a great many of earlier date, are available for consultation in the National Institute Library, whose librarian will be glad to assist enquirers at any time.

T.K.

NOTES

(1) Works are normally listed in chronological order within each section. Where items of cognate interest are grouped in a single entry, these also are in chronological order.

(2) The name of the publisher is given for works published since 1900. The place of publication is London unless otherwise indicated (works by university presses are ordinarily published from the university centre concerned, but the Oxford University Press publishes from London).

(3) The number of pages, which is given in the case of single-volume works only, includes any prefatory matter or appendices, whether these are numbered separately or not, and refers to the latest editions cited.

(4) The following general abbreviations are used:—

ASLIB	Association of Special Libraries and Information Bureaux.
B.B.C.	British Broadcasting Corporation.
B.I.A.E.	British Institute of Adult Education.
C.S.L.E.A.	Center for the Study of Liberal Education for Adults.
C.J.A.C.	Central Joint Advisory Committee on Tutorial Classes.
E.S.A.	Educational Settlements Association.
H.M.S.O.	Her Majesty's Stationery Office.
L.E.A.	Local Education Authority.
N.A.S.U.	National Adult School Union.
N.C.L.C.	National Council of Labour Colleges.
N.C.S.S.	National Council of Social Service.
N.F.C.A.	National Federation of Community Associations.
N.F.W.I.	National Federation of Women's Institutes.
N.F.A.E.	National Foundation for Adult Education.
N.I.A.E.	National Institute of Adult Education.
N.U.T.G.	National Union of Townswomen's Guilds.
N.S.	New Series.
P.	Press.
S.I.	Statutory Instrument.
S.R.O.	Statutory Rules and Orders.
UNESCO	United Nations Educational, Scientific and Cultural Organisation.
U.C.A.E.	Universities Council for Adult Education.
U.P.	University Press.
W.E.A.	Workers' Educational Association.
Y.M.C.A.	Young Men's Christian Association.
Y.W.C.A.	Young Women's Christian Association.

(5) The periodicals most frequently cited are abbreviated as follows:—

A.E.	..	Adult Education.	L.A.R.	..	Library Association Record.
B.J.E.P.	..	British Journal of Educational Psychology.	R.H.P.	..	Rewley House Papers.
B.J.E.S.	..	British Journal of Educational Studies.	S.A.E.	..	Scottish Adult Education.
B.J.P.	..	British Journal of Psychology.	T.B.	..	Tutor's Bulletin.
C.R.	..	Common Room.	Univs.Q.	..	Universities Quarterly.
F.A.E.	..	Fundamental and Adult Education.	Univs.Rev.		Universities Review.
F.E.	..	Further Education.	V.A.	..	The Vocational Aspect of Secondary and Further Education.
F.P.	..	Foundation Papers.	W.A.B.	..	Bulletin of the World Association for Adult Education.
Hwy.	..	Highway.			
J.A.E.	..	Journal of Adult Education.	Y.A.E.	..	International Journal of Youth and Adult Education.
J.E...	..	Journal of Education.			

CONTENTS

xii

I. GENERAL

(a) BIBLIOGRAPHIES

1. CANNONS, H. G. T. *Bibliography of Library Economy, 1876-1920*. Pp. 680. American Library Association, Chicago, 1927. Continued as *Library Literature, 1921-32*, pp. 442, 1934, with supplementary volumes published by Wilson, New York. Now quarterly with periodical cumulative volumes.
   An index to professional periodical literature.

2. *The Education Index*. Monthly with triennial cumulative volumes. Wilson, New York since 1929.
   Author and subject index to writings on education in English. A fuller list for British periodicals is the *British Education Index*, compiled by librarians of Institutes of Education and issued thrice yearly with periodical cumulative volumes (Vol. I, 1954-58, Library Association 1961).

3. HEADICAR, B. M., and FULLER, C. *A London Bibliography of the Social Sciences*. 4v. London School of Economics and Political Science, 1931-2, with 6 supplementary vols. 1934-58.
   A subject catalogue of various London University libraries.

4. BURTON, M., and VOSBURGH, E. *A Bibliography of Librarianship*. Pp. 182. Library Association, 1934.

5. CONGDON, W. H., and HENRY, D. D. *Adult Education: a Bibliography*. Pp. 40. Michigan School Service Co., Lansing, 1934.
   Annotated list, mainly of American publications.

6. PROCTOR, W. M. (ed.). *Annotated Bibliography on Adult Education*. Pp. 124. Stanford Univ. School of Education, Los Angeles, 1934.
   A world bibliography.

7. BEALS, R. A., and BRODY, J. *The Literature of Adult Education*. Pp. 511. American Assocation for Adult Education, New York, 1941.
   Primarily concerned with American adult education.

8. NATIONAL INSTITUTE OF ECONOMIC AND SOCIAL RESEARCH. *Register of Researches in the Social Sciences, and Directory of Research Institutions*. Annually or biennially, Nos. 1-13, 1943-56/7. Nos. 1-4 privately published, Nos. 5-12 Cambridge U.P., No. 13 ASLIB.

9. BLACKWELL, A. M. *A List of Researches in Education and Educational Psychology presented for higher degrees in the Universities of the United Kingdom, Northern Ireland, and the Irish Republic from 1918 to 1948*. Pp. 173. Newnes for National Foundation for Educational Research, 1950. *A Second List of Researches in Education and Educational Psychology (1949-51)*. Pp. 127. 1952. *Supplement I (1952-53)*. Pp. 57. 1954. *Supplement II (1954-55)*. Pp. 62. 1956. *Supplement III (1956-57)*. Pp. 64. 1958.
   These lists include both published and unpublished material. The most important items bearing on adult education are listed below under the appropriate headings.

10. HARRISON, J. F. C. *The Materials for the Early History of Adult Education*, in *A.E.*, Vol. XXIII, 1950-1, pp. 273-8.

11. BARON, G. *A Bibliographical Guide to the English Educational System.* Pp. 97. Athlone P., 1951, 2nd edn. 1960.

12. LEGGE, C. D., and WALLER, R. D. (eds.). *First Handlist of Studies in Adult Education*, 1951. Pp. 31. N.I.A.E., 1952. *Second Handlist of Studies in Adult Education*, 1952. Pp. 32. N.I.A.E., 1952. Continued as

13. LEGGE, C. D. (ed.). *Guide to Studies in Adult Education*, annually for the years 1953-60 (N.I.A.E., 1954-61). The *Guide* for 1959 appeared in duplicated form, and that for 1960 is incorporated in *Adult Education in 1961* (**40**).
These annual lists supplement the first edition of the present *Bibliography* (1952), and include many items which for various reasons have not been embodied in the revised edition.

14. BRITISH BROADCASTING CORPORATION. *British Broadcasting: a Bibliography.* Pp. 39. 1954.

15. UNESCO. Educational Studies and Documents No. VII. *Education for Community Development: a Selected Bibliography.* Pp. 50. Paris, 1954.

16. ────── *A Preliminary Survey of Bibliographies on Adult Education*, pp. 26, in *Education Abstracts* (**63**), Vol. VI, 1954.

17. INTERNATIONAL LABOUR ORGANISATION. *Bibliography on Workers' Education.* Pp. 47. I.L.O. Geneva, 1956.

18. THOMPSON, M., and IRONSIDE, D. J. *A Bibliography of Canadian Writings in Adult Education.* Pp. 62. Canadian Association for Adult Education, Toronto, 1956.

19. MEZIROW, J. D., and BERRY, D. *The Literature of Liberal Adult Education*, 1945-1957. Pp. 48. Scarecrow P., New York, 1960.

20. CANADIAN ASSOCIATION FOR ADULT EDUCATION. *The Literature of Adult Education.* Pp. 89 (duplicated). Toronto, 1961.
A select list of holdings in the Research Library of the Association.

(b) YEARBOOKS AND DIRECTORIES

21. *Official Year-book of the Scientific and Learned Societies of Great Britain and Ireland.* Griffin, annually 1884-1939. Superseded by

22. BRITISH COUNCIL. *Scientific and Learned Societies of Great Britain.* Pp. 219. Allen and Unwin, 1951, 60th edn. 1962.

23. *The Libraries Museums and Art Galleries Year Book* (originally *The Library Year Book*). Published at irregular intervals since 1897. Latest edition for 1954-55, Clarke.

24. NATIONAL ADULT SCHOOL UNION. *Adult School Year-book and Directory.* 1901, 1903, annually 1905-15, and thereafter at intervals to 1955 (current).

25. *The Education Authorities Directory and Annual.* School Government Pub. Co., annually since 1903.
Directory of officials, covering universities, libraries, education associations, etc., as well as Education Authorities.

26. HOWARTH, E., and PLATNAUER, H. M. *Directory of Museums and Art Galleries in the British Isles.* Pp. 400. Museums Association, 1911, 3rd edn., ed. MARKHAM, S. F., 1948. Superseded by

27. *Museums Calendar.* Museums Association, annually since 1955.

28. WORKERS' EDUCATIONAL ASSOCIATION. *The W.E.A. Education Year Book.* Pp. 507. 1918.
   Includes useful information on adult educational organisations, with essays by several distinguished hands and a prefatory essay by G. B. Shaw.

29. *Handbook of Settlements in Great Britain.* Pp. 46. n.d. [*c.* 1922].

30. KANDEL, I. L. (ed.). *Educational Yearbook of the International Institute of Teachers' College, Columbia University.* New York, annually 1924-44.
   General review of world developments.

31. BRITISH INSTITUTE OF ADULT EDUCATION. *The Handbook and Directory of Adult Education, 1926-1927.* Pp. 178. 1927. *The Handbook and Directory of Adult Education, 1928-1929.* Pp. 232. 1929.

32. LIBRARY ASSOCIATION. *The Year's Work in Librarianship.* Annually, 1927-50, thereafter quinquennially under the title *Five Year's Work in Librarianship.*

33. NATIONAL COUNCIL OF SOCIAL SERVICE. *Voluntary Social Services: Handbook and Directory.* Pp. 154. 1928, 5th edn. 1960.

34. WORLD ASSOCIATION FOR ADULT EDUCATION. *International Handbook of Adult Education.* Pp. 492. 1929.

35. [VARIOUS EDITORS]. *The Year Book of Education.* Evans, annually 1932-40 and from 1948.
   Review of progress and problems throughout the world. Notable contributions concerning adult education are listed below.

36. CENTRAL COUNCIL FOR HEALTH EDUCATION. *Health Education Year Book, 1937-8.* Pp. 144. 1938. *Health Education Year Book, 1939-40.* Pp. 148. 1940.
   Directory of associations concerned with health education, with list of publications and teaching aids.

37. *Informational Film Year Book.* 1947, 1948. Albyn P., Edinburgh.

38. NATIONAL FOUNDATION FOR ADULT EDUCATION. *Voluntary Agencies in Adult Education.* Pp. 35. Foundation Papers, Suppl. No. I, 1947. Superseded by

39. NATIONAL INSTITUTE OF ADULT EDUCATION. *Adult Education in the United Kingdom: a Directory of Organisations.* Pp. 80. 1950, 3rd edn. 1956. Superseded by

40. NATIONAL INSTITUTE OF ADULT EDUCATION. *Adult Education in 1961.* Pp. 88. 1961 (current).

41. CENTRAL OFFICE OF INFORMATION. *Britain: an Official Handbook.* H.M.S.O., annually since 1950.
   Includes much valuable background information regarding education, the press, broadcasting, etc.

42. UNESCO. *International Directory of Adult Education.* Pp. 324. Paris, 1952.

3

43. *Museums and Art Galleries in Great Britain and Northern Ireland.* Index Publishers, annually since 1955.
A popular illustrated guide.

44. SOCIETY FOR EDUCATION IN FILM AND TELEVISION. *Film Teachers' Handbook* (from 1960-1 *Screen Education Yearbook*). Annually from 1956-7.

45. *Physical Education Year Book.* Physical Education Association, 1958, and annually from 1959-60.

46. LYSAGHT, A. (ed.). *Directory of the Natural History and other Field Study Societies in Great Britain.* Pp. 229. British Association for Carnegie U.K. Trust, 1959.
Embraces natural history, archaeology, astronomy, meteorology, geology, and cognate subjects.

(c) ENCYCLOPAEDIAS

47. *Encyclopaedia Britannica.* Latest edn. 24v., Chicago U.P., 1961. (The last completely new edn. was the 14th, 1929, but each annual printing embodies certain revisions.)
s.v. Adult Education, etc. See next entry.

48. *Chambers's Encyclopaedia.* Latest edn. 15v., Newnes, 1959.
s.v. Adult Education, etc. Earlier editions of the *Britannica* (from the 5th edn. 1815-17) and of *Chambers's* (from the 1st edn. 1860-8) are of considerable value for the history of adult education.

49. WATSON, F. (ed.). *The Encyclopaedia and Dictionary of Education.* 4v. Pitman, 1921-2.

50. SELIGMAN, E. R. A., and JOHNSON, A. (eds.). *Encyclopaedia of the Social Sciences.* 15v. Macmillan, New York, 1930-5.
s.v. Adult Education, Further Education, etc.

51. MONROE, W. S. (ed.). *Encyclopaedia of Educational Research.* Pp. 1596. Macmillan, New York, 1941, 3rd edn., ed. HARRIS, C. W., 1960.
Mainly concerned with American education, but the bibliographies appended to the various articles, e.g. Adult Education, are often of general interest.

(d) PERIODICALS
(i) Educational

52. *Journal of Education.* Monthly, Vols. I-XC (last vol. incomplete), 1868-1958. Published latterly by Pergamon P.

53. *Education.* Weekly, 1903-61 (current). Association of Education Committees.

54. *Times Educational Supplement.* Weekly, 1910-61 (current). Times Publishing Co.

55. *University Bulletin.* Thrice yearly, Vols. I-VII, 1922-8. Continued as

56. *Universities Review.* Thrice yearly, Vols. VIII-XXIII, half-yearly Vols. XXIV-XXXIII, 1928-61 (current). Association of University Teachers.

57. *British Journal of Educational Psychology.* Half-yearly, Vols. I-XXXI, 1931-61 (current). Originally British Psychological Society and Training College Association, now Methuen.

4

58. *Sight and Sound*. Quarterly, Vols. I-XVIII, 1932-49; monthly, Vols. XIX-XX, 1950-1; quarterly, Vols. XXI-XXX, 1951-61 (current). British Film Institute (Vols. I-II published by B.I.A.E.).

59. *Universities Quarterly*. Vols. I-XV, 1946-61 (current). Turnstile P.

60. *BACIE Journal*. Bi-monthly, Vols. I-X, 1947-56; quarterly, Vols. XI-XV, 1957-61 (current). British Association for Commercial and Industrial Education.

61. *Look and Listen*. Monthly, Vols. I-VII, 1947-53. Pound.

62. *The Vocational Aspect of Secondary and Further Education*. Half-yearly, Vols. I-XIII, 1948-61 (current). Published by the Training Colleges for Teachers of Technical Subjects in Bolton, Huddersfield and London.

63. *Education Abstracts*. Ten issues yearly, Vols. I-XIII, 1949-61 (current). UNESCO. Bulletins of information and documentation, each dealing with a particular topic.

64. *Visual Education*. Monthly, 1950-61 (current). National Committee for Audio-Visual Aids in Education. July issue each year is entitled *Visual Aids Year Book*.

65. *British Journal of Educational Studies*. Half-yearly, Vols. I-IX, 1952-61 (current). Faber.

66. *International Review of Education*. Quarterly. Vols. I-VII, 1955-61 (current). Nijhoff, The Hague.

67. *Technology*. Monthly, Vols. I-V, 1957-61 (current). Times Publishing Co.

68. *Educational Research*. Thrice yearly, Vols. I-III, 1958-61 (current). Newnes for National Foundation for Educational Research.

69. *OVAC Bulletin*. Half-yearly, Nos. 1-4, 1960-1 (current). Overseas Visual Aids Centre. Designed for overseas work but contains much material of general interest.

70. *Technical Education Abstracts from British Sources*. Quarterly from April 1961. National Foundation for Educational Research.

(ii) Adult Educational

Periodicals relating only to the work of particular organisations are listed under the appropriate headings below.

71. *Bulletin of the World Association for Adult Education*. Quarterly, 1st. Ser., Nos. 1-50, 1919-31; 2nd Ser., Nos. 1-44, 1935-45.

72. *Tutors' Bulletin*. Nos. 1-105, 1922-56. Association of Tutors in Adult Education. Published at irregular intervals and not always numbered. During 1941-3 appeared in duplicated form as *Tutors' Newsletter*. Incorporated in *Adult Education* (74) since 1958.

73. *Journal of Adult Education*. Half-yearly, Vols. I-VI, 1926-34. B.I.A.E. Continued as

74. *Adult Education*. Quarterly, Vols. VII-XXXIII, 1934-60; bi-monthly, Vol. XXXIV, 1960-1 (current). B.I.A.E. till 1949, then N.I.A.E.

75. *Rewley House Papers.* Annually (publication irregular 1944-54), Vols. I-II, 1927-49; Vol. III (current), 1949-61. Oxford Univ. Extra-Mural Delegacy.

76. *International Quarterly of Adult Education.* Vols. I-II, 1932-5. World Association for Adult Education.

77. *Food for Thought.* 8 issues yearly, Vols. I-XXI, 1940-61. Canadian Association for Adult Education, Toronto. (Succeeded from Jan. 1962 by *Continuous Learning.*)

78. *Foundation Papers.* Quarterly, Nos. 1-8, 1948-9. N.F.A.E.

79. *Further Education.* Monthly, Vol. I, 1948-9; quarterly, Vols. II-IV, 1948-51. Turnstile P.

80. *Quarterly Bulletin of Fundamental Education,* from Vol. I, No. 4 *Fundamental Education,* from Vol. IV, No. 3 *Fundamental and Adult Education,* from Vol. XIII *International Journal of Youth and Adult Education.* Quarterly, Vols. I-XIII, 1949-61 (current). UNESCO.

81. *Adult Education.* Bi-monthly, Vols. I-IV, 1950-4; quarterly, Vols. V-XI, 1954-61 (current). Adult Education Association of the U.S.A., Chicago.

82. *Scottish Adult Education.* Thrice yearly, Nos. 1-33, 1951-61 (current). Scottish Institute of Adult Education.

83. *Adult Leadership.* 11 issues yearly, Vols. I-II, 1952-4; 10 issues yearly, Vols. III-IX, 1954-61 (current). Adult Education Association of the U.S.A., Chicago.

84. *Notes and Studies.* 2-3 issues yearly, Nos. 1-18, 1955-61 (current). European Bureau of Adult Education.
A bulletin of events, with occasional short articles.

85. *Television and Adult Education.* Quarterly, 1960-1 (current). Télévision et Culture and UNESCO, Paris.
An international bulletin.

86. *Australian Journal of Adult Education.* Half-yearly, Vol. I, 1961 (current). Australian Association of Adult Education.

II. THE SOCIAL AND EDUCATIONAL BACKGROUND

(a) GENERAL WORKS ON RELIGIOUS, SOCIAL AND ECONOMIC HISTORY

NOTE. Much of our information both on the general background of adult education and on specific details of its history has still to be sought in more general works dealing with religious, social and economic history. A complete bibliography cannot be provided here, but the fourteen volumes of the *Oxford History of England* (ed. Sir George Clark, 1936-61), furnish a general guide and contain full bibliographies. The booklists attached to the *Pelican Guide to English Literature* (ed. B. Ford, 7v. 1954-61), though less specialised, are also valuable.

Works on religious history are most important for the period up to 1800, before the movement for organised secular adult education gets under way. Standard works include J. R. H. Moorman, *History of the Church in England* (1953); J. H. S. Burleigh, *A Church History of Scotland* (1960); H. W. Clark, *History of English Nonconformity* (2v. 1911-13); A. C. Underwood, *History of the English Baptists* (1947); R. W. Dale (ed. A. W. W. Dale), *History of English Congregationalism* (1907); W. J. Townsend, H. B. Workman, and G. Eayrs (Eds.), *A New History of Methodism* (2v. 1909); A. H. Drysdale, *History of the Presbyterians in England* (1889); W. C. Braithwaite, *The Beginnings of Quakerism* (1912, 2nd edn. 1955), and *The Second Period of Quakerism* (1919, 2nd edn. 1961); and R. M. Jones, *The Later Periods of Quakerism* (2v. 1921). C. Smyth, *The Art of Preaching, 747-1939* (1940), is a useful short sketch.

Works on social and economic history become increasingly important from the fifteenth century onwards. G. M. Trevelyan, *English Social History* (1944) is an illuminating general conspectus, and R. J. Mitchell and M. D. R. Leys, *A History of the English People* (1950) is also useful, especially on social history before 1700. On the economic side Sir John Clapham and W. H. B. Court, *A Concise Economic History of Britain* (2v. 1951-4), is an up-to-date guide, and for some periods we also have volumes in the new *Economic History of England*, ed. T. S. Ashton (1955-). The progress of technology is dealt with in detail in the five-volume *History of Technology* ed. C. Singer, E. J. Holmyard, A. R. Hall, and T. I. Williams (1954-8), and is conveniently summarised by T. K. Derry and T. I. Williams in *A Short History of Technology* (1960).

The social and economic history of the period since about 1750 is particularly significant for the development of adult education, and here there are a number of well-known works to guide us: C. R. Fay, *Life and Labour in the Nineteenth Century* (1920, 4th edn. 1947); L. C. A. Knowles, *The Industrial and Commercial Revolutions in in Great Britain during the Nineteenth Century* (1921, 4th edn. 1926); Sir John Clapham, *Economic History of Modern Britain* (3v. 1926-38); P. Mantoux, *The Industrial Revolution in the Eighteenth Century* (1928); G. Slater, *The Growth of Modern England* (1932); E. Halévy, *History of the English People in the Nineteenth Century* (2nd edn., 6v. 1949-52); and the great series by J. L. and B. Hammond—*The Village Labourer* (1911, 4th edn.

1927); *The Town Labourer* (1917, 2nd edn. 1925); *The Skilled Labourer* (1919, 2nd edn. 1920); *The Rise of Modern Industry* (1925, 8th edn. 1951); and *The Age of the Chartists* (1930). To these we may now add A. Briggs, *The Age of Improvement* (1959). For the most recent period R. C. Mowat, *Britain between the Wars* (1955), assembles much information not readily found elsewhere.

The study of local history is also important. Many of the older town histories, e.g. W. H. Wylie, *Old and New Nottingham* (1853), J. A. Langford, *A Century of Birmingham Life* (2v. 1868), J. A. Picton, *Memorials of Liverpool* (2v. 1873), and W. E. A. Axon, *Annals of Manchester* (1886), contain much useful material; and there are also more modern studies such as W. H. Chaloner, *The Social and Economic Development of Crewe* (1950), and A. T. Patterson, *Radical Leicester* (1954).

The list that follows comprises a selection of more specialised works which are in various ways helpful in relation to the history of adult education.

The Middle Ages

87. CUTTS, E. L. *Parish Priests and their People in the Middle Ages in England.* Pp. 597. S.P.C.K., 1888, new edn. 1914.
For the teaching work of the clergy see especially Ch. xiv. Cf. GASQUET, F. A., *Parish Life in Medieval England*, pp. 299, Methuen, 1906; and for a sceptical view the works of COULTON, G. G., especially *Ten Medieval Studies*, pp. 313, Simpkin Marshall, 1906, 3rd edn. Cambridge U.P., 1930 (Ch. vii), and *The Medieval Village*, pp. 633, Cambridge U.P., 1925 (Ch.xix).

88. GAIRDNER, J. *Lollardy and the Reformation.* 4v. Macmillan, 1908–13.
Out of date in some respects, but still useful on the early phases. Cf. McFARLAND, K. B., *John Wycliffe and the Beginnings of English Nonconformity*, pp. 197, English Univs. P., 1952.

89. ABRAM, A. *Social England in the Fifteenth Century.* Pp. 259. Routledge, 1909.
See also the same author's *English Life and Manners in the Later Middle Ages*, pp. 368, Routledge, 1913. These and other works relating to the late medieval period are of interest for the development of education and the growth of literacy.

90. DEANESLY, M. *The Lollard Bible.* Pp. 503. Cambridge U.P., 1920.
A most valuable study, which throws much light on the popular culture of the period.

91. BENNETT, H. S. *The Pastons and their England.* Pp. 309. Cambridge U.P., 1922.

92. DAVIS, H. W. C. (ed.). *Medieval England.* Clarendon P., Oxford, 1924, new edn., ed. POOLE, A. L., 2v., 1958.

93. KINGSFORD, C. L. *Prejudice and Promise in XVth Century England.* Pp. 224. Oxford U.P., 1925.

94. OWST, G. R. *Preaching in Medieval England.* Pp. 399. Cambridge U.P., 1926.

95. SMITH, H. M. *Pre-Reformation England.* Pp. 572. Macmillan, 1938.

96. MOORMAN, J. R. H. *Church Life in England in the Thirteenth Century.* Pp. 472. Cambridge U.P., 1945.

97. BENNETT, H. S. (ed.). *Chaucer and the Fifteenth Century.* Pp. 326. Clarendon P., Oxford, 1947, 3rd edn. 1954.

98. RICKERT, E. (ed.). *Chaucer's World.* Pp. 478. Oxford U.P., 1948.

99. THRUPP, S. L. *The Merchant Class of Medieval London.* Pp. 421. Chicago U.P., 1948.

100. EDWARDS, K. *The English Secular Cathedrals in the Middle Ages.* Pp. 431. Manchester U.P., 1949.

101. PANTIN, W. A. *The English Church in the Fourteenth Century.* Pp. 291. Cambridge U.P., 1955.

Sixteenth and Seventeenth Centuries

102. WOODWARD, J. *An Account of the Rise and Progress of the Religious Societies in the City of London.* Pp. 190. 1697, 4th edn. 1712. Abridged by JENKINS, D. E., as *Religious Societies: Dr. Woodward's "Account"*, pp. 88, Evans, Liverpool, 1935.
These societies in some respects anticipated the work of the Y.M.C.A.

103. NEAL, D. *History of the Puritans.* 4v. 1732-8; new edn., ed. TOULMIN, J., 5v., Bath, 1793-7; repr. 3v. 1837.
Confused and inaccurate but still useful for detail.

104. BROWN, J. *John Bunyan.* Pp. 539. 1885, 5th edn., Hulbert, 1928.
Still a standard work. A useful recent sketch, with bibliography, is SHARROCK, R., *John Bunyan*, pp. 163, Hutchinson, 1954. On Bunyan's significance for adult education see **334**.

105. OVERTON, J. H. *Life in the English Church (1660-1714).* Pp. 390. 1885.

106. SYDNEY, W. C. *Social Life in England, 1660-1690.* Pp. 467. 1892.

107. GODFREY, E. *Social Life under the Stuarts.* Pp. 297. Grant Richards, 1904.

108. LEGG, J. W. *English Church Life from the Restoration to the Tractarian Movement.* Pp. 448. Longmans, 1914.

109. ONIONS, C. T. (ed.). *Shakespeare's England.* 2v. Clarendon P., Oxford, 1916.

110. COATE, M. *Social Life in Stuart England.* Pp. 200. Methuen, 1924.

111. POWICKE, F. J. *Life of the Reverend Richard Baxter.* 2v. Cape, 1924-7.
Baxter's autobiography, *Reliquiae Baxterianae*, ed. SYLVESTER, M., 3 pts., 1696, is available in an abridged form as *The Autobiography of Richard Baxter*, ed. THOMAS, J. M. LL. pp. 352, Dent, 1925, new edn. 1931.

112. PEARSON, A. F. S. *Thomas Cartwright and Elizabethan Puritanism.* Pp. 527. Cambridge U.P., 1925.

113. JAMES M. *Social Problems and Policy during the Puritan Revolution, 1640-1660.* Pp. 438. Routledge, 1930.

114. HENDERSON, G. D. *Religious Life in Seventeenth-Century Scotland.* Pp. 311. Cambridge U.P., 1937.

115. HALLER, W. *The Rise of Puritanism.* Pp. 472. Columbia U.P., New York, 1938.

116. KNAPPEN, M. M. *Tudor Puritanism.* Pp. 567. Chicago U.P., 1939.

117. SCHLATTER, R. B. *Social Ideas of the Religious Leaders, 1660-1688.* Pp. 262. Oxford U.P., 1940.

118. CAMPBELL, M. *The English Yeomen under Elizabeth and the Early Stuarts.* Pp. 466. Yale U.P., 1942, Merlin P., 1960.

119. SMITH, H. M. *Henry VIII and the Reformation.* Pp. 496. Macmillan, 1948.
Especially valuable on the impact of the printed English Bible.

120. ROWSE, A. L. *The England of Elizabeth.* Pp. 563. Macmillan, 1950.

121. HALLER, W. *Liberty and the Reformation in the Puritan Revolution.* Pp. 426. Columbia U.P., New York, 1955.

122. ELLIS, A. *The Penny Universities: a History of the Coffee Houses.* Pp. 308. Secker and Warburg, 1956.
Carries the story of the coffee houses into the nineteenth century. See also TIMBS, J., *Club Life in London,* 2v., 1866; ROBINSON, E. F., *The Early History of Coffee Houses in England,* pp. 256, 1893.

Eighteenth and Nineteenth Centuries

123. PORTER, G. R. *The Progress of the Nation.* 2v. 1836-8, 3rd edn., pp. 871, 1851.
Includes useful information on adult literacy (Sect. VII, Ch. iv). Cf. the revised edn. by HIRST, F. W., pp. 753, Methuen, 1912 (Ch.vii).

124. ENGELS, F. *The Condition of the Working Class in England in 1844.* Pp. 418. 1845, first English edn. 1885, new edn. by HENDERSON, W. D., and CHALONER, W. H., Blackwell, Oxford, 1958.

125. MARTINEAU, H. *History of the Thirty Years' Peace.* 2v. 1849, new edn. 4v. 1877.
Valuable on reforming movements of the early 19th century.

126. LUDLOW, J. M., and JONES, Ll. *The Progress of the Working Class, 1832-1867.* Pp. 320. 1867.
Part IV,§§ 3-5 deals with progress in adult education.

127. ABBEY, C. J., and OVERTON, J. H. *The English Church in the Eighteenth Century.* 2v. 1878, abridged edn., pp. 511, 1896.

128. ASHTON, J. *Social Life in the Reign of Queen Anne.* 2v. Chatto and Windus, 1882, 1v., pp. 496, 1883, repr. Scribners, New York, 1929.

129. SYDNEY, W. C. *England and the English in the Eighteenth Century.* 2v. 1892.
For Scotland see GRAHAM, H. G., *Social Life of Scotland in the Eighteenth Century,* pp. 557, Black, 1899, 4th edn. 1937.

130. WEBB, S., and B. *The History of Trade Unionism.* Pp. 592. Longmans, 1894, new edn. 1920.

131. ALLEN, W. O. B., and McCLURE, E. *Two Hundred Years: the History of the Society for Promoting Christian Knowledge, 1698-1898.* Pp. 557, 1898.
Useful on the educational work of the Society among adults. A more recent account is CLARKE, W. K. L., *A History of the S.P.C.K.,* pp. 244, S.P.C.K., 1959.

132. KENT, C. R. B. *The English Radicals.* Pp. 463. 1899.
Still useful, in spite of the fuller and more recent study by MACCOBY, S., *English Radicalism,* 6v., Allen and Unwin, 1935-61.

133. WEBB, C. (ed.). *Industrial Co-operation.* Pp. 309. Co-operative Union, Manchester, 1904, 10th edn. 1926.
A survey of history, theory and practice. See also HALL, F., and WATKINS, W. P., *Co-operation: a Survey of the History, Principles and Organisation of the Co-operative Movement in Great Britain,* pp. 408, Co-operative Union, Manchester, 1937; COLE, G. D. H., *A Century of Co-operation,* pp. 432, Co-operative Union, Manchester, 1944, 2nd edn. Allen & Unwin, 1946; BONNER, A., *British Co-operation,* pp. 548, Co-operative Union, Manchester, 1961.

134. SMILES, S. (ed. MACKAY, T.). *The Autobiography of Samuel Smiles.* Pp. 470. Murray, 1905.
Smiles was a fervent advocate of popular education, and his *Self-Help*, pp. 386, Murray 1859, new edn. 1958, was a classic for the self-educator. For its significance see Introduction by Professor A. Briggs to the 1958 edn.

135. VEITCH, G. S. *The Genesis of Parliamentary Reform.* Pp. 429. Constable, 1913.
Includes account of Radical reform societies before 1832.

136. HOVELL, M. *The Chartist Movement.* Pp. 365. Manchester U.P., 1918.
See also DOLLEANS, E., *Le Chartisme*, pp. 350, Rivière, Paris, 1914, 2nd edn. 1949; WEST, J., *History of the Chartist Movement*, pp. 328, Constable, 1920; COLE, G. D. H., *Chartist Portraits*, pp. 386, Macmillan, 1941; WRIGHT, L. C., *Scottish Chartism*, pp. 250, Oliver and Boyd, Edinburgh, 1953; BRIGGS, A. (ed.), *Chartist Studies*, pp. 435, Macmillan, 1960.

137. BEER, M. *A History of British Socialism.* 1912, 1st English edn. 2v. Bell 1919-20, 3rd edn. IV. Allen & Unwin, 1940, repr. 2v. 1953.
See also GRAY, A., *The Socialist Tradition: Moses to Lenin*, pp. 533, Longmans, 1946, 2nd edn. 1947; COLE, G. D. H., *A History of Socialist Thought*, 5v. in 7, Macmillan, 1953-60.

138. COLE, G. D. H. *Robert Owen.* Pp. 267. Bell, 1925.
Owen's activities as co-operator, trade unionist, and social reformer touched adult education at many points, and much adult educational work was done by his followers. There are earlier lives by JONES, LL., pp. 455, Allen and Unwin, 1899, 6th edn. 1919, and PODMORE, F., 2v., Hutchinson, 1906, repr. IV, pp. 710, Allen and Unwin, 1923. For his own views see his autobiography, *The Life of Robert Owen*, 2v. 1857-8, new edn. IV, pp. 368, Bell, 1920; and his *New View of Society and other Works*, ed. COLE, G. D. H., pp. 318, Dent, 1927. A short study by DAVIES, A. T., pp. 84, C.W.S., Manchester, 1948, is concerned particularly with his educational work.

139. ———. *A Short History of the British Working Class Movement.* 3v. Allen and Unwin, 1925-7, 4th edn. IV., pp. 512, 1948.
Documentary illustration is provided by COLE, G. D. H., and FILSON, A. W., *British Working Class Movements: Select Documents, 1789-1875*, pp. 651, Macmillan, 1951.

140. GEORGE, M. D. *London Life in the XVIIIth Century.* Pp. 464. Kegan Paul, 1925, repr. London School of Economics and Political Science, 1951.

141. WARNER, W. J. *The Wesleyan Movement in the Industrial Revolution.* Pp. 309. Longmans, 1930.
See especially Ch. vii on education and Ch. viii on leadership.

142. GEORGE, M. D. *England in Transition: Life and Work in the Eighteenth Century.* Pp. 160. Routledge, 1931, rev. edn. Penguin, 1953.

143. TURBERVILLE, A. S. *English Men and Manners of the Eighteenth Century.* Pp. 575. Oxford U.P., 1933.

144. ——— (ed.). *Johnson's England.* 2v. Clarendon P., Oxford, 1933.

145. McLACHLAN, H. *The Unitarian Movement in the Religious Life of England: I. Its Contribution to Thought and Learning, 1700-1900.* Pp. 317. Allen and Unwin, 1934.

146. YOUNG, G. M. (ed.). *Early Victorian England.* 2v. Oxford U.P., 1934.
Part of this work appeared in an expanded form as YOUNG, G. M., *Portrait of an Age*, pp. 223, Oxford U.P., 1936.

147. WEARMOUTH, R. F. *Methodism and the Working-Class Movements of England, 1800-1850.* Pp. 336. Epworth P., 1937.
This and the same author's later work, *Some Working-Class Movements of the Nineteenth Century,* pp. 350, Epworth P., 1948, throw valuable light on the organisation of certain working-class educational movements.

148. COLE, G. D. H., and POSTGATE, R. *The Common People, 1746-1938.* Pp. 752. Methuen, 1938, 4th edn. 1949.

149. QUINLAN, M. J. *Victorian Prelude: a History of English Manners, 1700-1830.* Pp. 311. Columbia U.P., New York, 1941.
See especially Ch. vii, The Improvement of the Masses.

150. GREGG, P. *A Social and Economic History of Britain, 1760-1950.* Pp. 584. Harrap, 1950.
One of the few general histories to devote adequate attention to adult education.

151. CLOW, A. and N. L. *The Chemical Revolution.* Pp. 696. Batchworth, 1952.
Ch. xxv is interesting on the development of scientific education.

152. EVANS, J. *John Ruskin.* Pp. 447. Cape, 1954.
The standard modern life. Earlier works of interest for Ruskin's associations with adult education are COLLINGWOOD, W. G., *The Life and Work of John Ruskin,* 2v., Methuen, 1893; HOBSON, J. A., *John Ruskin: Social Reformer,* pp. 348, Nisbet, 1898, 3rd edn. 1904.

153. JAEGER, M. *Before Victoria.* Pp. 224. Chatto and Windus, 1956.
A study of the development of Victorian ideals as illustrated in the lives of such people as Hannah More, Lord Brougham, T. B. Macaulay and Harriet Martineau.

154. MARSHALL, D. *English People in the Eighteenth Century.* Pp. 304. Longmans, 1956.

155. McCLATCHEY, D. *Oxfordshire Clergy, 1777-1869.* Clarendon P., Oxford, 1960.
Has a valuable chapter on the educational work of the clergy.

156. MECHIE, S. *The Church and Scottish Social Development, 1780-1870.* Pp. 193. Oxford U.P., 1960.

157. NEW, C. W. *The Life of Henry Brougham to 1830.* Pp. 470. Clarendon P., Oxford, 1961.
Brougham was active in many forms of adult education, including mechanics' institutes and educational publishing. See Chs. xvii and xviii. Of earlier accounts the best is ASPINALL, A., *Lord Brougham and the Whig Party,* pp. 342, Manchester U.P., 1927 (Ch. xii). There are unpublished theses on Brougham's educational work by ROSS, B. W. (1951), and McMANNERS, T. (1952) (for details see 9). See also below, **281, 429-30.**

158. Lives of working-class reformers and self-educated working men, e.g.
BAMFORD, S. *Passages in the Life of a Radical.* 2v. 2nd edn. Middleton, 1842, new edn. 1893.
SOMERVILLE, A. *The Autobiography of a Working Man.* Pp. 307. 1848, new edn. Turnstile P., 1951.
COOPER, T. *The Life of Thomas Cooper.* Pp. 408. 1872, 4th edn. 1873. Cf. PEERS, R., *Thomas Cooper—the Leicester Chartist,* in *J.A.E.,* Vol. V, 1930-2, pp. 239-52.
LOVETT, W. *The Life and Struggles of William Lovett in his Pursuit of Bread, Knowledge and Freedom.* 1876, new edn. with Introd. by TAWNEY, R. H., 2v. Bell, 1920.
BARKER, J. [ed. BARKER, J. T.]. *Life of Joseph Barker.* Pp. 399. 1880.
FROST, T. *Forty Years' Recollections.* Pp. 355. 1880.

HOLYOAKE, G. J. *Sixty Years of an Agitator's Life.* 2v. 1892, 3rd edn. 1906. See also MCCABE, J., *Life and Letters of George Jacob Holyoake*, 2v., Watts, 1908.
BONNER, H. B. *Charles Bradlaugh: a Record of his Life and Work.* 2v. Fisher Unwin, 1894, 7th edn. 2v. in 1, 1908.
ARCH, J. *Joseph Arch: the Story of his Life.* Pp. 432. 1898.
WALLAS, G. *Life of Francis Place.* Pp. 429. Longmans, 1898, 2nd edn. 1918.
COLE, G. D. H. *The Life of William Cobbett.* Pp. 467. Collins, 1924, 3rd edn. Home and Van Thal, 1947. See also REITZEL, W. (ed.), *The Autobiography of William Cobbett*, pp. 272, Faber, 1933, 2nd edn. 1957; COLE, G. D. H. and M. (eds.), *The Opinions of William Cobbett*, pp. 340, Cobbett Pub. Co., 1944.
TIBBLE, J. W. and A. *John Clare: a Life.* Pp. 468. Cobden-Sanderson, 1932.
WRIGHT, E. M. *Life of Joseph Wright.* 2v. Oxford U.P., 1932.
ASHBY, M. K. *Joseph Ashby of Tysoe, 1859-1919.* Pp. 317. Cambridge U.P., 1961.

For other such biographies see bibliography to **285.**

Twentieth Century

159. BOOTH, C. *Life and Labour of the People in London.* 2v. 1889-91, 3rd ed. 17v., Macmillan, 1902-03.
The first of the great modern social surveys. See SIMEY, T. S. and M. B., *Charles Booth, Social Scientist*, pp. 292, Oxford U.P., 1960.

160. ROWNTREE, B. S. *Poverty: a Study of Town Life.* Pp. 482. Macmillan, 1901, 3rd edn. 1902.
The first of three surveys of social life in York, its successors being ROWNTREE, B. S., *Poverty and Progress: a Second Social Survey of York*, pp. 560, Longmans, 1941; and ROWNTREE, B. S., and LAVERS, G. R., *English Life and Leisure: a Social Study*, pp. 498, Longmans, 1951.

161. SHEFFIELD—ST. PHILIP'S SETTLEMENT. *The Equipment of the Workers.* Pp. 350. Allen and Unwin, 1919.
An enquiry into the educational equipment of workers in Sheffield.

162. CARR-SAUNDERS, A. M., and JONES, D. C. *A Survey of the Social Structure of England and Wales.* Pp. 324. Clarendon P., Oxford, 1927, 2nd edn. 1937, 3rd edn., ed. CARR-SAUNDERS, A. M., JONES, D. C., and MOSER, C. A., *A Survey of Social Conditions in England and Wales*, 1958.

163. SMITH, H. LL. (ed.). *New Survey of London Life and Labour.* 9v. King, 1930-5. See especially Vol. IX, *Life and Leisure* (1935).

164. JONES, D. C. (ed.). *Social Survey of Merseyside*, 3v. Liverpool U.P., 1934.

165. COLE, G. D. H., and M. I. *The Condition of Britain.* Pp. 471. Gollancz, 1937.

166. THOMAS, F. G. *The Changing Village.* Pp. 188. Nelson 1939.
A study of village life and institutions. Cf. BAKER, W. P., *The English Village*, pp. 232, Oxford U.P., 1953; BRACEY, H. E., *English Rural Life*, pp. 272, Routledge and Kegan Paul, 1959. All three works make reference to educational facilities.

167. GLASS, R. (ed.). *The Social Background of a Plan: a Study of Middlesbrough.* Pp. 282. Routledge and Kegan Paul, 1948.

168. KUPER, L., and Others. *Living in Towns.* Pp. 379. Cresset P., 1953.
Studies of community life and leisure in the West Midlands. Cf. the three studies by WHITE, L. E.: *Community or Chaos*, pp. 47, 1950; *Small Towns*, pp. 63, 1951; and *New Towns*, pp. 100, 1951 (all N.C.S.S.). The most recent survey is NICHOLSON, J. H., *New Communities in Britain*, pp. 191, N.C.S.S., 1961.

169. BRENNAN, T., COONEY, E. W., and POLLINS, H. *Social Change in South Wales.* Pp. 208. Watts, 1954.
A study undertaken with the help of adult students (cf. **1186**).

170. GARDINER, R. K., and JUDD, H. O. *The Development of Social Administration.* Pp. 208. Oxford U.P., 1954.

171. COLE, G. D. H. *The Post-War Condition of Britain.* Pp. 507. Routledge and Kegan Paul, 1956.

172. SAVILLE, J. *Rural Depopulation in England and Wales, 1851-1951.* Pp. 269. Routledge and Kegan Paul, 1957.
A study of internal migration and its effects.

173. MARSH, D. C. *The Changing Social Structure of England and Wales, 1871-1951.* Pp. 280. Routledge and Kegan Paul, 1958.

174. SANDERSON, W. A. *The Changing Population Structure,* in *A. E.,* Vol. XXXII, 1959-60, pp. 137-44.

175. BRUCE, M. *The Coming of the Welfare State.* Pp. 319. Batsford, 1961.
Traces the welfare state to its nineteenth-century origins.

176. ZWEIG, F. *The Worker in the Affluent Society.* Pp. 286. Heinemann, 1961.
An examination of the effect of prosperity upon the living conditions and social attitudes of factory workers. Earlier studies by the same author are *Life, Labour and Poverty,* pp. 214, Gollancz, 1948; *Women's Life and Labour,* pp. 184, Gollancz, 1952; *The British Worker,* pp. 244, Penguin, 1952.

(b) HISTORY OF EDUCATION

(i) Official Government Publications

The works listed are those which have specific reference to adult education or provide useful background material. Works having reference to one only of the topics listed under III (b) are included in that section.

Annual Reports

177. COMMITTEE OF COUNCIL ON EDUCATION. *Minutes.* Annually for 1839/40 to 1857/8 (the date of publication in each case is usually within the succeeding educational year).

178. ——— *Reports.* Annually for 1858/9 to 1898/9.
These and the preceding *Minutes* contain occasional references to the education of adults, e.g. in Sunday schools and evening institutes, but they do not become an important source until after the introduction of the 1893 Code of Regulations for Evening Schools. The *Reports* cover Great Britain until 1872/3, thereafter England and Wales only.

179. BOARD OF EDUCATION. *Reports.* Annually for 1899/1900 to 1925/6. (For 1924/5 and 1925/6 the title was *Education in England and Wales.*) H.M.S.O.

180. ——— *Statistics of Public Elementary Day Schools, Evening Continuation Schools, and Certified Efficient Schools.* 1900 and annually (with some variation of title) to 1903. H.M.S.O.

181. ——— *Statistics of Public Education in England and Wales, 1903-05.* Also for 1904/6 and 1905/7, then annually for 1907/8 to 1925/6. H.M.S.O.

182. —— *Report and Statistics of Public Education in England and Wales.* Annually for 1926/7 to 1937/8. H.M.S.O.

183. MINISTRY OF EDUCATION. *Education in 1947,* etc. (Report and Statistics for 1946-47, etc.). Annually, in progress. H.M.S.O. Report for 1950 has the title *Education, 1900-1950.*

184. SCOTTISH (originally SCOTCH) EDUCATION DEPARTMENT. *Reports of the Committee of Council on Education in Scotland.* Annually for 1873/4 to 1938. H.M.S.O. Edinburgh.

185. —— *Education in Scotland: Summary Report for the Years 1939 and 1940.* 1941, and thereafter annually. H.M.S.O. Edinburgh.

Reports of Royal Commissions and Parliamentary Committees

These reports frequently provide information regarding the education of adults in Sunday schools, evening institutes, mechanics' institutes, University Extension courses, and so forth.

186. ROYAL COMMISSION ON POPULAR EDUCATION. *Report.* 6v. 1861.

187. ROYAL COMMISSION ON SCHOOLS IN SCOTLAND. *First, Second* and *Third Reports.* 10 pts. 1865-7.

188. SELECT COMMITTEE ON INSTRUCTION IN SCIENCE FOR THE INDUSTRIAL CLASSES. *Report.* Pp. 598. 1868.

189. ROYAL COMMISSION ON SCHOOL EDUCATION [Schools Inquiry Commission]. *Report.* 21v. 1868-70.

190. ROYAL COMMISSION ON SCIENTIFIC INSTRUCTION AND THE ADVANCEMENT OF SCIENCE. *First, Second, Third, Fourth, Fifth, Sixth, Seventh* and *Eighth Reports.* 10 pts. 1872-5.

191. ROYAL COMMISSION ON TECHNICAL EDUCATION. *First* and *Second Reports.* 6 pts. 1882-4.

192. ROYAL COMMISSION ON A UNIVERSITY FOR LONDON. *Report.* Pp. 331. 1889.
This Report and the two following afford information not only about university extramural work but also about such institutions as Birkbeck College, the Working Men's College, the Polytechnics, and Toynbee Hall.

193. ROYAL COMMISSION ON THE PROPOSED GRESHAM UNIVERSITY IN LONDON. *Report.* Pp. 1457. 1894.

194. ROYAL COMMISSION ON UNIVERSITY EDUCATION IN LONDON. *First, Second, Third, Fourth, Fifth* and *Final Reports.* 11 pts. 1910-13.

Other Reports

195. COMMITTEE OF COUNCIL ON EDUCATION. *Reports of the Commissioners of Inquiry into the State of Education in Wales.* Pp. 540. 1848.

196. CENSUS OF GREAT BRITAIN, 1851. *Education: England and Wales.* Pp. 482. 1854. (Sessional Papers, 1952-3, Vol. XC). *Religion and Education: Scotland.* Pp. 123. 1854 (Sessional Papers, 1854, Vol. LIX).
These two volumes are a mine of statistical information on all forms of education.

197. BOARD OF EDUCATION. *General Report of H.M. Inspectors on the Provision of Further Education in Yorkshire.* Pp. 106. H.M.S.O., 1927.

198. BOARD OF EDUCATION—COMMITTEE ON EDUCATION IN RURAL WALES. *Education in Rural Wales.* Pp. 190. H.M.S.O., 1930.

199. BOARD OF EDUCATION. *Educational Problems of the South Wales Coalfield.* Pp. 81. H.M.S.O., 1931.

200. —— *Educational Reconstruction.* Pp. 36. H.M.S.O., 1943.

201. MINISTRY OF EDUCATION. Pamphlet No. 2. *A Guide to the Educational System of England and Wales.* Pp. 61. H.M.S.O., 1945.

202. —— Pamphlet No. 8. *Further Education: the Scope and Content of its Opportunities under the Education Act, 1944.* Pp. 200. H.M.S.O., 1947.
Ch.iii, relating liberal adult education to other forms of further education, is particularly important.

203. SCOTTISH EDUCATION DEPARTMENT—ADVISORY COUNCIL ON EDUCATION IN SCOTLAND. *Further Education.* Pp. 176. H.M.S.O., Edinburgh, 1952.

204. MINISTRY OF EDUCATION—CENTRAL ADVISORY COUNCIL FOR EDUCATION (ENGLAND). *Early Leaving: a Report.* Pp. 99. H.M.S.O., 1954.
See below (**207**).

205. TREASURY. *Government and the Arts in Britain.* Pp. 32. H.M.S.O., 1958.
Report on government support for the arts in the post-war years.

206. MINISTRY OF EDUCATION—CENTRAL ADVISORY COUNCIL FOR EDUCATION (ENGLAND). *15 to 18* [the Crowther Report]. 2v. H.M.S.O., 1959-60.
See next entry.

207. MINISTRY OF EDUCATION. *The Youth Service in England and Wales* [the Albemarle Report]. Pp. 140. H.M.S.O., 1960.
This Report, and Nos. **204** and **206**, throw much light on the impact of social and educational change among adolescents, and the extent to which able boys and girls are failing to secure higher education.

Acts of Parliament

208. Acts affecting adult education:—
Elementary Education Act, 33 and 34 Vict. c. 75, 1870.
Education (Scotland) Act, 35 and 36 Vict. c. 62, 1872.
Technical Schools (Scotland) Act, 50 and 51 Vict. c. 64, 1887.
Technical Instruction Act, 52 and 53 Vict. c. 41, 1889.
Local Taxation (Customs and Excise) Act, 53 and 54 Vict. **c.** 60, 1890.
Technical Instruction (Amending) Act, 54 and 55 Vict. c. 4, 1891.
Education Act, 2 Edw. VII, c. 42, 1902.
Education (Scotland) Act, 8 Edw. VII, c. 63, 1908.
Education Act, 8 and 9 Geo. V, c. 39, 1918.
Education (Scotland) Act, 8 and 9 Geo. V, c. 48, 1918.
Education (Consolidating) Act, 11 and 12 Geo. V, c. 51, 1921.
Education Act, 7 and 8 Geo. VI, c. 31, 1944.
Education (Scotland) Act, 8 and 9 Geo. VI, c. 37, 1945.
Education (Scotland) Act, 9 and 10 Geo. VI, c. 72, 1946.
The English Act of 1944 and the corresponding Scottish Act of 1945 were the first to incorporate adult education fully into the national system of education.

(ii) Other Works

209. CRAIK, Sir H. *The State in its Relation to Education.* Pp. 210. Macmillan, 1882, 3rd edn. 1914.
Includes Scotland as well as England and Wales, and is still useful on the administrative side.

210. MONTMORENCY, J. E. G. de. *State Intervention in English Education.* Pp. 398. Cambridge U.P., 1902.
A history of developments prior to 1833.

211. WATSON, F. *The Beginnings of the Teaching of Modern Subjects in England.* Pp. 611. Pitman, 1909.

212. ADAMSON, J. W. *Education,* in *Cambridge History of English Literature,* Vol. IX (1912), Ch. xv; Vol. XIV (1916), Ch. xiv.
The appended bibliographies are particularly valuable.

213. —— *A Short History of Education.* Pp. 529. Cambridge U.P., 1919, 3rd edn. 1930.

214. BOYD, W. *The History of Western Education.* Pp. 485. Black, 1921, 6th edn. 1954.
A general survey from the Greeks to the present day.

215. MANSBRIDGE, A. *The Older Universities of England.* Pp. 320. Longmans, 1923.
A historical study by one specially interested in the extension of university education to able working people. Ch. x deals with extra-mural developments.

216. MILLIS, C. T. *Technical Education: its Development and Aims.* Pp. 191. Arnold, 1925.

217. BENNETT, C. A. *History of Manual and Industrial Education to 1870.* Pp. 461. 1926. *History of Manual and Industrial Education 1870 to 1917.* Pp. 566. 1937. Manual Arts P., Peoria.

218. MORGAN, A. *The Rise and Progress of Scottish Education.* Pp. 246. Oliver and Boyd, Edinburgh, 1927.

219. BRITISH ASSOCIATION FOR THE ADVANCEMENT OF SCIENCE. *London and the Advancement of Science.* Pp. 327. 1931.
Includes chapters on learned societies, education and museums.

220. ADAMSON, J. W. *"The Illiterate Anglo-Saxon."* Pp. 175. Cambridge U.P., 1946.
Essays on medieval and modern education.

221. CURTIS, S. J. *History of Education in Great Britain.* Pp. 645. University Tutorial P., 1948, 4th ed. 1957.
Includes excellent short accounts of history of adult education and education in H.M. Forces.

222. SMITH, W. O. L. *Education in Great Britain.* Pp. 225. Oxford U.P., 1949, 3rd ed. 1958.

223. JARMAN, T. L. *Landmarks in the History of Education.* Pp. 331. Cresset P., 1951.
Ch. xv covers briefly the early history of adult education.

224. CURTIS, S. J., and BOULTWOOD, M. E. A. *A Short History of Educational Ideas.* Pp. 627. University Tutorial P., 1953, 3rd edn. 1961.

225. KNOX, H. M. *Two Hundred and Fifty Years of Scottish Education.* Pp. 267. Oliver and Boyd, Edinburgh, 1953.

226. ARMYTAGE, W. H. G. *Civic Universities.* Pp. 328. Benn, 1955.
Surveys the development of higher learning outside Oxford and Cambridge from the Middle Ages onwards.

227. DENT, H. C. *Universities in Transition.* Pp. 176. Cohen and West, 1961.
A historical sketch with a more detailed study of recent developments and problems.

Early History

228. EDGAR, J. *History of Early Scottish Education.* Pp. 345. Edinburgh, 1893.

229. ADAMSON, J. W. *Pioneers of Modern Education, 1600-1700.* Pp. 307. Cambridge U.P., 1905.

230. LEACH, A. F. *The Schools in Medieval England.* Pp. 355. Methuen, 1915.

231. PARRY, A. W. *Education in England in the Middle Ages.* Pp. 272. Clive, 1920.

232. VINCENT, W. A. L. *The State and School Education, 1640-1660.* Pp. 156. S.P.C.K., 1950.

Eighteenth and Nineteenth Centuries

233. MANCHESTER STATISTICAL SOCIETY. *Report of a Committee on the State of Education in the Borough of Manchester in 1834.* Pp. 52. Manchester, 1834, 2nd edn. 1837.
This and similar reports for Bury, 1835, Liverpool, 1835-6, York, 1836-7, Pendleton (Lancs.), 1838, and Kingston-upon-Hull, 1840, contain valuable statistical material on the extent of educational provision, including evening schools and Sunday schools.

234. HILL, F. *National Education; its Present State and Prospects.* 2v. 1836.
Includes much useful information on adult education.

235. NATIONAL ASSOCIATION FOR THE PROMOTION OF SOCIAL SCIENCE. *Transactions.* Annually 1857-84.
The section on Education in each volume contains interesting papers on current educational developments, including developments in adult education, e.g. mechanics' institutes, evening schools, University Extension.

236. BARTLEY, G. C. T. *The Schools for the People.* Pp. 598. 1871.
Historical and descriptive account of schools for the poorer classes, including schools for adults.

237. BALFOUR, G. *The Educational Systems of Great Britain and Ireland.* Pp. 339. Clarendon P., Oxford, 1898, 2nd edn. 1903.
A comprehensive and detailed factual description.

238. ROBERTS, R. D. (ed.). *Education in the Nineteenth Century.* Pp. 286. Cambridge U.P., 1901.
Includes chapters on industrial education and the Extension movement.

239. BIRCHENOUGH, C. *History of Elementary Education in England and Wales from 1800 to the Present Day.* Pp. 402. University Tutorial P., 1914.

240. DOBBS, A. E. *Education and Social Movements, 1700-1850.* Pp. 271. Longmans, 1919.
Full of interesting material about adult education, much of it not to be found elsewhere.

241. ARCHER, R. L. *Secondary Education in the Nineteenth Century.* Pp. 377. Cambridge U.P., 1921.

242. ADAMSON, J. W. *English Education 1789-1902.* Pp. 529. Cambridge U.P., 1930.

243. McLACHLAN, H. *English Education under the Test Acts.* Pp. 356. Manchester U.P., 1931.
A history of the Dissenting academies. See also the same author's *Warrington Academy,* pp. 159, (Chetham Society, *Transactions,* 2nd Ser., Vol. CVII) Manchester, 1943, and SMITH, J. W. A., *The Birth of Modern Education,* pp. 329, Independent P., 1954.

244. SMITH, F. *A History of English Elementary Education, 1760-1902.* Pp. 368. Univ. of London P., 1931.

245. ABBOTT, A. *Education for Industry and Commerce in England.* Pp. 242. Oxford U.P., 1933.

246. JONES, M. G. *The Charity School Movement in the XVIIIth Century.* Pp. 460, Cambridge U.P., 1938.
Includes the best short account of the Welsh circulating schools.

247. BARNARD, H. C. *A History of English Education from 1760.* Pp. 382. Univ. of London P., 1947, 2nd edn. 1961.

248. MATHEWS, H. F. *Methodism and the Education of the People, 1791-1851.* Pp. 215. Epworth P., 1949.

249. WEBB, R. K. *Working Class Readers in Victorian England,* in *English Historical Review,* Vol. LXV, 1950, pp. 333-51.
A study of the extent of literacy. See also the same author's *Literacy among the Working Classes in Nineteenth-Century Scotland,* in *Scottish Historical Review,* Vol. XXXIII, 1954, pp. 100-14.

250. HANS, N. *New Trends in Education in the Eighteenth Century.* Pp. 261. Routledge and Kegan Paul, 1951.
Includes much new material on adult education, especially popular lecturing.

251. JUDGES, A. V. (ed.). *Pioneers of English Education.* Pp. 251. Faber, 1952.
Owen, Bentham, Kay-Shuttleworth, Newman, Spencer, Matthew Arnold, W. E. Forster.

252. PETERSON, A. D. C. *A Hundred Years of Education.* Pp. 272. Duckworth, 1952.
Includes a brief account of adult education.

253. HUDSON, D., and LUCKHURST, K. W. *The Royal Society of Arts, 1754-1954.* Pp. 429. Murray, 1954.
The latest history of a society which has played an important part in adult and technical education.

254. EAGLESHAM, E. *From School Board to Local Authority.* Pp. 220. Routledge and Kegan Paul, 1956.
Includes account of evening schools 1851-1902.

255. CARDWELL, D. S. L. *The Organisation of Science in England.* Pp. 214. Heinemann, 1957.
A survey of scientific and technological education from the eighteenth century onwards.

256. KELLY, E. and T. (eds.). *A Schoolmaster's Notebook, being an Account of a Nineteenth-Century Experiment in Social Welfare by David Winstanley of Manchester, Schoolmaster.* Pp. 128. Chetham Society, *Transactions,* 3rd Ser., Vol. VIII, Manchester, 1957.
Includes many references to adult educational work, especially at the Miles Platting Mechanics' Institute.

257. COTGROVE, S, F. *Technical Education and Social Change.* Pp. 220. Allen and Unwin, 1958.
Mainly concerned with modern developments, but Chs. i-iv sketch the nineteenth-century background.

258. SIMMONS, J. *New University.* Pp. 233. Leicester U.P., 1959.
Primarily a history of Leicester University, but includes a valuable short history of other modern universities, and a survey of earlier cultural developments in Leicester. For other university histories see **514.**

259. SIMON, B. *Studies in the History of Education, 1780-1870.* Pp. 375. Lawrence and Wishart, 1960.
Valuable on adult educational movements of late eighteenth and early nineteenth centuries.

Twentieth Century

260. WEBB, S. *London Education.* Pp. 229. Longmans, 1904.
Includes chapters on polytechnics and public libraries.

261. ASHBY, A. W., and BYLES, P. G. *Rural Education.* Pp. 227. Oxford U.P., 1923.
A later study is BURTON, H. M., *The Education of the Countryman,* pp. 263, Kegan Paul, 1943.

262. SELBY-BIGGE, L. A. *The Board of Education.* Pp. 329. Putnam, 1927.
Cf. WILLIAMS, Sir G., *The First Ten Years of the Ministry of Education,* in *B.J.E.S.,* Vol. III, 1954-5, pp. 101-13.

263. SMITH, H. B. (ed.). *Education at Work.* Pp. 173. Manchester U.P., 1927.
Includes a chapter on adult education by CAVENAGH, F. A.

264. WILSON, J. D. (ed.). *The Schools of England.* Pp. 408. Sidgwick and Jackson, 1928.
Includes chapters on adult and Forces education.

265. WARD, H. *The Educational System of England and Wales.* Pp. 264. Cambridge U.P., 1935.

266. LOWNDES, G. A. N. *The Silent Social Revolution: an Account of the Expansion of Public Education in England and Wales, 1895-1935.* Pp. 286. Oxford U.P., 1937.

267. SPENCER, F. H. *Education for the People.* Pp. 313. Routledge, 1941.

268. DENT, H. C. *A New Order in English Education.* Pp. 92. Univ. of London P., 1942.
On educational reconstruction.

269. —— *Education in Transition: a Sociological Study of the Impact of War on English Education, 1939-43.* Pp. 256. Kegan Paul, 1944.

270. WELLS, M. M., and TAYLOR, P. S. *The New Law of Education.* Pp. 655. Butterworth, 1944, 5th edn. 1961.
A detailed commentary on the 1944 Act. Includes grant regulations.

271. CURTIS, S. J. *Education in Britain since 1900.* Pp. 317. Dakers, 1952.

272. ALEXANDER, W. P. *Education in England: the National System—How it Works.* Pp. 159. Newnes, 1954.

273. DENT, H. C. *Growth in English Education, 1946-1952.* Pp. 220. Routledge and Kegan Paul, 1954.

274. ARMFELT, R. *The Structure of English Education.* Pp. 207. Cohen and West, 1955.

275. LOWNDES, G. A. N. *The British Educational System.* Pp. 155. Hutchinson, 1955.

276. VENABLES, P. F. R. *Technical Education: its Aims, Organisation and Future Development.* Pp. 657. Bell, 1955.
A detailed and comprehensive survey.

277. SMITH, W. O. L. *Education: an Introductory Survey.* Pp. 240. Penguin, 1957.

278. DENT, H. C. *The Educational System of England and Wales.* Pp. 224. Univ. of London P., 1961.

(c) THE MASS MEDIA

279. LAWS, F. (ed.). *Made for Millions.* Pp. 142. Contact, 1947.
Essays on the mass media of information and entertainment, including books, films, and television.

Books

NOTE.—The history of books and publishing is of course an enormous subject. We have included here only works which have special interest from the point of view of adult education.

280. MARTINEAU, H. (ed. CHAPMAN, M. W.). *Autobiography.* 2v. Windermere, 1857, 3rd edn. 3v. 1877.
Valuable as giving the viewpoint of an educational author, and for many sidelights on educational literature. See also WHEATLEY, V., *Life and Work of Harriet Martineau,* pp. 421, Secker and Warburg, 1957.

281. CAVENAGH, F. A. *Lord Brougham, with a list of the publications of the Society for the Diffusion of Useful Knowledge,* in *J.A.E.,* Vol. IV, 1929-30, pp. 3-37.
There are unpublished theses on the history of the Society by JARMAN, T. L. (B.Litt. Oxford, 1933) and GROBEL, M. C. (M.A. London, 1933).

282. STEINBERG, S. H. *Five Hundred Years of Printing.* Pp. 277. Penguin, 1955.

283. WEBB, R. K. *The British Working Class Reader, 1790-1848: Literacy and Social Tension.* Pp. 202. Allen and Unwin, 1955.
Deals among other matters with the work of the Society for the Diffusion of Useful Knowledge.

284. —— *The Victorian Reading Public,* in *Univs. Q.,* Vol. XII, 1957-8, pp. 24-44.

285. ALTICK, R. D. *The English Common Reader.* Pp. 448. Chicago U.P., 1957.
A study of the emergence and development of the mass reading public in the nineteenth century.

286. Lives of publishers and booksellers, e.g.
LACKINGTON, J. *Memoirs of the Forty-five First Years of the Life of James Lackington.* Pp. 352. 1791, 13th edn. 1810.
KNIGHT, C. *Passages of a Working Life.* 3v. 1864-65. (Knight was publisher to the Society for the Diffusion of Useful Knowledge. Cf. JARMAN, T. L., *Charles Knight: an Educational Pioneer,* in *J.A.E.,* Vol. VI, 1932-4, pp. 176-85).
CHAMBERS, W. *Memoir of Robert Chambers, with Autobiographic Reminiscences of William Chambers.* Pp. 344. Edinburgh, 1872, and many later edns. (The Chambers brothers and Knight were the leading pioneers of cheap educational publishing.)
DENT, J. M. *Memoirs of J. M. Dent.* Pp. 272. Dent, 1928.

287. Histories of publishing houses, e.g.
   WAUGH, A. *A Hundred Years of Publishing: being the story of Chapman and Hall Ltd.* Pp. 279.
   Chapman and Hall, 1930.
   MORGAN, C. *The House of Macmillan (1843-1943).* Pp. 260. Macmillan, 1943.
   WILLIAMS, W. E. *The Penguin Story.* Pp. 124. Penguin, 1956.
   NOWELL-SMITH, S. *The House of Cassell, 1848-1958.* Pp. 309. Cassell, 1958.

Newspapers

288. GRANT, J. *The Newspaper Press.* 3v. 1871-72.

289. BOURNE, H. R. F. *English Newspapers: Chapters in the History of Journalism.* 2v. 1887.

290. COLLETT, D. C. *History of the Taxes on Knowledge, their Origin and Repeal.* 2v. 1899. Abridged edn. pp. 247, Watts, 1933.
   The classic account of the nineteenth-century struggle against the newspaper taxes. For earlier phases of the movement against restrictions on the press see WICKWAR, W. H., *The Struggle for the Freedom of the Press, 1819-1832*, pp. 325, Allen and Unwin, 1928; CLYDE, W. M., *The Struggle for the Freedom of the Press from Caxton to Cromwell*, pp. 376, Oxford U.P., 1934; SIEBERT, F. S., *The Freedom of the Press in England, 1476-1776*, pp. 425, Illinois U.P., 1952.

291. POLITICAL AND ECONOMIC PLANNING. *Report on the British Press.* Pp. 332. 1938.
   See also subsequent reports on various aspects of the press in the P.E.P. journal *Planning*, 1949 and 1955-6.

292. *Hulton Readership Survey.* Hulton P., annually 1947-55, and in summary form 1956.
   See also the Readership Surveys published (under slightly varying titles) by the Institute of Practitioners in Advertising, 1947, 1954, and 1956, with periodical supplements 1957-60 (in progress). These surveys provide valuable detailed information regarding the reading public for newspapers and periodicals.

293. ROYAL COMMISSION ON THE PRESS. *Report.* Pp. 370. H.M.S.O., 1949.
   A general review dealing with such matters as ownership, the freedom of the press, and accuracy of reporting, with a detailed study of content and methods of presentation during the preceding twenty years.

294. HERD, H. *The March of Journalism.* Pp. 352. Allen and Unwin, 1952.
   A history of the press from 1622 to 1950. See also WILLIAMS, F., *Dangerous Estate*, pp. 304, Longmans, 1957.

Films

295. MANVELL, R. *Film.* Pp. 288. Penguin, 1944, 3rd edn. 1950.
   A general study of the art and social influence of the film. See further, by the same author, *The Film and the Public*, pp. 352, Penguin, 1955.

296. HARDY, F. (ed.). *Grierson on Documentary.* Pp. 256. Collins, 1946.
   Selected essays by the founder of the documentary movement on the cinema as an educational force. "HIGHWAYMAN", *Documentary Films*, in *Hwy.*, Vol. XLVII, 1955-6, pp. 117-21, 148-52, traces the story to 1952; and ROBINSON, D., *Looking for Documentary*, in *Sight and Sound*, Vol. XXVII, 1957-8, pp. 6-11, 70-5, is an informative review of the present state of film and television documentary.

297. MAYER, J. P. *Sociology of the Film.* Pp. 328. Faber, 1946.
   A useful study made when the film was at the height of its popularity. *British Cinemas and their Audiences*, by the same author, pp. 280, Dobson, 1948, is a sequel.

298. WRIGHT, B. *The Use of the Film.* Pp. 72. Bodley Head, 1948.

299. POLITICAL AND ECONOMIC PLANNING. *The British Film Industry.* Pp. 308. 1952.
Report on history, economic organisation, and audiences. A later P.E.P. survey, in
Planning, Vol. XXIV, 1958, pp. 131-70, reviews changes 1951-8.

Broadcasting

300. COOPER, G. *Caesar's Mistress: the B.B.C. on Trial.* Pp. 113. Venture Publications,
1948.
A criticism of policy and organisation.

301. BROADCASTING COMMITTEE, 1949. *Report.* Pp. 335. H.M.S.O., 1951.
The most recent of a series of reports beginning with that of the Broadcasting Committee,
1923. See especially Ch. xi, and memoranda submitted by B.B.C., N.I.A.E., and W.E.A.
in App. H. For a complete list of reports see **14**.

302. GORHAM, M. *Broadcasting and Television since 1900.* Pp. 274. Dakers, 1952.

303. SIMON OF WYTHENSHAWE, Lord. *The B.B.C. from Within.* Pp. 360. Gollancz,
1953.
A survey of principles, organisation and problems.

304. PAULU, B. *British Broadcasting: Radio and Television in the United Kingdom.*
Pp. 472. Minnesota U.P., Minneapolis, 1956.
A full discussion and appraisal. The same author's *British Broadcasting in Transition*, pp. 256,
Macmillan, 1961, considers the impact of commercial television.

305. CROZIER, M. *Broadcasting (Sound and Television).* Pp. 236. Oxford U.P., 1958.
A historical survey and evaluation.

306. POLITICAL AND ECONOMIC PLANNING. *Television in Britain*, in *Planning*, Vol.
XXIV, 1958 pp. 38-67.
Reviews the development of television, the viewing audience, programme content and
finance. Future possibilities are dealt with in *Prospects for Television, ibid.*, pp. 227-54.

307. BELSON, W. A. *Television and the Family.* Pp. 172. B.B.C. Audience Research
Dept., 1959.
Cf. TRENAMAN, J., *The Effects of Television*, in *Twentieth Century*, Nov. 1959, pp. 332-42;
HOGGART, R., *The Uses of Television*, in *Encounter*, Vol. XIV, 1960, pp. 38-45.

308. GRANADA T.V. NETWORK. *Granada Viewership Survey.* Half-yearly from 1959.
Provides valuable information regarding audiences for Independent Television.

309. BRIGGS, A. *History of Broadcasting in the United Kingdom.* Vol. I. *The Birth of
Broadcasting.* Pp. 440. Oxford U.P., 1961.
Carries the story to 1926.

310. TRENAMAN, J., and McQUAIL, D. *Television and the Political Image: a Study of
the Impact of Television on the 1959 General Election.* Pp. 287. Methuen, 1961.

See also **14, 37, 41, 44, 157-8, 323, 342, 898,** and for adult educational
aspects Section III(c)(vii).

III. HISTORY AND ORGANISATION OF ADULT EDUCATION

(a) GENERAL HISTORICAL AND DESCRIPTIVE SURVEYS

311. HUDSON, J. W. *The History of Adult Education.* Pp. 254. 1851.
A mine of information on adult schools, mechanics' institutes, etc., with valuable statistical tables.

312. HORRABIN, J. F. and W. *Working-Class Education.* Pp. 93. Labour Publishing Co., 1924.
Useful survey from a Marxist standpoint.

313. ROWSE, R. C. *An Introduction to the History of Adult Education.* Pp. 35. Mary Ward Settlement, 1933.

314. KELLY, M. *Village Theatre.* Pp. 189. Nelson, 1939.
A historical account from ancient times, with useful review of dramatic work in rural adult education.

315. POOLE, H. E. *The Growth of Adult Education.* Pp. 16. Bureau of Current Affairs, 1948.

316. DENT, H. C. *Part-Time Education in Great Britain: an Historical Outline.* Pp. 81. Turnstile P., 1949.

317. ALLAWAY, A. J. *Adult Education in England: a brief history.* Pp. 46 (duplicated). Vaughan College, Leicester, 1951, rev. edn. 1957.

318. NETTEL, R. *The Englishman Makes Music.* Pp. 258. Dobson, 1952.

319. STERN, H. H. *Parent Education in the Past,* in UNIVERSITY OF HULL, *Studies in Education,* Vol. II, 1954, pp. 175-95.
A historical survey from the seventeenth century.

320. GRATTAN, C. H. *In Quest of Knowledge: a Historical Perspective on Adult Education.* Pp. 351. Association P., New York, 1955.
History of adult education in Britain and America, with introduction on classical and medieval times.

321. NETTEL, R. *The Orchestra in England.* Pp. 272. Cape, 1956.
A historical survey.

322. PEERS, R. *Adult Education: a Comparative Study.* Pp. 379. Routledge and Kegan Paul, 1958.
On the history and problems of English adult education, with chapters on teaching methods and a review of developments in other countries. A section was reprinted as *The Future of Adult Education,* in *F.A.E.,* Vol. X, 1958, pp. 151-63.

323. SMITH, H. P. Adult Education and Society Series. Documentary No. 1: *The Origins of English Culture: the Part of the Grammar School and of Adult Education.* Pp. 50. 1959. No. 2: *The First Phase of Adult Education: an Encounter of Cultures.* Pp. 44. 1960. No. 3: *Literature and Adult Education a Century Ago: Panto-pragmatics and Penny Readings.* Pp. 39. 1960. No. 4: *Education and Social Purpose: Adult Learning Takes the Stage.* Pp. 38. 1961. No. 5: *Adult Education and the Working Class: Workers' Control and University Provision.* Pp. 41. 1961. All these are duplicated and published by the author at Oxford.
Documentary material, with commentary, on various phases of the history of adult education.

324. HARRISON, J. F. C. *Learning and Living, 1790-1960.* Pp. 420. Routledge and Kegan Paul, 1961.
"A social history of adult education" based on a detailed study of developments in the West Riding of Yorkshire.

325. KELLY, T. *A History of Adult Education in Great Britain.* Pp. 368. Liverpool U.P., 1962.
A general survey from the Middle Ages to the twentieth century.

See also **221, 223**.

Early History

326. WARD, J. *The Lives of the Professors of Gresham College.* Pp. 520. 1740.
Includes a life of Gresham and a history of the College. See also BURGON, J. W., *Life and Times of Sir Thomas Gresham*, 2v., 1839.

327. WRIGHT, L. B. *Middle Class Culture in Elizabethan England.* Pp. 747. N. Carolina U.P., 1935, 2nd edn. Cornell U.P., 1958.
A valuable and comprehensive survey.

328. JOHNSON, F. R. *Thomas Hood's Inaugural Address as Mathematical Lecturer to the City of London (1588)*, in *Journal of the History of Ideas*, Vol. III, 1942, pp. 94-106.
Describes an early venture in secular adult education.

329. HAMILTON, L. (ed.). *Gerrard Winstanley: Selections from his Works.* Pp. 204. Cresset P., 1944.
Winstanley's *Law of Freedom* (1652) contains the first fully developed scheme for adult education. There is a complete edition of his works by G. H. Sabine (pp. 686, Cornell U.P., Ithaca, 1941).

330. GIBBS, F. W. *George Wilson (1631-1711)*, in *Endeavour*, Vol. XII, 1953, pp. 182-5.
An account of the first public lecturer in chemistry. Recent volumes of this journal and of the *Annals of Science* contain a number of papers on early public lecturers in science.

331. TAYLOR, E. G. R. *The Mathematical Practitioners of Tudor and Stuart England.* Pp. 454. Cambridge U.P., 1954.
Valuable on provision for teaching of mathematics and allied subjects.

332. *Rules of a Society, which met once a week, for their improvement in useful Knowledge, and for the promoting of Truth and Christian Charity*, in R.H.P., Vol. III, III, 1954-5, pp. 62-3.
An early example of a mutual improvement society, *c.* 1690. The Rules were first printed in *A Collection of several Pieces of Mr. John Locke* [ed. P. des Maizeaux], 1720.

333. SMITH, H. P. *Adult Education in England—an Introductory Chapter,* in *R.H.P.,* Vol. III, IV, 1955-6, pp. 28-70.
Discussion of More's *Utopia* and the new learning as a starting point for adult education.

334. ———— *Adult Education Emerges,* in *R.H.P.,* Vol. III, v, 1956-7, pp. 35-52.
On sixteenth- and seventeenth-century developments, with special reference to Winstanley and Bunyan.

Eighteenth and Nineteenth Centuries

335. OPSINOUS. *History of the Robin Hood Society.* Pp. 258. 1764.
The fullest account of a famous eighteenth-century debating society. The early history is probably imaginary. The history of another early debating society is recounted in RAYLEIGH, P., *History of Ye Antient Society of Cogers* [1903], 2nd edn. *The Cogers of Fleet Street,* pp. 352, Elliot Stock, 1908.

336. NICHOLS, J. *Literary Anecdotes of the Eighteenth Century.* 9v. 1812-15.
See Vol. VI, Pt. I, for an account of gentlemen's literary and antiquarian societies. One such society, still existing, is chronicled in MOORE, W., *The Gentlemen's Society at Spalding: its Origin and Progress,* pp. 16, Spalding, 1909.

337. [CRAIK, G. L.]. *The Pursuit of Knowledge under Difficulties.* 2v. 1830-31, new edn., pp. 565, Bell, 1906.

338. ROSCOE, H. *Life of William Roscoe.* 2v. 1833.
Roscoe was a leading figure in the cultural life and societies of Liverpool in the late eighteenth and early nineteenth centuries. There are modern lives by MATHEWS, G. W., pp. 55, Mitre P. 1931; and CHANDLER, G., pp. 496, Batsford, 1953.

339. CURWEN, J. S. *Memorials of John Curwen.* Pp. 332. 1882.
This and the next entry are important for the development of the sol-fa movement in the mid-nineteenth century.

340. [HULLAH, F. R.]. *Life of John Hullah.* Pp. 306. 1886.

341. BUISSON, M. F. (ed.) *L'éducation populaire des adultes en Angleterre.* Pp. 336. Paris, 1896.
Accounts of the principal adult educational institutions of the period contributed by their officials.

342. PRATT, E. A. *Notable Masters of Men.* Pp. 320. Andrew Melrose [1901].
Popular accounts of Andrew Carnegie, Sir Josiah Mason, George Cadbury, George Birkbeck, Sir George Williams, Quintin Hogg, Thomas Cook, W. and R. Chambers, etc.

343. SANDAGEN, A. *Ideen englischer Volkserziehung und Versuche zu ihrer Verwirklichung.* Pp. 148. Comenius-Gesellschaft, Berlin, 1911.
General review of English adult educational development, with particular reference to the London Working Men's College.

344. PATON, J. L. *John Brown Paton: a Biography.* Pp. 558. Hodder and Stoughton, 1914.
A noted Congregational churchman who was a pioneer in many forms of adult education, e.g. University Extension, the National Home Reading Union, and the Recreative Evening Schools Association. See also MARCHANT, J., *J. B. Paton, Educational and Social Pioneer,* pp. 332, Clarke, 1909.

345. CAWTHORNE, H. H. *The Spitalfields Mathematical Society (1717-1845),* in *J.A.E.,* Vol. III, 1928-9, pp. 155-66.
An outstanding example of an early working-class cultural society, a forerunner of the mechanics' institutes.

346. HARRISON, J. F. C. *Adult Education and Self-Help*, in *B.J.E.S.*, Vol. VI, 1957-8, pp. 37-50.
On the idea of self-help in adult education in the nineteenth century.

347. BIBBY, C. T. H. *Huxley: Scientist, Humanist and Educator*. Pp. 352. Watts, 1959.
Huxley was an indefatigable adult educator, and for thirteen years Principal of the South London Working Men's College (see **482**). Cf. HUXLEY, L., *Life and Letters of Thomas Henry Huxley*, 2v. Macmillan, 1900, 2nd edn. 3v. 1903.

See also **234, 240, 250, 252.**

Twentieth Century

348. MANSBRIDGE, A. *A Survey of Working-class Educational Movements in England and Scotland*. Pp. 40. W.E.A., 1906. Reprinted from *Co-operative Wholesale Society Annual*, 1906.
Useful, especially on co-operative education.

349. MINISTRY OF RECONSTRUCTION—ADULT EDUCATION COMMITTEE. *First Interim Report: Industrial and Social Conditions in relation to Adult Education*. Pp. 32. 1918. *Second Interim Report: Education in the Army*. Pp. 10. 1918. *Third Interim Report: Libraries and Museums*. Pp. 19. 1919. *Final Report*. Pp. 415. 1919. H.M.S.O.
The *Final Report* is a most valuable comprehensive survey of the history, current position, and future prospects of adult education in Great Britain, and its recommendations exerted a decisive influence on subsequent development. These recommendations were summarised by A. GREENWOOD, *The Education of the Citizen*, pp. 64, N.A.S.U., 1920, and also provided a starting-point for YEAXLEE, B. A., *An Educated Nation*, pp. 80, Oxford U.P., 1920 (W.E.A. edn. 1921). An abridged edition was published by the Adult Education Association of the U.S.A., the Canadian Association for Adult Education, and the National Institute of Adult Education, under the title *A Design for Democracy*, pp. 222, Parrish, 1956, with an introduction by WALLER, R. D.

350. PARRY, R. St. J. (ed.). *Cambridge Essays on Adult Education*. Pp. 238. Cambridge U.P., 1920.
Essays on Purpose and Meaning; History; Organisation; Democracy and Adult Education; Labour and Adult Education; Women and Adult Education; University Extension; Tutorial Class Movement; A Student's Experience.

351. SWEENEY, C. P. *Adult Working Class Education in Great Britain and the United States*. Pp. 101. Bulletin of the U.S. Bureau of Labour Statistics, Washington, 1920.

352. BOARD OF EDUCATION—ADULT EDUCATION COMMITTEE. Paper No. 5. *British Music*. Pp. 72. 1924. Paper No. 6. *The Drama in Adult Education*. Pp. 220. 1926. Paper No. 9. *Pioneer Work and other Developments in Adult Education*. Pp. 88. 1929. Paper No. 10. *The Scope and Practice of Adult Education*. Pp. 102. 1930. H.M.S.O.

353. HODGEN, M. T. *Workers' Education in England and the United States*. Pp. 326. Kegan Paul, 1925.
Chs. i-vii on England are valuable, though confused and inaccurate. Long but unselective bibliography.

354. DANSETTE, A. *L'éducation populaire en Angleterre*. Pp. 171. Sagot, Paris, 1926.
Interesting account, with emphasis on working-class adult education. Brief historical introduction.

355. HADER, J. J., and LINDEMAN, E. C. *What do Workers Study?* Pp. 66. Workers' Education Bureau, New York, 1929.
Subject analysis of provision by various agencies in U.S.A. and Great Britain 1920-7.

356. YEAXLEE, B. A. *Lifelong Education.* Pp. 168. Cassell, 1929.
Deals with the need for adult education and some of its problems; two chapters on historical development.

357. HANSOME, M. *World Workers' Educational Movements: their Social Significance.* Pp. 594. Columbia U.P., 1931.
Analytical description of various types of workers' education.

358. BROWN, J. W. *The Adult Education Movement,* in *Year Book of Education,* 1932 (**35**), pp. 464-78.
Followed by note on *Adult Education in Scotland* by Ewen, J. T.

359. DAVIES, W. R. *The Concern of the State with Adult Education in England and Wales,* in *International Quarterly of Adult Education,* Vol. I, 1932-3, pp. 36-50.

360. BAILEY, S. H. *International Studies in Great Britain.* Pp. 140. Oxford U.P., 1933.
Ch. ii describes the provision for international studies in adult education. See also the same author's *International Studies in Modern Education,* pp. 327, Oxford U.P., 1938 (Ch. v).

361. PEERS, R. (ed.). *Adult Education in Practice.* Pp. 315. Macmillan, 1934.
Chapters on Character and Aims; Historical Background; Present Organisation; The Adult Student; Breaking New Ground; Adult Classes; Methods of Teaching; Supply of Books; Extra-class Activities; Full-time Studies; The Tutor. Useful bibliography and appendices.

362. WILLIAMS, W. E. *The Auxiliaries of Adult Education: a Brief Survey of those Movements which are Contributing, in the more Informal and Incidental Ways, to the Education of Adults in England.* Pp. 34. B.I.A.E., 1934.

363. MOLESWORTH, B. H. *Adult Education in America and England.* Pp. 72. Oxford U.P., 1935.

364. WILLIAMS, W. E., and LANGAARD, J. *Art on Circuit,* in *W.A.B.,* 2nd Ser., No. II, Aug. 1935, pp. 17-21.
On the British Institute scheme for circulating art exhibitions. See further GORDON, C., *Art for the People: the Fifth Year,* in *A.E.,* Vol. XII, 1939-40, pp. 3-12.

365. THOMAS, Sir B. B. (ed.). *Harlech Studies: Essays presented to Dr. Thomas Jones.* Pp. 361. Univ. of Wales P., 1938.
Includes valuable essays on R. D. Roberts and on science and music in adult education.

366. WILLIAMS, W. E. (ed.). *Adult Education in Great Britain and the United States of America.* Reprinted from *Year Book of Education* (**35**). Pp. 102. B.I.A.E., 1938.
Essays by various distinguished workers in adult education, mainly about Great Britain: the universities, the L.E.A.s, clubs for the unemployed, community centres, public libraries, the churches.

367. KANDEL, I. L. (ed.). *Columbia Educational Yearbook,* 1940 (**30**). Columbia U.P.
A world survey of adult education, including PEERS, R., on England and PEDDIE, J. R., on Scotland.

368. *War-Time Chronicles,* in *A.E.,* Vol. XIII, 1940-1, pp. 187-223.
Nine brief articles describing war-time experiences.

369. HIGGINSON, N. and J. H. *Great Adventure.* Pp. 146. Univ. of London P., 1945.
Reflections and reminiscences, mainly concerned with adult education.

370. MANSBRIDGE, A. *Fellow Men: a Gallery of England, 1876-1946.* Pp. 128. Dent, 1948.
Includes sketches of such adult educational personalities as Reuben George, William Temple, Charles Gore, Samuel Barnett, H. H. Turnor, G. W. Hudson Shaw.

371. JONES, T. *Welsh Broth.* Pp. 178. Griffiths, 1952.
Includes recollections, 1900-1920, of adult educational work in Glasgow, Ireland and Wales.

372. LINDSAY, J. *British Achievement in Art and Music.* Pp. 36. n.d.
An account of the work of various cultural agencies, and especially C.E.M.A., during the Second World War.

See also **263-4, 271.**

Recent Developments

373. ARTS ENQUIRY. *The Visual Arts.* Pp. 183. Political and Economic Planning, 1946.
See especially Ch. v, Public Art Galleries, Ch. vi, Art in General Education.

374. WALLER, R. D. *Learning to Live.* Pp. 63. Art and Educational Publishers, 1946.
Description of facilities for adult education and discussion of some problems.

375. ARTS ENQUIRY. *Music: a Report on Musical Life in England.* Pp. 224. Political and Economic Planning, 1949.
See especially Ch. iv, Amateur Music Making; Ch. vi, Music in General Education.

376. EVANS, B. I., and GLASGOW, M. C. *The Arts in England.* Pp. 138. Greywalls P., 1949.
Survey of developments in the promotion of the arts by C.E.M.A. and the Arts Council, local authorities, and private enterprise.

377. CAWSON, F. H. *The Education of the Adult.* Pp. 32. British Council [1951].
A useful brief general description.

378. NATIONAL COUNCIL OF SOCIAL SERVICE—STANDING CONFERENCE OF COUNTY MUSIC COMMITTEES. *Music and the Amateur.* Pp. 68. N.C.S.S., 1951.
A factual survey of provision and organisation.

379. LEGGE, C. D. *Facts and Figures in Further Education—the Place of the Responsible Bodies,* in *A.E.,* Vol. XXVI, 1953-4, pp. 269-75.
Analysis of statistics in the Ministry report for 1952. Discusses the provision made by L.E.A.s and Responsible Bodies.

380. ADAM, Sir R. *Problems in Adult Education.* Pp. 19. Birkbeck College, 1956.
A survey of existing provision and a statement of some problems.

381. RAYBOULD, S. G. *Adult Education in Transition,* in *Political Quarterly,* Vol. XXVIII, 1957, pp. 243-53.
Review of changes, especially in the position and work of the W.E.A. and the universities.

382. RAYBOULD, S. G. (ed.). *Trends in English Adult Education.* Pp. 272. Heinemann, 1959.
Discusses the work of the W.E.A., university extra-mural departments, trade unions, local authorities, residential colleges, broadcasting, and women's organisations.

383. STERN, H. H. *Parent Education: an International Survey*. Pp. 163. Hull University Institute of Education and Unesco Institute for Education, Hamburg. Hull, 1960.
Describes work in thirty-five countries.

Local and Regional Studies

384. JONES, J. *Historical Sketch of the Art and Literary Institutions of Wolverhampton*. Pp. 174. 1897.

385. BOARD OF EDUCATION. Educational Pamphlet No. 59. *Report on Adult Education in the County of Yorkshire*. Pp. 54. 1928. Educational Pamphlet No. 73. *Report on Adult Education in Lancashire and Cheshire*, Pp. 70. 1929. H.M.S.O.

386. MILLER, H. C. *The History and Development of Adult Education in North Stafford-shire*. Unpublished M.Ed. thesis, Manchester Univ., 1928.

387. JONES G. P. *A Report on the Development of Adult Education in Sheffield*. Pp. 38. Sheffield Social Survey Committee 1932.

388. BOARD OF EDUCATION—WELSH DEPARTMENT. Memorandum No. 5. *Report on Adult Education in Wales*. Pp. 86. H.M.S.O., 1936.
Cf. UNIVERSITY OF WALES EXTENSION BOARD, *Survey of Adult Education in Wales*, pp. 143, Cardiff, 1940 (publication restricted); and for an earlier study *Adult Education in Wales*, in *W.A.B.*, 1st Ser., No. VII, Feb. 1921, pp. 1-14.

389. CONSULTATIVE COMMITTEE ON ADULT EDUCATION IN BRISTOL. *Survey of Adult Education in Bristol*. Pp. 35. Bristol, 1937.

390. COCHRANE, C., and STEWART, D. M. *Survey of Adult Education in Scotland, 1938-9*. Pp. 40. B.I.A.E. (Scottish Branch), Edinburgh, 1944.
A valuable statistical survey. See also MARWICK, W. H., *Adult Education in Scotland*, in *W.A.B.*, 2nd Ser., No. XL, Feb. 1945; and for an examination of Scotland's relative weakness in this field SHEARER, J. G. S., *Scottish Adult Education*, in *A.E.*, Vol. XXVI, 1953-4, pp. 115-24.

391. NETTEL, R. *Music in the Five Towns, 1840-1914*. Pp. 130. Oxford U.P., 1945.
A study of the social influence of music.

392. BROWNE, H. B. *Chapters of Whitby History, 1823-1946*. Pp. 355. Brown and Sons, Hull, 1946.
Deals particularly with the Literary and Philosophical Society and the Museum, but also with other adult educational organisations.

393. MacGREGOR, J. *History of Adult and Technical Education in Skipton-in-Craven during the Nineteenth Century*. Unpublished M.Ed. thesis, Leeds Univ., 1949.

394. GRIFFIN, J. *The Development of Adult Education in Scotland*. Unpublished Ph.D. thesis, St. Andrews Univ., 1953.
A valuable pioneering study in a previously little explored field. A comprehensive history, with many references to parallel developments in England, and with supplementary chapters on student personnel, teaching methods, and other topics.

395. ALLAWAY, A. J. *Adult and Further Education in Leicester and Leicestershire*, in *Victoria County History*, Leicester, Vol. III, 1955, pp. 252-68.

396. HAGGAR, R. G. *Some Adult Educational Institutions in North Staffordshire*, in *R.H.P.*, Vol. III, VI, 1957-8, pp. 12-26.
Account of various institutions, especially mechanics' institutes, during the nineteenth century.

397. KELLY, T., and Others. *Three Ventures in Adult Education in Lancashire in the Reign of George III.* Reprinted from *Transactions of the Lancashire and Cheshire Historic Society,* Vol. CX, 1958, pp. 127-56.
Accounts of an adult school at Chorley, a book society at Colne, and a book club at St. Helens.

398. STEPHENS, W. B. *The History of Adult Education in Warrington during the Nineteenth Century.* Unpublished M.A. (Educ.) thesis, Exeter Univ., 1959.

399. WALLER, R. D., WILSON, A., and RUDDOCK, R. *After Work: Leisure and Learning in Two Towns.* Pp. 63. N.I.A.E., 1959.
Surveys of adult educational provision in Rochdale and Bolton.

400. BARCLAY, J. B. *Adult Education in South-East Scotland.* Unpublished Ph.D. thesis, Edinburgh Univ., 1960.
A comprehensive and in the later phases detailed historical survey from the earliest times, with chapters on teaching techniques and statistical and other appendices.

401. KELLY, T. *Adult Education in Liverpool: a Narrative of Two Hundred Years.* Pp. 48. Liverpool University Extra-Mural Department, 1960.

(b) PARTICULAR MOVEMENTS AND ORGANISATIONS

(i) Adult Education in Association with Day Schools and Sunday Schools

402. *Welch Piety.* Annually 1740-76.
These reports on the Welsh circulating schools, written and published till 1761 by the founder, Rev. Griffith Jones of Llanddowror, are the principal original source. The Reports for 1740-52 were published in 2v. 1753, Reports for 1752-60 in IV. 1760. National Library of Wales has the only complete set. WILLIAMS, W. M. (ed.), *Selections from the Welch Piety,* pp. 128, Univ. of Wales P., Cardiff, 1938, gives some key passages. For the adult educational work of the schools see **408.**

403. MATHEWS, W. *A Sketch of the Principal Means which have been employed to ameliorate the Intellectual and Moral Condition of the Working Classes at Birmingham.* Pp. 34. 1830.
Describes adult education societies deriving from the Sunday school movement.

404. MORE, M. (ed. ROBERTS, A.). *The Mendip Annals.* Pp. 258. 1859, 2nd edn. 1859.
Describes the philanthropic and educational work of Hannah and Martha More in the Mendip villages in the late eighteenth century. JONES, M. G., *Hannah More, 1745-1833,* pp. 296, Cambridge U.P., 1952, is now the standard biography.

405. EVANS, D. *The Sunday Schools of Wales.* Pp. 414. 1883.
On adult educational work see especially Ch. x. Cf. JONES, L. S., *Church and Chapel as Sources and Centres of Education in Wales during 1850-1900,* unpublished M.A. thesis, Liverpool Univ., 1940.

406. HARRIS, J. H. *The Story of the Sunday School.* Pp. 144. Culley, 1901.

407. JENKINS, D. E. *Life of the Rev. Thomas Charles of Bala.* 3v. Jenkins, Denbigh, 1908, 2nd edn. 1910.
Includes an account of the Sunday schools and adult schools promoted by Charles in North Wales.

408. KELLY, T. *Griffith Jones, Llanddowror, Pioneer in Adult Education.* Pp. 56. Univ. of Wales P., Cardiff, 1950.
The most recent study of the adult educational work of the Welsh circulating schools, with full bibliography. Of earlier biographies the most important are those by JONES, D., pp. 308, S.P.C.K., 1902; JONES, D. A., pp. 176, Hughes, Wrexham, 1923 (Welsh); CAVENAGH, F. A., pp. 72, Univ. of Wales P., Cardiff, 1930 (reprinted from *J.A.E.*, Vol. I, 1926-8); and JENKINS, R. T., pp. 62, Univ. of Wales P., Cardiff, 1930 (English and Welsh).

409. SMITH, H. P. *The Origins of Adult Education,* in *R.H.P.*, Vol. III, II, 1953, pp. 44-65.
A survey of pioneering efforts in the eighteenth and early nineteenth centuries, with particular reference to the origins of the adult school movement.

See also **233, 246.**

(ii) Adult Schools and Evening Schools

410. POLE, T. *A History of the Origin and Progress of Adult Schools.* Pp. 134. Bristol, 1814, 2nd edn. 1816.

411. [GODDARD, C.]. *An Account of the Origin, Principles, Proceedings and Results of an Institution for Teaching Adults to Read, established in the contiguous parts of Buckinghamshire and Berkshire, in 1814.* Pp. 156. Windsor, 1816.
An important though little-known source.

412. WINKS, J. F. *History of Adult Schools.* Pp. 69. 1821.
Only known copies are at Leicester City Library. N.I.A.E. has transcript.

413. ROWNTREE, J. W. and BINNS, H. B. *A History of the Adult School Movement.* Pp. 100. 1903. Reprinted from *Present Day Papers*, Vol. V, 1902.
Includes valuable statistical material.

414. NATIONAL ADULT SCHOOL UNION. *Annual Reports,* 1907-58, thereafter incorporated in *One and All* (**422**). *Adult School Lesson Handbook.* Annually 1911-45. Continued as *Adult School Study Handbook.* Annually from 1946.

415. HOBLEY, E. F., and MERCER, T. W. *The Adult School Movement: what it is and what it may become.* Pp. 80. Headley, 1911.
See also *The Friend,* Vol. LXII, 1922, pp. 691-703; and articles by GILLMAN, F. J., in *Friends' Quarterly Examiner,* Vols. LVII, 1923, pp. 52-65; LVIII, 1924, pp. 213-20; and LXIV, 1930, pp. 241-57.

416. MARTIN, G. C. *The Adult School Movement: its Origin and Development.* Pp. 453. N.A.S.U., 1924.
The standard history, with full bibliography.

417. CHAMPNESS, E. *Adult Schools: a Study in Pioneering.* Pp. 79. Religious Education P., Wallington, 1941.
Study of current problems with brief historical introduction. See further PORTEOUS, G., *Adult School Education in the New Age,* pp. 24, N.A.S.U. [1948]; N.A.S.U., *Adult Schools and how to Establish Them,* pp. 16, n.d.; N.A.S.U., *The Adult Schools of the Future,* pp. 16, 1957.

418. *The City of London College, 1848-1948.* Pp. 42. The College, 1948.
Traces the origin of the College in evening classes for young men promoted by a group of London clergy.

419. BEDALE, JOAN. *The Colne Iron School*, in *A.E.*, Vol. XXIV, 1951-2, pp. 207-14. Interesting account of an adult evening school in the 1860s and 1870s.

420. Biographies of adult school pioneers:
MORLAND, O. *William White*. Pp. 175. Morland, Birmingham, 1903.
DONCASTER, P. *Joseph Stephenson Rowntree*. Pp. 456. Headley, 1908.
WEDMORE, E. T. *Thomas Pole. Journal of the Friends' Historical Society*, Suppl. 7, 1908.
ROBSON, S. E. *Joshua Rowntree*. Pp. 190. Allen and Unwin, 1916.
GARDINER, A. G. *George Cadbury*. Pp. 338. Cassell, 1923.
THOMAS, A. Ll.B., and EMMOTT, E. B. *W. C. Braithwaite*. Pp. 186. Longmans, 1931.
DAVIES, G. M. Ll. *J. R. Gillett*. Pp. 158. Allen and Unwin, 1942.
VERNON, A. *A Quaker Business Man: the Life of Joseph Rowntree, 1836-1925*. Pp. 207. Allen and Unwin, 1958.

421. Histories of local adult schools:
WHITE, W. *The Story of Severn Street and Priory First-Day Schools* [Birmingham]. Pp. 127. Jones, Birmingham, 1895.
GILLMAN, F. J. *The Story of the York Adult Schools*. Pp. 64. Delittle Fenwick, York, 1907.
CHOLERTON, A. F. (ed.). *Fifty Years of Adult School Work in Leicestershire, 1861-1910*. Pp. 58. Wallin and Rowe, Leicester, 1910.
See also local supplements issued with *One and All* by the various County Unions. For Chorley see **397**.

422. Periodicals:
The Monthly Record, 1882-91. (Concerned with Quaker adult schools).
The Adult School. Monthly, 1887-92.
One and All. Monthly, Vols. I-LI, 1891-1940; N.S. Vols. I-XXI, 1941-61. (The current adult school journal.)
References to adult school work are also to be found in Quaker journals: *The British Friend*, monthly 1843-1913; *The Friend*, monthly 1843-91, weekly 1892-1961 (current); The *Friends' Quarterly Examiner*, 1867-1946; *The Friends' Quarterly*, 1947-61 (current).

See also **24, 233, 235-6, 311, 342, 397, 407, 409, 605,** and for evening schools under the auspices of local education authorities Section III(b)(xiii).

(iii) Literary and Philosophical Societies
and other Learned Societies

NOTE. These societies have their place in the history of adult education because most of them originally partook more of the character of middle-class or upper-class mutual improvement societies than of learned societies such as we are familiar with to-day. This was true even of the Royal Society in its early years.

423. JONES, H. B. *The Royal Institution: its Founder and its first Professors*. Pp. 441. 1871.
See also MARTIN, T., *The Royal Institution*, pp. 69, Longmans for British Council, 1942, 3rd edn. Royal Institution, 1962; and for a detailed account of the early years SPARROW, W. J., *Benjamin Thompson, Count von Rumford*, unpublished Ph.D. thesis, Birmingham Univ., 1953, Ch. xi. For a provincial Royal Institution see ORMEROD, H. A., *The Liverpool Royal Institution: a Record and a Retrospect*, pp. 93, Liverpool U.P., 1953; and **401**.

424. PRIESTLEY, J. (ed. BOLTON, H. C.). *Scientific Correspondence of Joseph Priestley*. Pp. 248. New York, 1892.
See App. II for the Lunar Society of Birmingham, predecessor of the literary and philosophical societies. Cf. SCHOFIELD, R. E., *Membership of the Lunar Society of Birmingham*, in *Annals of Science*, Vol. XII, 1956, pp. 118-36; HOLT, A., *Life of Joseph Priestley*, pp. 239, Oxford U.P., 1931; PEARSON, H., *Doctor Darwin*, pp. 254, Dent, 1930; and **259**.

33

425. LYONS, Sir H. *The Royal Society, 1660–1940.* Pp. 364. Cambridge U.P., 1944.
The fullest recent history. For the early years see also STIMSON, D., *Scientists and Amateurs: a History of the Royal Society*, pp. 286, Sigma, 1949; HARTLEY, Sir H. (ed.) *The Royal Society: its Origins and Founders*, pp. 275, The Society, 1960.

426. EVANS, J. *A History of the Society of Antiquaries.* Pp. 503. The Society, 1956.
Includes an account of the Elizabethan society of this name, as well as the modern Society founded in 1717.

427. Histories of individual literary and philosophical institutions:
Derby. ROBINSON, E. *The Derby Philosophical Society*, in *Annals of Science*, Vol. IX, 1953, pp. 359–67.
Edinburgh. MILLER, W. A. S. *The Philosophical: a Short History of the Edinburgh Philosophical Institution, 1846–1948.* Pp. 96. Cousland, Edinburgh, 1949.
Halifax. HALIFAX LITERARY AND PHILOSOPHICAL SOCIETY. *Centenary Handbook, 1830–1930.* Pp. 86. The Society, 1930.
Leeds. CLARKE, E. K. *History of 100 Years of the Leeds Philosophical Society.* Pp. 249. Jowett and Sowry, Leeds, 1924.
Leicester. LOTT, F. B. *Centenary Book of the Leicester Literary and Philosophical Society.* Pp. 271. The Society, Leicester, 1935.
Manchester. SMITH, R. A. *A Centenary of Science in Manchester*, in *Memoirs of the Literary and Philosophical Society of Manchester*, 3rd Ser., Vol. IX, 1883. NICHOLSON, F. *The Literary and Philosophical Society, 1781–1851*, in *Memoirs*, 8th Ser., Vol. LXVIII, 1923–4, pp. 97–148. BARNES, C. L. *The Manchester Literary and Philosophical Society.* Pp. 15. [The Society], Manchester, 1938.
Newcastle. WATSON, R. S. *The History of the Literary and Philosophical Society of Newcastle-upon-Tyne (1793–1896).* Pp. 400. 1897.
Sheffield. PORTER, W. S. *Sheffield Literary and Philosophical Society. A Centenary Retrospect.* Pp. 106. The Society, Sheffield, 1922.
For the Whitby society see **392**.

428. Histories of other learned societies, e.g.
WOODWARD, H. B. *History of the Geological Society of London.* Pp. 356. The Society, 1907.
SIDDALL, J. D. *The Chester Society of Natural Science, Literature and Art from 1871 to 1911.* Pp. 63. The Society, Chester, 1911.
MOORE, T. S., and PHILIP, J. C. *The Chemical Society, 1841–1941.* Pp. 235. The Society, 1947.
JESSUP, F. W. *Kent Archaeological Society*, pp. 43, reprinted from *Archaeologia Cantiana*, Vol. LXX, 1956.
For lists of societies see HUME, A., *Learned Societies and Printing Clubs of the United Kingdom*, pp. 339, 1847; *Encyclopaedia Britannica*, 11th edn., *s.v.* Societies, Learned; and **21**.
See also **21, 22, 46, 219, 226, 259**.

(iv) Mechanics' Institutes and Similar Bodies

429. BROUGHAM, H. *Practical Observations upon the Education of the People.* Pp. 33. 1825 (20 edns.).
Did much to promote the spread of mechanics' institutes. Originally printed in *Edinburgh Review*, Vol. XLI, Oct. 1824, and later reprinted in Brougham's *Speeches* (4v, Edinburgh, 1838), Vol. III. The opposition view is represented by such works as A COUNTRY GENTLEMAN, *The Consequences of a Scientific Education to the Working Classes*, pp. 77, 1826.

430. *The Eloquent Speeches of Dr. Birkbeck and Mr. Brougham at the Opening of the London Mechanics' Institute New Lecture Room.* Pp. 16. 1825.
Typical of a large class of literature. Cf. the addresses to the Liverpool and Manchester Institutes in Vol. III of Brougham's *Speeches* (see previous entry); and HEYWOOD, B., *Addresses delivered at the Manchester Mechanics' Institution* [1825–40], pp. 124, 1843.

431. BURNS, D. *Mechanics' Institutions; their Objects and Tendency.* Pp. 84. Glasgow and Edinburgh, 1837.
Includes account of origins.

432. CENTRAL SOCIETY OF EDUCATION. *Papers.* 3v. 1837, 1838, 1839.
Includes essays on lyceums and mechanics' institutes.

433. CLAXTON, T. *Hints to Mechanics on Self Education and Mutual Instruction.* Pp. 238. 1839.
Important for the origins of mechanics' institutes. Gives list of institutes 1838. CLAXTON, T., *Memoir of a Mechanic*, pp. 179, Boston and New York, 1839, appears to be another edition of the same work.

434. [DUPPA, B. F.]. *A Manual for Mechanics' Institutions.* Pp. 332. Society for the Diffusion of Useful Knowledge, 1839.
A general account of the institutes.

435. [COATES, T.]. *Report of the State of Literary, Scientific, and Mechanics' Institutions in England.* Pp. 121. Society for the Diffusion of Useful Knowledge, 1841.
Includes list of institutes.

436. HOLE, J. *An Essay on the History and Management of Literary, Scientific, and Mechanics' Institutions.* Pp. 191. Society of Arts, 1853.
A valuable critical survey. Cf. HARRISON, J. F. C., *Social Reform in Victorian Leeds: the Work of James Hole, 1820–1895*, pp. 70, Thoresby Soc., Leeds, 1954.

437. SOCIETY OF ARTS. *Report of the Committee to inquire into the Subject of Industrial Instruction.* Pp. 232. 1853.
Discusses a proposal to convert mechanics' institutes into industrial colleges. Reprinted as *Middle Class Education and Class Instruction in Mechanics' Institutions*, 1857.

438. DAWES, R. *Mechanics' Institutes and Popular Education.* Pp. 48. 1856.

439. TRAICE, W. H. J. *Handbook of Mechanics' Institutions.* Pp. 94. 1856, 2nd edn. 1863.
A compendium of information prepared for the Yorkshire Union of Institutes.

440. COLLINS, P. A. W. *Dickens and Adult Education*, in *B.J.E.S.*, Vol. III, 1954-5, pp. 115-27. Re-issued in revised form, pp. 40 (duplicated), Leicester Univ., 1962.
On Dickens' contacts with mechanics' institutes and his ideas on adult education as shown in his novels, speeches and letters. His numerous addresses to mechanics' institutes and similar bodies are to be found in FIELDING, K. J. (ed.) *The Speeches of Charles Dickens*, pp. 480, Clarendon P., Oxford, 1960. Cf. COLLINS, P. A. W., *Dickens' Periodicals: Articles on Education*, pp. 36 (duplicated) Vaughan College Papers No. 3, Leicester, 1957.

441. KELLY, T. *George Birkbeck, Pioneer of Adult Education.* Pp. 394. Liverpool U.P., 1957.
Biography of Birkbeck and survey of the origins and history of the mechanics' institute movement, with full bibliography. See also GODARD, J. G., *George Birkbeck, the Pioneer of Popular Education*, pp. 264, London and Derby, 1884.

442. Biographies of pioneers:
HALEVY, E. *Thomas Hodgskin.* Pp. 205. Paris, 1903, transl. A. J. Taylor, Benn, 1956.
STYLER, W. E. *Rowland Detroisier*, in *A.E.*, Vol. XXI, 1948-9, pp. 133-8.
MUIR, J. (ed. MACAULAY, J. M.) *John Anderson, Pioneer of Technical Education, and the College he founded.* Pp. 174. Smith, Glasgow, 1950.
COPEMAN, W. S. C. *Andrew Ure*, in *Proc. of the Roy. Soc. of Medicine*, Vol. XLIV, 1951, pp. 655-62.

443. Regional histories:

MARWICK, W. H. *Mechanics' Institutes in Scotland*, in *J.A.E.*, Vol. VI, 1932-4, pp. 292-309.

UNION OF LANCASHIRE AND CHESHIRE INSTITUTES. *A Hundred Years of Educational Service.* Pp. 69. Manchester, 1939.

BRISCOE, H. K., *Nottinghamshire Mechanics' Institutes in the Nineteenth Century*, in *V.A.*, Vol. VI, 1954, pp. 151-62.

TYLECOTE, M. *The Mechanics' Institutes of Lancashire and Yorkshire before 1851.* Pp. 356. Manchester U.P., 1957. (Valuable not only for the North of England but for the movement as a whole.)

POPPLE, J. *The Mechanics' Institutes of the East and North Ridings and of York*, in *V.A.*, Vol. X, 1958, pp. 29-46.

—— *The Origin and Development of the Yorkshire Union of Mechanics' Institutes.* Unpublished M.A. thesis, Sheffield Univ., 1960.

444. Histories of individual mechanics' institutes and similar bodies (see also bibliographies to **441** and **443** (Tylecote)):

Aberdeen: FRASER, G. M. *Aberdeen Mechanics' Institution.* Pp. 72. Aberdeen, 1912.

Accrington. WILLIAMS, C. *The Accrington Mechanics' Institution, 1845-1895.* Pp. 48. Accrington, 1895. STONES, E. *The Growth of Technical Education in Nineteenth Century Accrington*, in *V.A.*, Vol. IX, 1957, pp. 26-37.

Birmingham. WATERHOUSE, R. E. *The Birmingham and Midland Institute, 1854-1954.* Pp. 212. The Institute, 1954.

Dumfries. NICOL, W. B. de B. *Dumfries and Maxwelltown Mechanics' Institute, 1825-1900*, in *Dumfriesshire and Galloway Nat. Hist. and Antiq. Soc. Trans.*, 3rd Ser., Vol. XXVIII, 1951, pp. 64-74.

Ebbw Vale. MILES, P. B. *Ebbw Vale Literary and Scientific Institute, 1849-1949.* Pp. 40. Pontypool [1949].

Edinburgh. MARWICK, W. H. *Early Adult Education in Edinburgh*, in *J.A.E.*, Vol. V, 1930-2, pp. 389-404.

Glasgow. SEXTON, A. H. *The First Technical College.* Pp. 206. Glasgow, 1894. MARWICK, W. H. *Early Adult Education in the West of Scotland*, in *J.A.E.*, Vol. IV, 1929-30, pp. 191-202. See also **442** (Muir).

Greenock. SMITH, R. M. *A Page of Local History . . . Greenock Mechanics' Library and Institution.* Pp. 129. Pollock, Greenock, 1904.

Hitchin. DYER, L. J. *Hitchin Mechanics' Institute*, in *A.E.*, Vol. XXIII, 1950-1, pp. 113-21, 212-20.

Leeds. LEEDS INSTITUTE OF SCIENCE, ART AND LITERATURE. *Historical Sketch of One Hundred Years' Work.* Pp. 26. The Institute, 1923.

Leicester. LOTT, F. B. *The Story of the Leicester Mechanics' Institute, 1833-1871.* Pp. 20. Thornley, Leicester, 1935. EAGLE, E. C. *The Leicester Mechanics' Institute, 1834-1870—I*, in *R.H.P.*, Vol. III, VII, 1958-9, pp. 48-73.

Lewes. TYNAN, A. *Lewes Mechanics' Institute*, in *R.H.P.*, Vol. III, IV, 1955-6, pp. 12-24.

Liverpool. TIFFEN, H. J. *A History of the Liverpool Institute Schools.* Pp. 190. Institute Old Boys' Assoc., 1935.

London. BURNS, C. D. *Short History of Birkbeck College.* Pp. 170. Univ. of London P., 1924.

Newcastle. DYER, L. J. *Newcastle Mechanics' Institute*, in *A.E.*, Vol. XXII, 1949-50, pp. 122-9, 205-12.

Nottingham. GREEN, J. A. H. *History of the Nottingham Mechanics' Institution, 1837-1887.* Pp. 56. The Institution, 1887. GRANGER, J. *Nottingham Mechanics' Institution: a Retrospect, 1837-1912.* Pp. 44. The Institution, 1912. NOTTINGHAM MECHANICS' INSTITUTION. Pp. 68. *Fifteen Years' Record, 1912-27.* The Institution, 1928.

Oldham. TAIT, A. *History of the Oldham Lyceum.* Pp. 137. Lee, Oldham, 1897.

Richmond (Surrey). BARKAS, A. A. *A Chapter in the History of our Local Institutions.* Pp. 19. Richmond, 1907.

Rotherham. REILLY H. P. *History of Technical Education in Rotherham.* Unpublished M.A. thesis, Sheffield Univ., 1952. (Includes account of Mechanics' Institute.)

St. Just. TODD, A. C. "Solely the Promotion of Useful *Knowledge*"—*a Cornish Literary Institute of the Nineteenth Century*, in *R.H.P.*, Vol. III, V, 1956-7, pp. 25-34.

36

Sheffield. TAYLOR, J. *A Nineteenth-Century Experiment in Adult Education*, in *A.E.*, Vol. XI, 1938-9, pp. 151-60.
Skipton. GIBBON, A. M. *One Hundred Years Old: the Story of the Skipton Mechanics' Institute, 1847-1947.* Pp. 20. The Institute, 1947.
Stourbridge. PALFREY, H. E. *The Story of the Stourbridge Institute and Social Club, 1834-1948.* Pp. 93. Mark and Moody, Stourbridge, 1948.
Taunton. HUDSON, A. K. *Taunton Mechanics' Institute,* in *Notes and Queries for Somerset and Dorset,* Vol. XXVI, Parts 251-2, Aug.-Dec., 1952, pp. 95-8, 101-4.
Thornton (Yorks.). DYER, L. J. *Thornton Mechanics' Institute,* in *A.E.,* Vol. XXI, 1948-9, pp. 15-22, 59-66.
Woolton (Liverpool). STEWART, D. P. *The Woolton Mechanics' Institute,* in *Trans. of the Unitarian Hist. Soc.,* Vol. X, 1951-4, pp. 66-90.

445. Periodicals:
The Mechanics' Magazine. Weekly, Vols. I-LXIX, 1823-58; N.S. Vols. I-XXVIII, 1859-72.
The Glasgow Mechanic's Magazine. Weekly, Vols. I-V, Glasgow, 1823-6.
The London Mechanics' Register. Weekly, Vols. I-IV, 1824-6.
The New London Mechanics' Register. Weekly, Vols. I-II, 1827-8.
The Scots Mechanic's Magazine. Weekly, Vols. I-II, Glasgow, 1825-6.

(v) Political and Religious Reform Societies

446. REID, W. H. *The Rise and Dissolution of the Infidel Societies in the Metropolis.* Pp. 125. 1800.

447. LOVETT, W., and COLLINS, J. *Chartism: a New Organisation of the People, embracing a plan for the education and improvement of the people.* Pp. 132. 1840, 2nd edn. 1841.

448. JONES, R. A. *Knowledge Chartism.* Unpublished M.A. thesis, Birmingham Univ., 1938.
On the influence of Chartism on nineteenth-century educational development.

449. SALT, J. *The Sheffield Hall of Science,* in *V.A.,* Vol. XII, 1960, pp. 133-8.
One of the few studies in this field. There is an unpublished Dip.Ed. dissertation by BLACK, A., on *Owenite Education, 1839-1851, with special reference to the Manchester Hall of Science,* Manchester Univ., 1953.
See also **132, 135-6, 139, 147, 158, 259.**

(vi) Co-operative Education

450. CO-OPERATIVE CONGRESS. *Annual Reports.* Co-operative Union, Manchester, from 1869 (except 1944).
See especially the reports and discussions on education in Reports for 1896-98, 1916-19, 1932, 1945, and 1948, and in the Report of a Special Congress at Blackpool, 1920. A paper by Arnold Toynbee on *The Education of Co-operators,* given to the 1882 Congress, is reprinted in his *Lectures on the Industrial Revolution* (1908 edn., pp. 239-48); and a paper by R. H. Tawney on *Education and Social Progress,* included in the Report of the 1912 Congress, was also published separately (pp. 12, Co-operative Union, 1912). From 1948, Congress Reports include annual reports of the National Co-operative Education Association (also published separately).

451. GREENWOOD, A. *The Educational Department of the Rochdale Equitable Pioneers Society.* Pp. 16. Central Co-operative Board, Manchester, 1877.

452. ACLAND, A. H. D., and JONES, B. *Working Men Co-operators.* Pp. 224. London, 1884, 9th edn., ed. MADAMS, J. P., Co-operative Union, Manchester, 1945.

453. HOLYOAKE, G. J. *The Essentials of Co-operative Education.* Pp. 20. Labour Association, 1898.

454. HALL, F. *The Co-ordination and Extension of Co-operative Education.* Pp. 22. Co-operative Union, Manchester, 1914.
One of a number of pamphlets by Hall, afterwards first Principal of the Co-operative College.

455. WEBB, S. and B. *The Consumers' Co-operative Movement.* Pp. 520. Longmans, 1921, students' edn. 1930.
Includes critical appraisal of educational work.

456. MERCER, T. W. (ed.). *Dr. William King and the Co-operator, 1828-30.* Pp. 198. Co-operative Union, Manchester, 1922, repr. as *Co-operations' Prophet, 1947.*
Reprint of King's educational journal *The Co-operator*, with letters and account of his life.

457. DAWSON, L. A. *Co-operative Education.* Pp. 17. Fabian Society, 1923.
A description and critical estimate.

458. TWIGG, H. J. *The Organisation and Extent of Co-operative Education.* Pp. 52. Co-operative Union, Manchester, 1924.
Statistical survey and description of machinery. Good bibliography.

459. —— *An Outline History of Co-operative Education.* Pp. 67. Co-operative Union, Manchester, 1924.
Contains useful bibliography, statistics and chronology. For an account of the activity of a local society, see PEAPLES, F. W., *History of the Education Department of the Bolton Co-operative Society, 1861-1914*, pp. 119, Bolton, 1915.

460. WEBB, C. *The Woman with the Basket.* Pp. 205. Co-operative Union, Manchester, 1927.
A history of the Women's Co-operative Guild, 1883-1927. See Ch. iii, Education. See also DAVIES, M. LL. (ed.), *Life as We Have Known It*, by Co-operative Working Women, pp. 182, Hogarth P., 1931.

461. BROUCKERE, L. DE. *Co-operative Education in the Changing Social Order.* Pp. 19. International Co-operative Alliance, 1934.
Useful study of the content of co-operative education.

462. CO-OPERATIVE UNION. *A Ten Year Plan for Co-operative Education.* Pp. 22. Manchester, 1936.

463. WATKINS, W. P. *The Organisation of Co-operative Education.* Pp. 36. International Co-operative Alliance, 1937.

464. CARR-SAUNDERS, A. M., FLORENCE, P. S., and PEERS, R. *Consumers' Co-operation in Great Britain.* Pp. 572. Allen and Unwin, 1938, 2nd edn. 1938.
Contains a critical chapter on co-operative education. 2nd edn. has appendix considering the theory of co-operative education and making proposals for development.

465. THOMAS, J. *Co-operation and Adult Education after the War.* Pp. 27. Co-operative Union, Manchester, 1943.
A plan for integrating co-operative adult education with wider movements.

466. MARSHALL, R. L. *Co-operative Education.* Pp. 21. Co-operative Union, Manchester, 1948.
A general survey against the historical background. For a more detailed review of current provision see the same author's article on *Co-operative Education* in the *People's Year Book*, 1950, pp. 93-109.

467. MAUDSLEY, S. R. *Co-operative Education, 1900-1950,* in *The Co-operator's Year Book, 1950,* pp. 53-60.

468. BAILEY, J. *The British Co-operative Movement.* Pp. 178. Hutchinson, 1955.
Description of the aims, organisation and problems of the co-operative movement. Has a chapter on co-operative education.

469. NATIONAL CO-OPERATIVE EDUCATION ASSOCIATION AND CO-OPERATIVE UNION EDUCATION EXECUTIVE. *A Plan and a Challenge addressed to Co-operative Education Committees.* Pp. 12. Loughborough, 1956.
Plan for concerted action in co-operative education as agreed by the 1956 Conference.

470. CO-OPERATIVE UNION—EDUCATION DEPARTMENT. *Co-operative Education: a Handbook of Practical Guidance for Co-operative Educationists.* Pp. 242. Loughborough, 1957.

471. CO-OPERATIVE INDEPENDENT COMMISSION. *Report.* Pp. 320. Co-operative Union, Manchester, 1958.
A survey of the whole co-operative field. For its educational significance see articles in *Co-operative Educational Bulletin,* Nos. 30, 38, and 41 (1957-9).

472. GROOMBRIDGE, B. *Report on the Co-operative Auxiliaries.* Pp. 84. Co-operative Union, Manchester, 1960.
A report on the purposes and organisation of the Co-operative Guilds.

473. Periodicals:
The Co-operative Educator. Vols. I-XXI. Co-operative Union, Manchester, 1917-38. (Incorporates an earlier journal, *The College Herald,* 1913-17.)
The Co-operative Educational Bulletin. Quarterly, Co-operative Union, 1948-60, thereafter absorbed into *Co-operative Review.*

See also **133, 138, 158, 348, 449, 610.**

(vii) Working Men's Colleges and Similar Institutions

474. CHADWICK, D. *On Working Men's Colleges.* Pp. 12. Reprinted from NATIONAL ASSOCIATION FOR THE PROMOTION OF SOCIAL SCIENCE, *Transactions,* 1859.
Useful on the early history of the colleges. See also *Working Men's College Magazine* **(476)** and for modern accounts **325** and **561.**

The London College

475. MAURICE, J. F. D. *Learning and Working.* Pp. 374. London and Cambridge, 1855.
Expounds Maurice's ideas for the London College. See also RAVEN, C. E., *Christian Socialism, 1848-1854,* pp. 408, Macmillan, 1920.

476. *The Working Men's College Magazine* [London]. Monthly. Vols. I-III, 1859-61.
An essential source for the early years of the movement. For a later period see the *Working Men's College Journal,* 1890-1932, continued as *The Journal,* 1933-date.

477. MAURICE, F. (ed.). *The Life of Frederick Denison Maurice.* 2v. 1884.
Vol. II is of particular value. For others specially associated with the London College, see FAYLE, C. E., *Charles Wright: a Memoir,* pp. 206, Allen and Unwin, 1943; KENDALL, G., *Charles Kingsley and his Ideas,* pp. 190, Hutchinson, 1948; MACK, E. C., and ARMYTAGE, W. H. G., *Thomas Hughes,* pp. 302, Benn, 1952.

478. HARRISON, J. F. C. *A History of the Working Men's College, 1854-1954.* Pp. 235. Routledge and Kegan Paul, 1954.
The standard history. The Jubilee volume, ed. DAVIES, J. LL., *The Working Men's College, 1854-1904*, pp. 306, Macmillan, 1904, is however still useful.

See also **192-4, 343.**

Other Colleges

479. ATKINS, E. (ed.). *The Vaughan Working Men's College, 1862-1912* [Leicester]. Pp. 154. Adams and Shardlow, Leicester, 1912.
See also ALLAWAY, A. J., *David James Vaughan: Liberal Churchman and Educationist,* reprinted from LEICESTERSHIRE ARCHAEOLOGICAL AND HISTORICAL SOCIETY, *Transactions,* Vol. XXXIII, 1957, pp. 45-58.

480. SMITH, G. C. M. *The Story of the People's College, Sheffield, 1842-1878.* P p. 85. Sheffield, 1912.
A thorough and valuable study of the earliest College.

481. HARRIS, R. M. *Frances Martin College,* in *F.E.*., Vol. I, 1947-8, pp. 225-6.
Brief record of what was once the College for Working Women.

482. BIBBY, C. *The South London Working Men's College,* in *A.E.*, Vol. XXVIII, 1955-6, pp. 211-21.

483. RICHARDS, D. *Offspring of the Vic: a History of Morley College.* Pp. 336. Routledge and Kegan Paul, 1958.
Though later in date Morley College had many features in common with the Working Men's Colleges. See also HOPKINSON, D., *Family Inheritance: a Life of Eva Hubback,* pp. 196, Staples, 1954.

For the Manchester College see **514** (Thompson), for the Wolverhampton College see **384**, and for South London see also **347**. There are annual reports for certain years for Colleges at Halifax, Ipswich, Nottingham and Salford.

(viii) Working Men's Clubs

484. WORKING MEN'S CLUB AND INSTITUTE UNION. *Annual Reports.* From 1862.
See also *The Club and Institute Journal,* monthly from 1875 (current).

485. SOLLY, H. *Working Men's Social Clubs and Educational Institutes.* Pp. 252. 1867, 2nd edn., ed. HALL, B. T., Simpkin Marshall, 1904.
See also Solly's autobiography, *These Eighty Years,* 2v. 1893.

486. HALL, B. T. *Our Sixty Years: the Story of the Working Men's Club and Institute Union.* Pp. 398. The Union, 1922.,
Revised edition of *Our Fifty Years* (1912). *A Short History of the Working Men's Club and Institute Union,* pp. 99, 1927, is a popular summary reprinted from the *Club and Institute Journal.* See also histories of local institutes, e.g. GARDINER, F. J., *The Fiftieth Birthday of a Model Institute* [Wisbech], pp. 128, Wisbech, 1914; DYER, L. J., *Leighton Buzzard Working Men's Club and Institute,* in *A.E.*, Vol. XXI, 1948-9, pp. 139-47, 200-9.

487. LEVITT, J. *Adult Education in Working Men's Clubs,* in *A.E.*, Vol. XXVIII, 1955-6, pp. 260-72.
Account of work in the Clubs both historically and at the present time.

(ix) University Extra-Mural Teaching

488. MOULTON, R. G. *The University Extension Movement*. Pp. 67. 1886.

489. MACKINDER, H. J., and SADLER, M. E. *University Extension, Past, Present and Future*. Pp. 152. 1891.
3rd and revised edition of Mackinder's *University Extension: has it a Future?* (1890). Sadler was Secretary to the Oxford Extension Delegacy.

490. ROBERTS, R. D. *Eighteen Years of University Extension*. Pp. 144. Cambridge, 1891.

491. ROYAL COMMISSION ON SECONDARY EDUCATION. *Report*. 9v. 1895.
Useful for the connections of University Extension with secondary education.

492. WENLEY, R. M. *The University Extension Movement in Scotland*. Pp. 54. Glasgow, 1895.
Historical record by the Secretary of the Glasgow Extension Board. A more recent assessment is MARWICK, W. H., *The University Extension Movement in Scotland*, in *University of Edinburgh Journal*, Vol. VIII, 1937, pp. 227-34.

493. ROBERTS, R. D. *University Extension under the Old and New Conditions*. Pp. 24. Cambridge U.P., 1908.
Valuable appraisal of the movement at that date.

494. HILL, A. (ed.). *Congress of the Universities of the Empire, 1912: Report of Proceedings*, Pp. 507. Hodder and Stoughton, 1912. *Second Congress of the Universities of the British Empire, 1921: Report of Proceedings*. Pp. 508. Bell, 1921.
Both volumes have sections on extra-mural teaching.

495. ROYAL COMMISSION ON UNIVERSITY EDUCATION IN WALES. *First, Second* and *Final Reports*. 6 parts. H.M.S.O., 1917-18.

496. UNIVERSITY GRANTS COMMITTEE. *Reports*. H.M.S.O., 1921, 1925, 1930, 1936, 1948, 1953, 1958 (in progress).
These reports, which from 1948 appear under the title *University Development*, often contain important comments on extra-mural work. The Committee's annual *Returns from Universities and University Colleges in receipt of Treasury Grant*, which begin with the session 1919/20 (1921), include statistics for extra-mural work.

497. ROYAL COMMISSION ON OXFORD AND CAMBRIDGE UNIVERSITIES. *Report*. Pp. 256. H.M.S.O., 1922.
Recommends the establishment of Boards of Extra-Mural Studies.

498. DRAPER, W. H. *University Extension: a Survey of Fifty Years, 1873-1923*. Pp. 163. Cambridge U.P., 1923.

499. UNIVERSITIES EXTRA-MURAL CONSULTATIVE COMMITTEE. *Reports*. Annually 1925/26 to 1938/39. *Report on the War Years, 1939/40 to 1944/45*. Continued as

500. UNIVERSITIES COUNCIL FOR ADULT EDUCATION. *Reports*. 1945/47, 1947/49 and then annually (in progress).
A general review of extra-mural work, with statistical tables. From 1956/57 each Report includes an account of a specific region or Department (see **512**).

501. KOLBE, P. R. *Urban Influences on Higher Education in England and the United States*. Pp. 262. Macmillan, New York, 1928.
Part I, England, gives a useful account of the development and current position of university adult education.

41

502. CROSSMAN, R. H. S. *The Universities and Adult Education*, in *A.E.*, Vol. XI, 1938-9, pp. 99-118.
A stimulating criticism of existing university provision. For later statements see SALT, W. E., *The Universities and Adult Education*, in *Univs. Rev.*, Vol. XXIII, 1950-1, pp. 48-55; KELLY, T., *The Extra-Mural Function of Universities*, in *Univs. Rev.*, Vol. XXV, 1952-3, pp. 99-103; and especially WILTSHIRE, H. C., *The Great Tradition*, in *A.E.*, Vol. XXIX, 1956-7, and the ensuing debate in the columns of the same journal.

503. POLITICAL AND ECONOMIC PLANNING. *The Universities and Adult Education*, in *Planning*, Vol. XVII, 1951, pp. 269-91.
Discusses the present provision, the administrative system, the teaching staff and the future of Extra-Mural work.

504. RAYBOULD, S. G. *The English Universities and Adult Education*. Pp. 188. W.E.A. 1951.
A critical review of recent developments, with valuable appendices on statistics and grant regulations. The discussion to which the book gave rise was maintained in the columns of *Adult Education, Highway, Cambridge Rev., Tutors' Bulletin*, and elsewhere, over the next two years.

505. UNESCO. Problems in Education. IV. *Universities in Adult Education*. Pp. 172. Paris, 1952.
See also two Unesco conference reports: UNESCO INSTITUTE FOR EDUCATION, *The Universities and Adult Education*, pp. 37 (duplicated), Hamburg, 1954; and WALLER, R. D. (ed.), *The Universities and Adult Education*, pp. 168, Ministry of Education, H.M.S.O., 1957.

506. SAUNDERS, J. W. *Extra-Mural Examinations*, in *A.E.*, Vol. XXVII, 1954-5, pp. 280-97.
A general study illustrated from a course in the history of drama.

507. JEPSON, N. A. *The Origin and Development of the Oxford and Cambridge University Extension Movement between 1873 and 1902*. Unpublished Ph.D. thesis, Leeds Univ., 1955.
The author has published articles on *Staffing Problems during the Early Years of the Oxford University Extension Movement*, in *R.H.P.*, Vol. III, III, 1954-5, pp. 20-33; and *Leeds and the Beginning of University Adult Education*, pp. 16, reprinted from LEEDS PHILOSOPHICAL SOCIETY, *Proceedings*, Vol. VIII, Pt. III, 1957.

508. GOLDMAN, F. (ed.). *Report on the International Conference on University and Adult Education*, in *Y.A.E.*, Vol. XIII, 1961, pp. 91-168.
On the Conference held at Sagamore, New York, 1960. Valuable discussion of principles and practice in many countries.

509. PRITCHARD, E. P. *University Extra-Mural Libraries*. Pp. 33. Library Association 1961.

510. UNIVERSITIES COUNCIL FOR ADULT EDUCATION. *The Universities and Adult Education*. Pp. 32. U.C.A.E., 1961.
Report of a Working Party: a re-assessment of the place of extra-mural work in the light of recent social and educational changes. For an American view on the same problem see PETERSEN, R. and W., *University Adult Education: a Guide to Policy*, pp. 310, Harper, New York, 1960.

511. Lives of leading figures, especially

ROSCOE, Sir H. E. *Life and Experiences*. Pp. 432. Macmillan, 1906. (Anticipated Extension work at Manchester.)

STUART, J. *Reminiscences*. Pp. 318. Privately printed, 1911. (The founder of University Extension.)

MOULTON, W. F. *Richard Green Moulton*. Pp. 148. Epworth P., 1926.

HERFORD, C. H. *Philip Henry Wicksteed*. Pp. 444. Dent, 1931.

MUIR, J. R. B. (ed. HODGSON, S.). *Ramsay Muir: an Autobiography and Some Essays*. Pp. 222. Lund Humphries, 1943.

MARRIOTT, Sir John. *Memories of Four Score Years*. Pp. 262. Blackie, 1946.

ROYDEN, M. R. (Mrs. HUDSON SHAW). *A Threefold Cord*. Pp. 125. Gollancz, 1947.

HARTOG, M. *P. J. Hartog: a Memoir*. Pp. 186. Constable, 1949.

SADLEIR, M. *Michael Ernest Sadler*. Pp. 436. Constable, 1949. See also GRIER, L., *Achievement in Education—The Work of Michael Ernest Sadler, 1885-1935*, pp. 295, Constable, 1952.

CRANAGE, D. H. S. *Not only a Dean*. Pp. 240. Faith P., 1952.

WALLER, R. D. (ed.). *Harold Pilkington Turner: Memories of his Life and Personality*. Pp. 99. Manchester U.P., 1953.

CANTOR, L. M. *Halford Mackinder: a Pioneer of Adult Education*, in *R.H.P.*, Vol. III, IX, 1960-1, pp. 24-9.

For R. D. Roberts see **365.**

512. Accounts of work in individual Extra-Mural Departments:

Birmingham. DUDLEY, D. R. *A Survey of New Developments, 1945-55*. Pp. 26. The Department, 1956.

Hull. MAYFIELD, G. E. T. *The University of Hull Department of Adult Education, 1928-1960*, in U.C.A.E., *Report*, 1959-60.

Leeds. Tenth Annual Report, 1955-56. Pp. 32. 1956 (A review of ten years' work.)

Liverpool. McPHEE, A. *A Short History of Extra-Mural Work at Liverpool University*. Pp. 18. The Department, 1949. WILLIAMS, V. *A History of the Society for University Extension in Liverpool and District, 1899-1910*. Unpublished Dip.Ed. dissertation, Manchester Univ., 1959.

London. Extra-Mural Education in London, in U.C.A.E., *Report*, 1958-9.

Manchester. KELLY, T. *Outside the Walls: Sixty Years of University Extension at Manchester, 1886-1946*. Pp. 136. Manchester U.P., 1950. (Includes Liverpool and Leeds to 1903). STYLER, W. E. *Post-War in the North-West* in *A.E.*, Vol. XXX, 1957-8, pp. 20-8.

Nottingham. PEERS, R. *Adult Education in the East Midlands, 1920-26*. Pp. 43. The Department, 1926. PEERS R. *The Nottingham Experiment in Adult Education, 1920-35*, in *W.A.B.*, 2nd Ser., No. II, Aug. 1935, pp. 1-16. PEERS, R. *Extra-Mural Adult Education in the East Midlands*, in U.C.A.E., *Report*, 1957-8.

Wales. REES, A. D. *Adult Education in Wales*, in U.C.A.E., *Report*, 1956-7.

Brief accounts of work in various universities are to be found in *T.B.*, Nos. 84-92, 1951-3. For the Scottish universities see *S.A.E.* Nos. 1-2, Mar.-July, 1951. See also Annual Reports: Cambridge, from 1873; London, from 1876/7; Oxford, from 1885/6; Liverpool, from 1900/1; Manchester, from 1909/10; Aberystwyth, from 1919/20; Nottingham, from 1920/1; Wales, from 1921/2; others post 1939.

513. Histories of local centres:

COLMAN, H. C. *University Extension Lectures in Norwich: Diamond Jubilee 1877-1937*. Pp. 43. University Extension Society, Norwich, 1937.

WOOD, I. M. *Southport and Birkdale University Extension Society, 1874-1954*. Pp. 20. University Extension Society, Southport, 1954.

514. Histories of universities, especially the modern universities:

Birmingham. VINCENT, E. W., and HINTON, P. *The University of Birmingham: its History and Significance*. Pp. 246. Cornish, Birmingham, 1947.

Bristol. COTTLE, B., and SHERBORNE, J. W. *The Life of a University*. Pp. 155. Arrowsmith, Bristol, 1951, 2nd edn. 1959.

Exeter. PARRY, H. LL. *History of the Royal Albert Memorial College, Exeter.* Pp. 35. The College, Exeter, 1946.

Leeds. SHIMMIN, A. N. *The University of Leeds: the First Half-Century.* Pp. 236. Cambridge U.P., 1954.

Manchester. THOMPSON, J. *The Owens College: its Foundation and Growth.* Pp. 687. Cornish, Manchester, 1886.

North Staffordshire. GALLIE, W. B. *A New University: A. D. Lindsay and the Keele Experiment.* Pp. 152. Chatto and Windus, 1960. Cf. MALBON, G., *Adult Education in North Staffordshire and the Foundation of the University College at Keele,* in *R.H.P.,* Vol. III, III, 1954-5, pp. 34-49.

Nottingham. WOOD, A. C. *A History of the University College, Nottingham, 1881-1948.* Pp. 192. Blackwell, Oxford, 1953.

Reading. CHILDS, W. M. *The Making of a University.* Pp. 328. Dent, 1933.

Sheffield. CHAPMAN, A. W. *The Story of a Modern University.* Pp. 567. Oxford U.P., 1955.

Wales. EVANS, D. E. *The University of Wales: a Historical Sketch.* Pp. 188. Univ. of Wales P., Cardiff, 1953.

For Leicester see **258**.

515. Periodicals:

Oxford University Extension Gazette. Monthly. Vols. I-V, 1890-5.

University Extension Journal. At first monthly, later nine issues annually. Originally sponsored by London, later also by Oxford, Cambridge, and for a time Victoria University. Vols. I-V, 1890-5; N.S. Vols. I-IX, 1895-1904. Continued as *University Extension,* Nos. 1-9, 1904-7; *University Extension Bulletin,* Nos. 1-52, 1907-26; *Cambridge Bulletin of Extra-Mural Studies,* Nos. 1-8, 1926-31.

Cf. BIRKHEAD, E., *Journals of the University Extension Movement: 1890-1914,* in *A.E.,* Vol. XXXII, 1959-60, pp. 45-9.

Outlook. Bulletin of the Liverpool Univ. Extra-Mural Department: Twice annually, Nos. 1-3, 1960-1 (current).

See also below, Section III(b)(xi), and Subject Index *s.v.* Universities.

(x) Workers' Educational Association

516. ASSOCIATION TO PROMOTE THE HIGHER EDUCATION OF WORKING MEN, from 1905 WORKERS' EDUCATIONAL ASSOCIATION. *Annual Reports.* From 1903/4.

For a fuller picture Annual Reports of the District and Branch organisations should also be consulted.

517. TAWNEY, R. H. *An Experiment in Democratic Education,* in *Political Quarterly,* May 1914, pp. 62-84.

States the aims and ideals of the Association. Cf. TAWNEY'S Jubilee address, *The W.E.A. and Adult Education,* pp. 12, Athlone P., 1953.

518. BEGBIE, H. *Living Water: Chapters from the Romance of the Poor Student.* Pp. 210. [1918].

The story of some early student-leaders of the W.E.A.

519. MANSBRIDGE, A. *An Adventure in Working-Class Education: being the Story of the Workers' Educational Association, 1903-1915.* Pp. 93. Longmans, 1920.

An intimate narrative by the founder. See also **910**, which includes the three articles by Mansbridge in the *University Extension Journal* of 1903 which led to the foundation of the W.E.A.

520. PRICE, T. W. *The Story of the Workers' Educational Association, 1903-1924.* Pp. 94. Labour Publishing Co., 1924.

521. "DATALLER, R." [EAGLESTONE, A. A.] *Oxford into Coalfield.* Pp. 212. Dent, 1934.

Reminiscences of a tutor-organiser.

522. WORKERS' EDUCATIONAL ASSOCIATION. *Report on the Purpose and Organisation of the Association.* Pp. 14. 1934.

523. IRVING, J. *Youth and Adult Education—A W.E.A. Experiment,* in *W.A.B.*, 2nd Ser., No. X, Aug. 1937, pp. 21-32.
Describes an experiment in the education of the 18-25 age group.

524. WORKERS' EDUCATIONAL ASSOCIATION. *Workers' Education in Great Britain.* Pp. 35. 1944, 2nd ed., 1945.
An account of the Association's work since 1918. See also the Association's record of service by W.E.A. students on public bodies, *The Adult Student as Citizen*, pp. 59, 1938.

525. RAYBOULD, S. G. *The W.E.A.—the Next Phase.* Pp. 120. W.E.A., 1949.
Reviews the position of the W.E.A. and develops the view that it should be concerned with providing facilities for the "educationally underprivileged". This view gave rise to much discussion, especially in *The Highway*, Oct. 1949 onwards. An article by Raybould on *University Extension and the W.E.A.*, in *Hwy.*, Vol. XLVIII, 1956-7, pp. 68-71, provoked further controversy.

526. MARWICK, W. H. *The Workers' Educational Association in Scotland,* in *S.A.E.*, No. 8, Aug. 1953, pp. 10-13.
Brief account of the history of the W.E.A. in Scotland.

527. STOCKS, M. D. *The Workers' Educational Association—The First Fifty Years.* Pp. 158. Allen and Unwin, 1953.
See also the Jubilee recollections and comments by various writers in *Hwy.*, Vols. XLIV and XLV, Apr. and Oct., 1953, and three other W.E.A. publications of the Jubilee year: *W.E.A. Retrospect*, pp. 24; *The Workers' Educational Association, 1946-1952: a Review*, pp. 84; and *Jubilee Addresses on Adult Education*, pp. 56. The two former include useful statistical material.

528. WORKERS' EDUCATIONAL ASSOCIATION. *Memorandum on Matters Within the Scope of the Terms of Reference of the Committee Appointed to Review the Present System* [i.e. the Ashby Committee]. Pp. 48. 1955.
Cf. the W.E.A. statement on *Implications of the Ashby Report*, pp. 12, 1955.

529. ——— *Education for a Changing Society: The Role of the W.E.A.* Pp. 12. 1958.
Statement adopted at the 1958 Annual Conference.

530. MALONE, E. W. F. *The W.E.A.—A New Phase,* in *A.E.*, Vol. XXXIII, 1960-1, pp. 78-82, 116-21.
A review of developments since 1948 (cf. **525**).

531. Lives of leading figures:
[SMITH, M. F.]. *Arthur Lionel Smith, Master of Balliol (1916-1924)*. Pp. 326. Murray, 1928.
MANSBRIDGE, A. *The Trodden Road.* Pp. 316. Dent, 1940. (Includes sketches of Lord Haldane, R. St. John Parry, Reuben George, Harold Wright, Lord Sanderson and others).
IREMONGER, F. A. *William Temple, Archbishop of Canterbury.* Pp. 679. Oxford U.P., 1948.
SMITH, H. P. *Edward Stuart Cartwright,* in *R.H.P.*, Vol. III, I, 1949-50, pp. 8-24.
——— *G. D. H. Cole—an Appreciation,* in *R.H.P.*, Vol. III, VII, 1958-9, pp. 3-11.
WILLIAMS, J. R., TITMUSS, R. M., and FISHER, F. *J. R. H. Tawney.* Pp. 35. [W.E.A. 1960].

532. W.E.A. Branch and District histories (published, unless otherwise stated, by the Branch or District concerned):

ALLAWAY, A. J., and RAWSON, J. *The Rossendale Branch of the Workers' Educational Association.* Pp. 66 (duplicated). 1954.

SOUCH, W. J. *History of the Reading Branch of the Workers' Educational Association, 1904-54.* Pp. 20. 1954.

HARRISON, J. F. C. *Workers' Education in Leeds.* Pp. 27. 1957.

ALLAWAY, A. J. *The First Fifty Years of the W.E.A. in Leicester.* Pp. 54 (duplicated). Univ. of Leicester, Vaughan Coll. Papers No. 6, 1959.

EAGLE, E. C. *The East Midland District of the Workers' Educational Association.* Pp. 12. Derby, 1954.

WILLIAMS, C. R. *The South Wales District of the Workers' Educational Association, 1907-1957.* Pp. 24. [Cardiff] 1957.

533. Periodicals:

The Highway. Monthly 1908-23, quarterly 1923-25, thereafter monthly during the winter months only, with summer issue 1950-3. Vols. I-L, 1908-59. (The journal of the Association, recording the growth of the movement and reflecting the views of tutors and students.)

International Bulletin of Workers' Education. Irregular, Nos. 1-23 (duplicated), 1951-61 (current). International Federation of Workers' Educational Associations.

W.E.A. News. Half-yearly, Nos. 1-5, 1959-61 (current).

See also next two Sections, and Subject Index *s.v.* Workers' Educational Association.

(xi) University Tutorial Classes

534. *Oxford and Working-Class Education, being the Report of a Joint Committee of University and Working-Class Representatives on the Relation of the University to the Higher Education of Workpeople.* Pp. 190. Oxford U.P., 1908, 2nd edn. 1909, repr. 1951.

A document of cardinal importance, stating the principles of co-operation on which the tutorial class movement was built. Its significance is discussed by BRUCE, M., in *A.E.*, Vol. XXV, 1952-3, pp. 270-9.

535. CENTRAL JOINT ADVISORY COMMITTEE ON TUTORIAL CLASSES. *Annual Reports.* 1909-58.

Further information may be had from the reports of Joint Committees for Tutorial Classes at the various universities. The first two Reports of the Oxford Committee (1908-10) are particularly valuable on the early history of tutorial classes.

536. MANSBRIDGE, A. *University Tutorial Classes.* Pp. 209. Longmans, 1913.

Full statement of aims and early development, with valuable documentary appendices.

537. *The University Tutorial Class Movement,* in *W.A.B.,* 1st Ser., No. 11, Nov. 1919, pp. 30.

See further COLE, G. D. H., *The Tutorial Class in British Working-Class Education,* in *International Quarterly of Adult Education,* Vol. I, 1932-3, pp. 127-48; NICHOLSON, J. H., *Why Adult Education?* in *W.A.B.,* 2nd Ser., No. X, Aug. 1937, pp. 1-13.

538. MACK, J. A. (ed.). *The History of Tunstall II Tutorial Class, 1913-1934.* Pp. 52. Tunstall, 1935.

For other early tutorial classes see *Hwy.,* Vol. XLIV, 1952-3, pp. 253-61; SMITH, H. P., *A Tutorial Class makes History,* in *A.E.,* Vol. XXXI, 1958-9, pp. 271-80 (Longton).

539. SMITH, H. P. *Labour and Learning: Albert Mansbridge, Oxford and the W.E.A.* Pp. 92. Blackwell, Oxford, 1956.

540. RAYBOULD, S. G. *The University Tutorial Class in the United Kingdom*, in *F.A.E.*, Vol. IX, 1957, pp. 145–8.
An account of history, methods and results. For some interesting experiments see BAKER, W. P., *A Residential Tutorial Class for Rural Workers*, in *Hwy.*, Vol. XLV, 1953-4, pp. 11-13; and BRANDT, M., *A Women's Class solves a Tough Problem*, in *Hwy.*, Vol. XLVIII, 1956-7, pp. 122-4.

See also previous Sections, and Subject Index *s.v.* Universities.

(xii) Trade Unions and Allied Organisations

541. TRADES UNION CONGRESS. *Annual Reports.* From 1873.
Important for the development of trade union ideas in relation to adult education, especially in recent years. See especially Reports for 1954 (on the Ashby Committee), and for 1959-61 (on proposals for the reorganisation of trade union education).

542. TRADE UNION ENQUIRY COMMITTEE. *Report on Educational Facilities for Trade Unionists.* Pp. 35. 1921.

543. FIRTH, A. S. *Adult Education and the Trade Union Movement*, in *J.A.E.*, Vol. V, 1930-2, pp. 74-8.
Describes the changed attitude of the unions after the First World War.

544. WORKERS' EDUCATIONAL TRADE UNION COMMITTEE. *Annual Reports.* From 1931.
Covers the joint work of the W.E.A. and trade unions. For earlier information regarding the work of the Committee see Annual Reports of the W.E.A., from 1920 (**516**).

545. —— *Workers' Education and the Trade Union Movement: a Post-War Policy.* Pp. 24. 1944.

546. WORKERS' EDUCATIONAL ASSOCIATION. *The W.E.A. and the Working Class Movement.* Pp. 12. 1944.

547. MILLAR, J. P. M. *Forty Years of Independent Working-Class Education*, in *A.E.*, Vol. XXI, 1948-9, pp. 210-15.
Useful review of the work of the National Council of Labour Colleges in this field. The history, policy and activities of the N.C.L.C. are described in a variety of pamphlets by MILLAR, J. P. M. and others, issued from 1922 onwards and in many cases frequently reissued, e.g. *More Production—and More Poverty, The Trained Mind—Trained for What? Education and Power, What is Workers' Education?* See also articles in the Jubilee issue of *Plebs*, Vol. LI., Feb. 1959.

548. WORKERS' EDUCATIONAL TRADE UNION COMMITTEE. *The Workers' Educational Trade Union Committee: Administration, Finance, and Structure.* Pp. 31. 1949.
This report was the basis of the revised constitution introduced 1950. Cf. GREGORY, W.C.E., *Three Aspects of the W.E.T.U.C.*, in *A.E.*, Vol. XXXI, 1958-9, pp. 210-15.

549. TURNER, H. A. *The N.C.L.C., the W.E.A. and the Unions*, in *Plebs*, Vol. XLIII, 1951, pp. 271-6, and Vol. XLIV, 1952, pp. 16-20.
On the work of the two organisations and effects of their rivalry, with interpolated editorial comment.

550. WINTERBOTTOM, A. *T.U.C. Training Courses*, in *Progress*, Vol. XLII, 1952, pp. 30-6.
Description of work of the London education centre of the T.U.C.

551. CHESTER, T. E. *Education for Trade Union Members—Some Approaches and Suggestions*, in *A.E.*, Vol. XXV, 1952-3, pp. 20-9.
For further accounts of experiments in trade union education, and for discussion of principles and methods, see STUTTARD, C. G., *Linked Week-end Schools*, in *Hwy.*, Vol. XLV, 1953-4, pp. 162-5; CYNOG-JONES, T. W., *Education for Trade Unionists*, in *Hwy.*, Vol. XLVII, 1955-6, pp. 106-9; ROLFE, R. W., *Shiftworkers' Tutorial*, in *Hwy.*, Vol. XLVIII, 1956-7, pp. 173-5; MARSH, A. I., *Trade Unions and Workers' Education*, in *R.H.P.*, Vol. III, VI, 1957-8, pp. 27-36, and *The New Workers' Education*, in *A.E.*, Vol. XXXI, 1958-9, pp. 126-30; CORFIELD, A. J., *Education in the Transport and General Workers' Union*, in *R.H.P.*, Vol. III, VIII, 1959-60, pp. 9-15; and numerous articles in *Trade Union Education* (558).

552. COLE, G. D. H. *An Introduction to Trade Unionism*. Pp. 324. Allen and Unwin, 1953.
On trade unions and education see pp. 188-205. Cf. COLE, G. D. H., *Organised Labour*, pp. 194, Allen and Unwin, 1924, pp. 112-16; ROBERTS, B. C., *Trade Union Government and Administration in Great Britain*, pp. 572, Bell, 1956, Ch. xiv.

553. WORKERS' EDUCATIONAL ASSOCIATION. *Trade Union Education*. Pp. 120. 1953.
Report of a Working Party set up by the W.E.A. in 1951.

554. WILLIAMS, J. E. *An Experiment in Trade Union Education*, in *A.E.*, Vol. XXVII, 1954-5, pp. 113-24.
On day-release courses for miners arranged by Sheffield Extra-Mural Department. Cf. THORNTON, A. H., *Day-Release for Liberal Studies*, in *A.E.*, Vol. XXIX, 1956-7, pp. 197-204, and *Liberal Studies for Factory Workers*, in *A.E.*, Vol. XXXIII, 1960-1, pp. 13-15; COLTHAM, S. W., *Adult Education for North Staffordshire Mineworkers*, in *R.H.P.*, Vol. III, VII, 1958-9, pp. 20-9.

555. INTERNATIONAL LABOUR ORGANISATION. *Review of the Past Activities of the I.L.O. in the Field of Workers' Education*. Pp. 30. *Methods and Techniques of Workers' Education*. Pp. 65. *The Scope and Content of Workers' Education Programmes*. Pp. 42. Geneva, 1957.
Documents prepared for 1957 conference on workers' education.

556. CLEGG, H. A., and ADAMS, R. *Trade Union Education*. Pp. 102. W.E.A. 1959.
Valuable independent report sponsored by the W.E.A. Discussed by BAYLISS, F. J., *The Future of Trade Union Education*, in *A.E.*, Vol. XXXII, 1959-60, pp. 109-15.

557. WORKERS' EDUCATIONAL ASSOCIATION AND WORKERS' EDUCATIONAL TRADE UNION COMMITTEE. *Statement submitted at the Invitation of the Trade Union Congress in connection with consideration of the 1957 Congress Motion calling for a co-ordinated Educational Policy with Affiliated Unions and other Educational Bodies*. Pp. 23. 1959.
Cf. *The N.C.L.C.'s Rationalisation Proposals*, in *Plebs*, Vol. LI, 1959, pp. 169-71, and articles on this subject by MILLAR, J. P. M., in the same journal from 1957 onwards.

558. Periodicals:
Plebs. Monthly. Vols. I-LIII, 1909-1961 (current). Published originally by Plebs League, from 1927 by National Council of Labour Colleges; at Oxford 1909-19, London 1919-40, Tillicoultry since 1940. (Informative on work of the National Council of Labour Colleges and the trade unions supporting it, with much general comment on trade union education.)
Trade Union Education. Nos. 1-8, 1955-61 (current), W.E.A. (Short articles on work in progress in trade unions and W.E.A. districts.)

See also **17, 129, 138-9, 382.**

(xiii) Adult Education under the auspices of
Local Education Authorities

559. WEBB, S. *The London Polytechnic Institutes*, in DEPARTMENT OF EDUCATION, *Special Reports on Educational Subjects*, Vol. II, 1898.
Cf. JOHNSON, F. *The London Polytechnic Movement*, unpublished M.A. thesis, London Univ., 1929.

560. WOOD, E. M. (*née* HOGG). *The Polytechnic and its Founder Quintin Hogg.* Pp. 383. Nisbet, 1904, rev. edn. 1932.
The story of the Regent Street Polytechnic. Cf. BAYLEY, E., *The Borough Polytechnic: its Origin and Development*, pp. 95, 1910; BROOKS, C., *An Educational Adventure: a History of the Woolwich Polytechnic*, pp. 165, 1955; and jubilee histories of the Chelsea Polytechnic (pp. 8, 1945), Northern Polytechnic (pp. 32, 1946), and Northampton Polytechnic (pp. 20, 1946).

561. SADLER, M. E. (ed.). *Continuation Schools in England and Elsewhere.* Pp. 805. Manchester U.P., 1907, 2nd edn. 1908.
Has long and valuable introductory survey of the history of adult education. (Ch. i). Bibliography.

562. BRITISH INSTITUTE OF ADULT EDUCATION. Report of Second Annual Conference. *Adult Education and the Local Education Authority.* Pp. 47. 1923.
Includes also papers on Public Libraries and Adult Education, Music and Drama in Adult Education.

563. MORRIS, H. *The Village College: a Memorandum.* Pp. 27. Cambridge, 1924.
On the development of village colleges in Cambridgeshire, foreshadowed in this memorandum, see further DENT, H. C., *The Countryman's College*, pp. 32, British Council, 1943; WILTSHIRE, H. C., *Impington and Adult Education*, in *A.E.*, Vol. XVII, 1944-5, pp. 125-34; HOLBROOK, D., *Sweetness and Light for Hodge*, in *J.E.*, Vol. LXXXVIII, 1956, pp. 138-42; HARVEY, J., *The Arthur Mellows Village College, Glinton*, in *The Village*, Vol. X, 1955, pp. 63-6; HUNTER, M., *Village College*, in *A.E.*, Vol. XXX, 1960-1, pp. 310-14. Cf. WILLIAMS, R. D., *A Pilot Project in Leicestershire*, in *A.E.*, Vol. XXVIII, 1955-6, pp. 273-8.

564. BOARD OF EDUCATION. *The Work of Men's Institutes in London.* Pp. 16. H.M.S.O., 1926.
See also MYERS, S., and RAMSAY, E., *London Men and Women: an Account of the L.C.C. Men's and Women's Institutes.* WILLIAMS, T. G., *Adult Education under the London County Council*, in *W.A.B.*, 2nd Ser., No. I, June 1935, pp. 3-21, is an informative general survey, 1870-1935.

565. LONDON COUNTY COUNCIL—EDUCATION COMMITTEE. *The Literary Institutes of London.* Pp. 24. 1929.
The story of the most famous of the Institutes is told in WILLIAMS, T. G., *The City Literary Institute*, pp. 60, St. Catherine P., 1960.

566. JAMES, C. *Adult Education in Rural Lancashire*, in *J.A.E.*, Vol. V, 1930-2, pp. 129-35.
A survey of developments 1928-31. See further MEADON, P., *The Work of the Local Education Authority in Adult Education with special reference to Rural Areas*, in *A.E.*, Vol. X, 1937-8, pp. 309-24.

567. BOARD OF EDUCATION—ADULT EDUCATION COMMITTEE. Paper No. 11. *Adult Education and the Local Education Authority.* Pp. 171. H.M.S.O., 1933.
A valuable survey of L.E.A. activity, with historical introduction.

49

568. THOMAS, B. B. *Adult Education in Wales and the Statutory Body*, in *A.E.*, Vol. XI, 1938-9, pp. 139-51.
Thoughtful survey of special needs and organisation in Wales.

569. KENT EDUCATION COMMITTEE. *Adult Education in Kent*. Pp. 36. Maidstone, 1945. Cf. JESSUP, F. W., *Post-War Developments in Adult Education in Kent*, in *A.E.*, Vol. XXIV, 1951-2, pp. 91-7.

570. WATKINS, H. M. *Unusual Students*. Pp. 143. Evans, Liverpool, 1947.
Experiences of a tutor in adult education in Glamorganshire, and sketches of students.

571. NATIONAL FOUNDATION FOR ADULT EDUCATION. *Adult Education in the Development Plans of L.E.A.s*. Pp. 80. 1948.
Report of the Foundation's First Annual Conference. The L.E.A. Schemes for Further Education, prepared at this time for submission to the Ministry, and often published, provide a useful record of existing facilities and plans for development under the 1944 Act. For examples of the work of particular authorities see numerous articles in *Adult Education*, e.g. FAIRLESS, T. A. A., *Blackburn People's College*, Vol. XXII, 1949-50, pp. 134-40; CHESSEL, H., *Adult Education in a Local Authority* [Croydon], Vol. XXIII, 1950-1, pp. 97-105; FLOWER, F. D., *Adult Education in the Technical College* [Hendon], Vol. XXIV, 1951-2, pp. 107-13; WILLIAMS, I. C., *The L.E.A. and Recreational Education* [Salford], Vol. XXIV, 1951-2, pp. 256-68; FAIRBAIRN, A. N., *The Whitefield Centre*, Vol. XXXIII, 1960-1, pp. 315-18.

572. NATIONAL INSTITUTE OF ADULT EDUCATION. *Social Aspects of Further Education: a Survey of Local Education Authority Action*. Pp. 59. N.I.A.E., 1952.
A statistical survey and consideration of problems arising.

573. MINISTRY OF EDUCATION. Pamphlet No. 28. *Evening Institutes*. Pp. 54. H.M.S.O., 1956.
Review of the work of evening institutes, with suggestions for further development. See comments by various writers in *A.E.*, Vol. XXIX, 1956-7, pp. 14-23.

574. EDWARDS, H. J. *The Evening Institute*. Pp. 192. N.I.A.E., 1961.
Valuable historical survey and review of current position. Cf. FIELDING, J. T., *The Place of the Evening Institute in Further Education in the East Midlands*, unpublished M.Ed. thesis, Nottingham Univ., 1951; FORTH, E. M., *Adult Education according to Women*, in *A.E.*, Vol. XXVIII, 1955-6, pp. 168-80 (history of the Stoke Newington Women's Institute, 1885-1955).

See also Subject Index, *s.v.* Evening Institute, Local Education Authorities.

(xiv) Non-residential Adult Education Centres

University and Social Settlements

575. WOODS, R. A. *English Social Movements*. Pp. 284. 1892.
An American view of university settlements and Extension work in England.

576. KNAPP, J. M. (ed.). *The Universities and the Social Problem*. Pp. 245. 1895.
An account of university settlements in East London.

577. REASON, W. (ed.). *University and Social Settlements*. Pp. 207. 1898.
Valuable survey by various authors, with directory of organisations.

578. PICHT, W. *Toynbee Hall und die englische Settlement-Bewegung*. Pp. 229. Tübingen, 1913. Eng. edn., *Toynbee Hall and the Settlement Movement*, pp. 260, Bell, 1914.
Full account of Toynbee Hall and general sketch of the movement elsewhere. Appendices on University Extension and the W.E.A. Bibliography.

579. FREEMAN, A. *Education through Settlements.* Pp. 63. Allen and Unwin [1919]. A detailed account of ideals, methods and organisation.

580. [YEAXLEE, B. A. (ed.)]. *Settlements and their Outlook.* Pp. 192. King, 1922. Proceedings of the First International Conference of Settlements.

581. BRITISH ASSOCIATION OF RESIDENTIAL SETTLEMENTS. Annual Reports for various years, 1930/1 to 1943/4.

582. Lives of pioneers, e.g.
ROWLEY. C. *Fifty Years of Work without Wages.* Pp. 260. Hodder and Stoughton, 1911. (On work at Ancoats, Manchester).
BARNETT, S. A. *Canon Barnett, His Life, Work and Friends.* 2v. Murray, 1918, 2nd edn. 1919. (First Warden of Toynbee Hall).

583. Histories of individual settlements:
[HOROBIN, I. M.]. *Mansfield House University Settlement.* Pp. 28. [1925].
RODGERS, J. *Mary Ward Settlement: a History, 1891-1931.* Pp. 19. The Settlement, 1931.
PIMLOTT, J. A. R. *Toynbee Hall: Fifty Years of Social Progress, 1884-1934.* Pp. 335. Dent, 1935.
STOCKS, M. D. *Fifty Years in Every Street* [Manchester University Settlement]. Pp. 152. Manchester U.P., 1945, 2nd edn. 1956.

See also **29, 192-4, 370.**

Educational Settlements and Centres

584. GILLMAN, F. J. *The Workers and Education.* Pp. 68. Allen and Unwin [1916]. Deals with early years at Woodbrooke, Fircroft, and settlements at Leeds, York, Wakefield, Leamington, and Birkenhead.

585. EDUCATIONAL SETTLEMENTS ASSOCIATION. *What Educational Settlements are Doing.* Pp. 20. 1921.
The first of a number of statements in which the Association argued the case for non-residential adult education centres.

586. BRITISH INSTITUTE OF ADULT EDUCATION. *The Guildhouse: a Co-operative Centre for Adult Education.* Pp. 111. 1924.
Report of a Commission on the educational functions of settlements, with bibliography. An *Interim Report*, pp. 12, was published in 1922.

587. *Educational Settlements in England*, in *W.A.B.*, 1st Ser., No. XXVII, Feb. 1926, pp. 1-11.
See further FLEMING, H., *Educational Settlements Association Retrospect, 1914-30*, in *Friends' Quarterly Examiner*, Vol. LXV, 1931, pp. 62-75; EDUCATIONAL SETTLEMENTS ASSOCIATION (from 1945 EDUCATIONAL CENTRES ASSOCIATION), *Annual Reports* (especially those for 1956-9).

588. WATKINS, Sir P. E. *Educational Settlements in South Wales and Monmouthshire.* Pp. 15. Privately published by Wardens' Group of South Wales Educational Settlements, Cardiff, 1940.
A valuable survey of a distinctive group of settlements.

589. ALLAWAY, A. J. *The Educational Centres Movement: a Comprehensive Survey.* Pp. 99. N.I.A.E., 1961.
A brief history of the movement, and an account of its spread.

590. Histories of individual centres:

BRAYSHAW, W. M. B. *The Wilmslow Beacon Guild, 1926-36.* Pp. 16. Privately pubd., 1936.

FLEMING, H. *Beechcroft: the Story of the Birkenhead Settlement. 1919-24.* Pp. 116. E.S.A., 1938.

HUGHES, M. W. (ed.). *An Experiment in Adult Education in the City of Leeds, 1909-1949.* Pp. 11. Swarthmore Centre, Leeds, 1949.

COULSON, S. J. *From Forces Centre to Folk House* [Bristol], in *A.E.,* Vol. XXIII, 1950-1, pp. 199-205.

MILTON, A. *Dartington Adult Education Centre, 1947-1950,* in *A.E.,* Vol. XXIII, 1950-1, pp. 206-11.

HAZELTON, W. *Maes-yr-Haf, 1927-1952.* Pp. 14. Maes-yr-Haf Settlement, Trealaw, 1952.

ROBERTS, H. D. *Oxford House, Risca, Jubilee Handbook.* Pp. 32. Oxford House, 1956.

ALDERTON, E. *Bexley Adult Education Centre: the First Decade.* Pp. 28. The Centre, 1960.

591. Periodicals:

The Common Room. Quarterly. Nos. 1-76, 1924-50. The journal of the Educational Settlements Association, afterwards Educational Centres Association. Succeeded by *Phoenix.* Twice yearly, Nos. 1-14, 1951-8. E.S.A.

See also **1074**, and for centres under L.E.A. auspices Section III (b) (xiii).

Community Centres

592. NATIONAL COUNCIL OF SOCIAL SERVICE. *New Housing Estates and their Social Problems.* Pp. 48. 1935, 3rd edn. 1950.
On the value of community centres, with a list of publications.

593. *Adult Education,* Vol. XI, No. 1, Sept. 1938.
A Community Centres number, with articles by various writers.

594. PEARSE, I. H., and CROCKER, L. H. *The Peckham Experiment.* Pp. 333. Allen and Unwin, 1943.
On the history and ideals of the Peckham Health Centre, and its educational significance.

595. NATIONAL ASSOCIATION OF WOMEN'S CLUBS. *Club Management.* Pp. 24. N.C.S.S., 1945, 4th edn. 1959.
Handbook for guidance of women's clubs or sections of community associations.

596. THOROLD, H. K., and FARROW, D. G. *Community Centres: Some Service Experiences.* Pp. 37. Home and Van Thal, 1945.
On an R.A.F. Education Centre.

597. MINISTRY OF EDUCATION. *Community Centres.* Pp. 40. H.M.S.O., 1946.
A report on purposes, organisation and methods.

598. HARRIS, E. S., and MOLLOY, P. N. *The Watling Community Association: the First 21 Years.* Pp. 63. Watling Community Association, 1949.
A history of one of the earliest associations.

599. MARKS, H. E. S. *Community Associations and Adult Education.* Pp. 43. N.F.C.A. and N.C.S.S., 1949.
Cf. HOLE, R. H., *Adult Education in a Community Centre* [Lymington], in *A.E.,* Vol. XXIV, 1951-2, pp. 128-34.

600. NATIONAL FEDERATION OF COMMUNITY ASSOCIATIONS. *Our Neighbourhood: a Handbook of Information for Community Centres and Associations.* Pp. 95. N.C.S.S., 1950, 2nd edn. 1955. *A Handbook on Administration for Community Associations.* Pp. 40. N.C.S.S., 1959.

601. MORIARTY, D. R. *Twenty Years a-Growing.* Pp. 8. N.C.S.S., 1952 (reprinted from *Social Service*, Vol. XXVI, 1952).
On the development and problems of community centres. See further TYLECOTE, M., *Old Towns and New*, in *A.E.*, Vol. XXVII, 1954-5, pp. 189-96; BLACKIE, J. E. H., *Culture and Environment*, pp. 16, N.F.C.A., 1955.

602. WILCOX, A. *Community Centres—the Consumers' View*, in *A.E.*, Vol. XXV, 1952-3, pp. 101-11.
Based on an inquiry in ten Community Associations in Manchester.

603. UNITED NATIONS. *Development of Community Welfare Centres in the United Kingdom.* Pp. 37. H.M.S.O., 1953.

604. Periodicals:
Community News. Monthly. Vols. I-II, 1948-50. N.F.C.A. Continued as
Community News Bulletin. Irregular, Nos. 1-47, 1950-61 (current).
The Neighbourhood Worker. Three or four issues yearly, 1957-61 (current).

See also **168, 366, 833, 846, 1068, 1098.**

(xv) Residential Colleges for Adult Education

605. HOERNER, M. *Die Heimschulen in der englischen Arbeiterbildung.* Pp. 110. Quelle und Meyer, Leipzig, 1930.
Useful factual review of residential adult education at this period, including Winter Schools of the National Adult School Union.

606. EDUCATIONAL SETTLEMENTS ASSOCIATION. *People's Colleges for Residential Adult Education.* Pp. 31. 1943.
Survey of past experience and proposals for the future.

607. SPEAK, L. *Residential Adult Education in Great Britain.* Unpublished M.A. thesis, Leeds Univ., 1949.
Useful survey of developments over the preceding fifty years.

See also **382, 867,** and prospectuses and annual reports of individual colleges, listed in **40.**

Long-Term Colleges

608. PLUMMER, A. *The Residential Colleges in Adult Education*, in *J.A.E.*, Vol. V, 1930-2, pp. 405-17.
See further THOMAS, B. B., *The Place of the Residential College in Adult Education*, in *A.E.*, Vol. VIII, 1935-6, pp. 100-10; DUDLEY, J., *The Residential College*, in *W.A.B.*, 2nd Ser., No. VIII, Feb. 1937, pp. 16-26; DUDLEY, J., *Residential Adult Education in Britain*, in *A.E.*, Vol. XIV, 1941-2, pp. 70-6; HUGHES, H. D., *The Long Term Residential Colleges and the L.E.A.s*, in *A.E.*, Vol. XXIV, 1951-2, pp. 143-9; and LYLE, E. A., *Reflections on Residential Adult Education*, in *A.E.*, Vol. XXVI, 1953-4, pp. 190-6.

609. EDUCATIONAL SETTLEMENTS ASSOCIATION. *Residential Colleges for Adult Education.* Pp. 16. 1934.
Brief account of each college. For the post-war situation see RESIDENTIAL COLLEGES COMMITTEE, *Colleges for Adult Students*, pp. 15, 1947.

610. Accounts of individual colleges:

Avoncroft. *Avoncroft College for Rural Workers*, in *W.A.B.*, 2nd Ser., No. VIII, Feb. 1937, pp. 31-7; Avoncroft College, *Avoncroft: an Experiment in Rural Education*, pp. 21, 1944.

Catholic Workers' College. Somerville, H., *A Catholic Labour College*, in *Studies*, Vol. X, 1921, pp. 392-400.

Coleg Harlech. Articles under this title in *W.A.B.*, 1st Ser., No. XXXIV, Nov. 1927, pp. 22-6, and 2nd Ser., No. VI, Aug. 1936, pp. 1-10. See also **365**.

Co-operative College. Hall, F., *The Co-operative College and its Work*. Pp. 18. Co-operative Union, Manchester, 1928. Marshall, R. L., *The Co-operative College*, in *A.E.*, Vol. XX, 1947-8, pp. 129-33. Garratt, R., *A New Appraisal of the Co-operative College*, in *Agenda*, Vol. III, 1956, pp. 21-31.

Fircroft. Wood, H. G., and Ball, A. E., *Tom Bryan: First Warden of Fircroft*. Pp. 156. Allen and Unwin, 1922. Pumphrey, M. E., *Recollections of Fircroft*. Pp. 84. Fircroft College, 1952. Leighton, W. H., *Fircroft, 1909-1959*. Pp. 71. Fircroft College, 1959.

Hillcroft. *Hillcroft College*, in *W.A.B.*, 1st Ser., No. XXXVII, Aug. 1928, pp. 21-7. Street, F., *An Experiment in Adult Education for Working Women*, in *J.A.E.*, Vol. III, 1928-9, pp. 186-91. McKay, S., *Hillcroft College, Surbiton*, in *W.A.B.*, 2nd Ser., No. XVII, May 1939, pp. 2-11. Paice, D. R., *Do you know Hillcroft?* in *A.E.*, Vol. XXVIII, 1955-6, pp. 254-9.

Newbattle Abbey. Mack, J. A., *Newbattle Abbey and What it is Accomplishing*. Pp. 18. B.I.A.E., 1938. For later history see notes in *S.A.E.*, Nos. 1, 2 and 4, 1951-2.

Ruskin College. Buxton, C. S., *Ruskin College: an Educational Experiment*, in *Cornhill Magazine*, Vol. XXV, 1958, pp. 192-200. Plebs League, *The Burning Question of Education*. Pp. 24. Oxford, 1909, 2nd edn. 1909. Furniss, H. S. (Lord Sanderson), *Memories of Sixty Years*. Pp. 274. Methuen, 1931. *The Story of Ruskin College*. Pp. 25. Oxford U.P., 1949, 2nd edn. 1955.

Woodbrooke. Rowntree, A. S., *Woodbrooke: its History and Aims*. Pp. 87. Woodbrooke Extension Committee, Birmingham, 1923. Davis, R. (ed.), *Woodbrooke 1903-1953: a Quaker Experiment in Religious Education*. Pp. 191. Bannisdale P., 1953.

William Temple College. Batten, E. M., *Report on William Temple College, 1955-1960*. Pp. 21. 1960.

See also **1019, 1130**.

Short-Term Colleges

611. Hunter, G. *Residential Colleges: some New Developments in British Adult Education*. Pp. 78. Fund for Adult Education, Occasional Papers No. 1, White Plains, N.Y., 1952.

Discussion of the development and policy of the short-term colleges. Cf. Ritchie, W. D., *Short-Term Residential Colleges for Adult Education*, in *S.A.E.*, No. 6, Dec. 1952, pp. 10-17.

612. Hughes, A. M. *Some Problems of the Short-Term Adult Residential College in Post-War Britain*. Unpublished M.A. thesis, Liverpool Univ., 1954.

613. Accounts of individual colleges:

Burton Manor. Newton, J. *Burton Manor: the First Ten Years*. Pp. 20. The College [1958].

Holly Royde. Waller, R. D., *Residential College: Origins of the Lamb Guildhouse and Holly Royde*. Pp. 69. Manchester U.P., 1954.

Pendley. Williams, D., *Pendley and a Pack of Hounds*. Pp. 191. Hodder and Stoughton, 1959.

Urchfont Manor. *Urchfont Manor: Reflections on the First Ten Years by the Governors*, in *A.E.*, Vol. XXX, 1957-8, pp. 110-117.

See also **620, 992**.

(xvi) Education in H.M. Forces

614. DAVIES, A. T. *Student Captives.* Pp. 29. 1917. *Student Captives II.* Pp. 36. 1918. British Prisoners of War Book Scheme.
An account of the operation of the scheme during the First World War. HOLLAND, R. W., *Adversis Major*, pp. 163, Staples, 1949, describes similar work during the Second World War.

615. GORELL, LORD. *Education and the Army.* Pp. 291. Oxford U.P., 1921.
On the beginnings of serious adult education in the Army from 1917 onwards.

616. WAR OFFICE. *Education in the War-time Army.* Pp. 8. 1940.
The starting-point of the war-time developments. Other War Office publications include *Army Education Scheme (Release Period)*, pp. 8, 1944 (described by PHILIPS, C. H., in *A.E.*, Vol. XVII, 1944-5, pp. 68-74); *The A.B.C.A. Handbook*, pp. 38, 1945 (on the Army Bureau of Current Affairs); *Organisation Handbook (Army Education Scheme)*, pp. 75, 1945; *Handbook of General Education*, pp. 166, 1948; and with CENTRAL OFFICE OF INFORMATION, *Education during National Service*, pp. 8, H.M.S.O., 1952. Except for the last item, publication was restricted.

617. SHAWYER, R. C. *The Army Fights Illiteracy*, in *A.E.*, Vol. XVII, 1944-5, pp. 74-83.
On this subject see also WALL, W. D., *Reading Backwardness among Men in the Army*, *B.J.E.P.*, Vol. XV, 1945, pp. 28-40, Vol. XVI, 1946, pp. 133-48; CUMMINS, A. J. E., *Historical Survey of Illiteracy in the Army*, in *Army Education*, Vol. XXVI, 1952, pp. 80-6, Vol. XXVII, 1953, pp. 14-19, 72-8.

618. BURGE, C. G. (ed.). *Window to a Fuller Life.* Pp. 44. Gale and Polden, 1945.
Essays on education by Sir R. Livingstone and others, with special reference to the R.A.F. Some of the contributions are reprinted from the *R.A.F. Quarterly*, 1944. Cf. POLLOCK, C. W., *Education in the Royal Air Force*, in *R.A.F. Quarterly*, Vol. XX, 1949, pp. 98-103.

619. CLARK, G. *Adult Education in the Royal Navy*, in *Education*, Vol. LXXXVI, July 1945, pp. 7-9.

620. *Formation Colleges*, in *A.E.*, Vol. XIX, 1946-7, pp. 63-7.
See further WILBE-JONES, K., CHAPMAN, H., and GARRARD, W. V., *And Then There was One*, in *Army Education*, Vol. XXIV, 1950, pp. 116-26.

621. HAWKINS, T. H., and BRIMBLE, L. J. F. *Adult Education: the Record of the British Army.* Pp. 428. Macmillan, 1947.
Though mainly concerned with the Second World War and after, gives the only published general account of historical development. See also HANCOCK, S. T. R., *Education and the Army*, unpublished M.Ed. thesis, Manchester Univ., 1949 (a careful history to 1939); BOWYER-BOWER, T. A., *A Survey of Some Early Developments in Army Education*, in *Army Education*, Vol. XXVII, 1953, pp. 5-12; and the same author's *Some Sources for the History of Education in the British Army during the 19th Century*, in *B.J.E.S.*, Vol. IV, 1954-5, pp. 71-7.

622. PAFFORD, J. H. P. *Books and Army Education, 1944-46: Preparation and Supply.* Pp. 72. ASLIB, 1947.

623. WAVELL, LORD. *Minerva's Owl, or Education in the Army.* Pp. 18. Birkbeck College, 1948.
A clear summary of the history and functions of Army Education.

624. WILSON, N. S. *Education in the Forces 1939-46: the Civilian Contribution.* Pp. 181. Evans [1949].
A detailed factual survey written for the Central Advisory Council for Adult Education in H.M. Forces. See also JOBEY, G., *Civilian Aid to Adult Education in the Army*, in *T.B.*, No. 95/96, June-Sept. 1954, pp. 5-11 (on work in the Durham area); MACGREGOR, J., *The Development of Adult Education in the Army, with special reference to the Organisation of Civilian Aid in Army Education since 1914*, unpublished Ph.D. thesis, Leeds Univ., 1954.

625. LLOYD, C. *British Services Education.* Pp. 95. British Council, 1950.
Describes provision in the three Services.

626. CENTRAL COMMITTEE FOR ADULT EDUCATION IN H.M. FORCES. *Annual Reports,* 1951/2 to 1960/1.

627. Periodical: *Army Education.* Quarterly, Vols. I-XXIX, 1924-57 (publication irregular during Second World War). Incorporated from 1957 in *Torch* (house journal of the Royal Army Education Corps, half-yearly, Vols. I-IV, 1953-61, current).

See also **221, 264, 349, 596, 656, 874, 947, 1155-6.**

(xvii) Adult Education in the Merchant Navy

628. SEAFARERS' EDUCATION SERVICE (from 1938 Seafarers' Education Service and College of the Sea). *Annual Reports,* from 1920. *The Ship's Library: Six Years' Experience,* pp. 36, 1926. Periodical: *The Seafarer,* quarterly, Nos. 1-112, 1934-61 (current) (see espec. No. 77, Jan. 1953, Memorial Issue on the founder, Albert Mansbridge).

629. FAYLE, C. E. *Harold Wright: a Memoir.* Pp. 187. Allen and Unwin, 1934.
See especially Ch. viii.

630. COOK, H. K. *In the Watch Below.* Pp. 181. Dent, 1937.

631. RYDER, R. *The College of the Sea,* in *W.A.B.,* 2nd Ser., No. XX, Feb. 1940, pp. 13-22.
See further HOPE, R., *Further Education for Merchant Seafarers,* pp. 8, reprinted from *F.E.,* Vol. I, 1947-8; HOPE, R., *International Understanding and the Seafarer,* in *A.E.,* Vol. XXVIII, 1955-6, pp. 38-45.

632. HOPE, R. *Spare Time at Sea.* Pp. 176. Maritime P., 1954.

(xviii) Adult Education in Hospitals

633. WILLIAMS, W. E. *A New Field of Provision: Adult Education in Hospitals,* in *A.E.,* Vol. IX, 1936-7, pp. 144-7.
Describes an experimental scheme in convalescent, T.B., and similar hospitals.

634. LAWLEY-WAKELIN, D. *The Epsom Experiment,* in *A.E.,* Vol. XXV, 1952-3, pp. 130-5.
Describes the achievements of a B.I.A.E. experiment in mental hospitals. Cf. the same author's *Adult Education by Mental Hospitals,* in *A.E.,* Vol. XX, 1947-8, pp. 145-51.

(xix) Adult Education in Prisons

635. DOUIE, C. O. G. *The Drama in Prisons,* in *J.A.E.,* Vol. I, 1926-7, pp. 56-9.
Cf. BELL, V. A., *Educational Classes in Prisons,* in *J.A.E.,* Vol. V, 1930-2, pp. 175-85; INGRAM, B., *Education in Prisons,* in *A.E.,* Vol. X, 1937-8, pp. 33-9; A TEACHER, *Students behind Bars,* in *Hwy,* Vol. L, 1948-9, pp. 100-2 (on women prisoners); SALKELD, P. T., *Prison Education To-day,* in *F.E.,* Vol. III, 1949-50, pp. 150-6; DOUIE, C. O. G., *The Unsolved Conflict: Prison,* in *J.E.,* Vol. LXXXII, 1950, pp. 74-8; and HOWARD, D. L., *Education as Social Rehabilitation at H.M. Prison, Eastchurch,* in *A.E.,* Vol. XXXI, 1958-9, pp. 190-202.

636. BANKS, F. *Teach Them to Live.* Pp. 295. Parrish, 1958.
The fullest study of educational work in English prisons. There are briefer accounts in two works by FOX, Sir L. W., *The Modern English Prison,* pp. 277, Routledge, 1934, and *The English Prison and Borstal Systems,* pp. 493, Routledge and Kegan Paul, 1952. For detailed information see annual *Reports of the Commissioners of Prisons* (H.M.S.O.).

(xx) Women's Organisations

Women's Institutes

637. NATIONAL FEDERATION OF WOMEN'S INSTITUTES. *Annual Reports,* from 1917; *Handbook,* annually from 1921; *Music Handbook,* pp. 47, 1954, rev. edn. 1960; *Drama Handbook,* pp. 38, 1957; *Introducing the Women's Institutes,* pp. 32, Gryphon Books, 1951. Periodical: *Home and Country,* monthly, Vols. I-XLIII, 1919-61 (current).

638. WATT, A., and LLOYD, N. (eds.). *The First Women's Institute School.* Pp. 168. Sussex Federation of W.I.s [1918].

639. BOARD OF EDUCATION. *Report of H.M. Inspectors on the Educational Work of Women's Rural Institutes.* Pp. 22. H.M.S.O., 1925.

640. SCOTT, J. W. R. *The Story of the Women's Institute Movement.* Pp. 306. Village P., Idbury, 1925.

641. COURTNEY, J. E. *Countrywomen in Council.* Pp. 203. Oxford U.P., 1933.

642. BLAIR, C. *Rural Journey.* Pp. 166. Nelson, 1941.
The story of the first twenty-one years of the Scottish Women's Rural Institutes.

643. DENEKE, H. *Grace Hadow.* Pp. 231. Oxford U.P., 1946.
A pioneer in the work of Women's Institutes. See also HUXLEY, G., *Lady Denman,* pp. 205, Chatto and Windus, 1961.

644. JENKINS, I. *History of the Women's Institutes of England and Wales.* Pp. 181. Oxford U.P., 1953.

645. SCOTTISH WOMEN'S RURAL INSTITUTES. Periodical: *Scottish Home and Country.* Monthly, Vols. I-XXXVII, 1924-61 (current).

Townswomen's Guilds

646. NATIONAL UNION OF TOWNSWOMEN'S GUILDS. *Annual Reports,* from 1930. *The Constitutions, Rules and Handbook,* pp. 135, 1938, latest edn. 1960. Periodical: *The Townswoman,* monthly, Vols. I-XXVIII, 1934-61 (current)—for a brief account of the history of the movement see Vol. XIX, pp. 154-5, and the Jubilee issue of May, 1958.

647. SMITH, E. M. *The National Union of Townswomen's Guilds,* in *W.A.B.,* 2nd Ser., No. IV, Feb. 1936, pp. 12-17.

Other Organisations

648. BOAS, F. S., *The Mothers' Union: its Educational Work,* in *J.A.E.,* Vol. I, 1926-7, pp. 70-9. See further FIELD, E. M., *Adult Religious Education: the Mothers' Union Scheme,* in *A.E.,* Vol. IX, 1936-7, pp. 267-71.

649. RAE, L. M. (ed.). *Ladies in Debate, being a History of the Ladies' Edinburgh Debating Society, 1865-1935*. Pp. 132. Oliver and Boyd, Edinburgh, 1936.

650. CRUICKSHANK, A. J., and STACK, P. *Movement is Life*. Pp. 251. Bell, 1937.
Biography of Mrs. M. B. Stack, founder of the Women's League of Health and Beauty, The activities of the movement are chronicled in its periodical *Health and Beauty*, monthly or bi-monthly till 1939, afterwards quarterly, Vols. I-IV, 1933-61 (current).

See also Section III (c) (iii), and Subject Index *s.v.* Women.

(xxi) Young People's Organisations

NOTE.—Organisations concerned only with adolescents have been excluded. For these see bibliographies in *Guide to Studies*, (**13**) 1955-9, Appendix B.

Young Farmers' Clubs

651. NATIONAL FEDERATION OF YOUNG FARMERS' CLUBS. *Annual Reports*, from 1929; *Young Farmers' Clubs: their Organisation and Formation*, pp. 24, 1949; TRESAWNA, N., *The Farmhouse: a Handbook of Suggestions for Work in Young Farmers' Clubs*, pp. 88, 1958; *The Things we Do: a Guide to Club Programmes and Young Farmers' Activities*, pp. 48, 1961. Periodical: *The Young Farmer*, monthly, 1929-32, quarterly 1932-9, bi-monthly from 1944, Vols. I-XXIX, 1929-39 and 1944-61 (current).

Young Men's Christian Associations

652. STEVENSON, G. J. *Historical Records of the Young Men's Christian Association from 1844 to 1884*. Pp. 218. [1884].
Not a collection of records, but a chronicle.

653. NATIONAL COUNCIL OF Y.M.C.A.s. *Annual Reports*, 1902-39, and from 1959 (there are also annual reports of various national and local organisations from 1844 onwards); WORT, R. S., *One Hundred Years: the Story of the Y.M.C.A.*, pp. 58, 1944; COLES, E. K. T., *Earning and Learning*, pp. 42, n.d. (a guide to local secretaries in the planning of educational work). Periodicals: *British Y.M.C.A. Review*, quarterly, Nos. 1-53, 1948-61 (current) (for earlier periodicals, 1907-39, see first edn. of the present work, pp. 21, 41).

654. WILLIAMS, J. E. H. *The Father of the Red Triangle: the Life of Sir George Williams, Founder of the Y.M.C.A.* Pp. 308. Hodder and Stoughton, 1918.

655. DOGGETT, L. L. *A History of the Young Men's Christian Association*. Pp. 405. Association P., New York, 1922.
Both this volume and SHEDD, C. P. and others, *History of the World Alliance of Young Men's Christian Associations*, pp. 766, S.P.C.K., 1955, are useful on the early history of the British movement.

656. WILLIS, Z. F. *The Y.M.C.A. and Adult Education*. Pp. 11. Reprinted from *J.A.E.*, Vol III, 928-9.
An article under the same title by BARKER, E., in *W.A.B.*, 2nd Ser., No. XXIII, Feb. 1943, pp. 1-7, has special reference to work with H.M. Forces.

See also **342.**

Young Women's Christian Association

657. YOUNG WOMEN'S CHRISTIAN ASSOCIATION OF GREAT BRITAIN. *Annual Reports*, from 1877. Periodical: *The Blue Triangle*, 11 issues annually, Vols. I-LXXIX, 1884-1961 (current).

658. DUGUID, J., *The Blue Triangle*. Pp. 191. Hodder and Stoughton, 1955. An account of the work of the Association during the past hundred years.

(xxii) Organisations for the Promotion of Music and the Arts

British Drama League

659. *Annual Reports*, from 1920. Periodical: *Drama*, quarterly, Vol. I, 1919-20; 10 issues yearly, N.S. Vols. I-XVII, 1920-39; quarterly, N.S. Nos. 1-63, 1946-61 (current).

British Film Institute

660. *Annual Reports*, from 1934; *The British Film Institute: the First Twenty-five Years*, pp. 39, 1958. Periodicals: *Sight and Sound* (**58**); *Monthly Film Bulletin*, Vols. I-XXVIII, 1934-61 (current); *Contrast* (a television quarterly), from Autumn 1961.
See also COMMITTEE ON THE BRITISH FILM INSTITUTE, *Report*, pp. 13, H.M.S.O., 1948.

Council for the Encouragement of Music and the Arts, from 1945 **Arts Council of Great Britain**

661. COUNCIL FOR THE ENCOURAGEMENT OF MUSIC AND THE ARTS. *Reports: The Arts in War-Time* (1942/3); *The Fifth Year of C.E.M.A.* (1944). ¡
See also PILGRIM TRUST, *9th and 10th Annual Reports*, 1939-40, and **376**.

662. ARTS COUNCIL OF GREAT BRITAIN. *Annual Reports*, from 1945/6; *The First Ten Years* (reprinted from *11th Report*), pp. 20, 1957.

English Folk Dance and Song Society

663. *Annual Reports*, from 1912; KENNEDY, H. and D., *Folk Dance History (1911-61)*, pp. 12, 1961. Periodical: *English Dance and Song*, bi-monthly, Vols. I-XXII, 1922-59; quarterly, Vols. XXIII-XXIV, 1959-61 (current).

Federation of Film Societies

664. EVANS, J., and HANCOCK, M. *Forming and Running a Film Society*. Pp. 24. Federation of Film Societies and British Film Institute 1948, 3rd edn. 1961. Periodical: *Film*, 4 issues yearly, Nos. 1-30, 1954-61 (current).

Rural Music Schools Association

665. *Annual Reports*, from 1935. Periodical: *Making Music*, thrice yearly, Nos. 1-47, 1946-61 (current).
See also IBBERSON, E. M., *Rural Music Schools*, in *W.A.B.*, 2nd Ser., No. X, Aug. 1937, pp. 38-41; *The Local Education Authority and the Rural Music School*, in *A.E.*, Vol. XXIV, 1951-2, pp. 305-7.

Scottish Community Drama Association

666. *Annual Reports*, from 1932. Periodical: *S.C.D.A. Bulletin*, thrice yearly, 1949-61 (current).

Scottish Country Dance Society, from 1952 **Royal Scottish Country Dance Society**

667. Periodical: (*Royal*) *Scottish Country Dance Society Bulletin*, annually, Nos. 1-39, 1932-61 (current) (includes annual reports).

Society for Education in Film and Television

668. Periodicals: *Screen Education*, Nos. 1-11, 1959-61 (current) with supplement *Film Society News*.

(xxiii) Other Organisations concerned with Adult Education

British Council

669. *Annual Reports*, from 1941 (see especially *Twenty-first Anniversary Report, 1934-1955* (1955)); *The British Council: What it is and What it does*, pp. 16, n.d.; SINKER, Sir P., *The Main Tasks*, pp. 24, reprinted from *Annual Report* for 1958-59.

Bureau of Current Affairs

670. FORD, B. *The Bureau of Current Affairs, 1946-1951.* Pp. 32. 1952. See also **1039.**

Catholic Social Guild

671. CLEARY, J. M., *Catholic Social Action in Britain, 1909-1959*, pp. 228, Oxford, 1961. Periodicals: *Christian Democrat*, monthly, Vols. I-XXIX and N.S. Vols. I-IV, 1921-53; 10 issues yearly, N.S. Vols. V-XII, 1954-61 (current); *C.S.G. Bulletin*, quarterly, Vols. I-VII, 1946-53.

Central Council for Health Education

672. *Annual Reports*, from 1928. Periodical: *Health Education Journal*, quarterly, Vols. I-XIX, 1943-61. See also **36.**

Central Office of Information

673. *Annual Reports*, 1947-50, H.M.S.O.; *An Outline of the Functions and Organisation of the Central Office of Information*, pp. 51, 1961 (publication restricted).

Council for the Promotion of Field Studies, from 1955 **Field Studies Council**

674. *Annual Reports*, from 1944. Periodical: *Field Studies*, annually from 1959.
See also FITTER, R. S. R., *Field Studies and Further Education*, in *A.E.*, Vol. XXXI, 1958-9, pp. 203-8.

English New Education Fellowship

675. *The Home and School Handbook,* pp. 48, n.d. (on parent-teacher associations, originally published by Home and School Council).

The English-Speaking Union

676. Periodical: *The English-Speaking World.* Monthly or bi-monthly (now bi-monthly), Vols. I-XLIII, 1919-61 (current).

Gilchrist Trust

677. SHUTTLEWORTH, LORD, and CRANAGE, D. H. S. *Pioneering Work in Education.* Pp. 36. Cambridge, 1930.
On the work of the trust from 1865, including its work for adult education.

Hansard Society

678. *Annual Reports,* from 1945; *The Story of the Hansard Society,* pp. 32, 1950; KING-HALL, Sir S., *The Hansard Society for Parliamentary Government, 1944-59* (reprinted from *Parliamentary Affairs,* Vol. XIII), pp. 10, 1960.

National Council of Social Service

679. *Annual Reports,* from 1919; *Music and Drama in the Counties,* pp. 119, 1949; *In the Service of the Community* (brief account of the work of the Council), pp. 12, 1959.
Numerous other N.C.S.S. publications are listed, as appropriate, in other sections of this bibliography, e.g. above, III(b)(xiv). Annual Reports include those of Associated Groups, e.g. National Association of Women's Clubs, National Federation of Community Associations, and Standing Conferences of Amateur Music, Councils of Social Service, Drama Associations, and Local History. For the Standing Conference of Local History see the article by TREHARNE, R. F., in *A.E.,* Vol. XXIII, 1950-1, 279-84.

680. Periodicals: *N.C.S.S. Monthly Bulletin,* Ser. I, 1920; continued as *British Institute and N.C.S.S. Monthly Bulletin,* Ser. II, 1920-1; continued as *Social Service Bulletin,* monthly, Ser. III, 1922, Vols. III-XX, 1923-39; resumed as *Social Service,* quarterly, Vols. XXI-XXXV, 1947-61 (current); *The Village* (originally *The Village Hall*), quarterly, Nos. 1-35, 1932-44, N.S. Vols. I-XVI, 1947-61 (current).

National Home Reading Union

681. Periodicals: *The General Readers' Magazine.* Monthly. Vols. I-II, 1889-91. Continued under varying titles in three divisions (the General Course, the Special Courses, and the Young People's section), Vols. III-XXV, 1891-1914. Recombined as *The Home Reading Magazine,* Vols. XXVI-XXXVI, 1914-25. Succeeded by *The Reader,* Nos. 1-12, 1925-6, and *The Young Reader,* Nos. 1-6, 1925-6. Recombined as *The Reader,* Vols. II-V, 1926-30.

National Society

682. Periodical: *The Teaching Church Review,* monthly, Vols. I-XVI, 1930-48; continued as *The Teaching Church,* Vol. I (2 issues only), 1949 (Church of England Council for Education).

Physical Education Association

683. Periodical: *Physical Education*. Thrice yearly, under various titles, Vols. I-LIII, 1908-61 (current).

See also Annual Reports of Central Council for Physical Recreation (from 1936), Church of England Council for Education (from 1948), Council of Industrial Design (from 1946), United Nations Association (from 1946). For other associations engaged wholly or partly in adult education see lists in **40**.

(xxiv) Libraries

Before 1850

684. SELECT COMMITTEE ON PUBLIC LIBRARIES. *Reports*. 1849 and 1850.
Report for 1849 surveys public library provision before the 1850 Act, and includes much material on mechanics' institute libraries.

685. [BROWN, S.] *Some Account of the Itinerating Libraries and their Founder*. Pp. 125. Edinburgh, 1856.
Describes an interesting early nineteenth-century experiment by Samuel Brown of Haddington, which had imitators in many parts of the country.

686. MCKILLOP, A. D. *English Circulating Libraries, 1725-50*, in *The Library*, 4th Ser., Vol. XIV, 1933-4, pp. 477-85.
On this subject see also HAMLYN, H. M., *Eighteenth-Century Circulating Libraries in England*, in *The Library*, 5th Ser., Vol. I, 1947, pp. 197-222.

687. BECKWITH, F. *The Eighteenth-Century Proprietary Library in England*, in *Journal of Documentation*, Vol. III, 1947-8, pp. 81-98.
An account of early private subscription libraries, with bibliography.

688. THOMPSON, H. P. *Thomas Bray*. Pp. 127. S.P.C.K., 1954.
Bray was a pioneer in the provision of parochial libraries.

689. IRWIN, R. *The Origins of the English Library*. Pp. 255. Allen and Unwin, 1958.
Mainly a study of private collections.

690. OLDMAN, C. B., MUNFORD, W. A., and NOWELL-SMITH, S. *English Libraries, 1800-1850*. Pp. 78. Lewis, 1958.
Lectures on the British Museum Library, mechanics' institute libraries, and the London Library.

691. WORMALD, F. and WRIGHT, C. E. (eds.). *The English Library before 1700*. Pp. 285. Athlone P., 1958.

692. CENTRAL COUNCIL FOR THE CARE OF CHURCHES. *The Parochial Libraries of the Church of England*. Pp. 125. Faith P., 1959.
A valuable history and directory of parochial libraries past and present.

693. Histories of early libraries, e.g.
TOVEY, C. *The Bristol City Library*. Pp. 96. 1853.
CHRISTIE, R. C. *The Old Church and School Libraries of Lancashire*. Pp. 236. (Chetham Society, *Transactions*, N.S. Vol. VII, Manchester, 1885).
BORRAJO, E. M. *The Guildhall Library* [London] in *L.A.R.*, Vol. X (1908), pp. 381-95.
STEPHEN, G. A. *Three Centuries of a City Library*. Pp. 90. Public Library, Norwich, 1917.

694. *Public Libraries Acts.* 13 and 14 Vict. c. 65, 1850; 18 and 19 Vict. c. 70, 1855; 55 and 56 Vict. c. 53, 1892; Edw. VII c. 19, 1901; 9 and 10 Geo. VI, c. 93, 1919.

695. EDWARDS, E. *Free Town Libraries.* Pp. 650. 1869.
An important work dealing with public library development in Europe and the United States. Other early accounts of the public libraries are GREENWOOD, T., *Public Libraries* (originally *Free Public Libraries*), pp. 604, 1886, 4th edn. 1894; OGLE, J. J., *The Free Library: its History and Present Condition*, pp. 364, 1897.

696. BROWN, J. D. *Manual of Library Economy.* Pp. 319. Scott Greenwood, 1903, 7th edn., rewritten by LOCK, R. N., Grafton, 1961.
Successive editions of this work record the development of the library system since 1903.

697. CARNEGIE UNITED KINGDOM TRUST. *Annual Reports*, from 1914/15. Edinburgh.
Cf. HENDRICK, B. J., *Life of Andrew Carnegie*, pp. 764, Heinemann, 1933; *Centenary of the Birth of Andrew Carnegie: the British Trusts and their Work*, pp. 165, Pillans and Wilson, Edinburgh, 1935.

698. [ADAMS, W. G. S.]. *A Report on Library Provision and Policy.* Pp. 104. Carnegie U.K. Trust, Edinburgh, 1915.
An important and influential report.

699. LIBRARY ASSOCIATION. *Public Libraries: their Development and Future Organisation.* Pp. 123. 1917.

700. [MITCHELL, J. M.]. *The Public Library System of Great Britain and Ireland, 1921-23.* Pp. 147. Carnegie U.K. Trust, Edinburgh, 1924.
A sequel to **698**.

701. BOARD OF EDUCATION—PUBLIC LIBRARIES COMMITTEE. *Report on Public Libraries in England and Wales* [the Kenyon Report]. Pp. 356. H.M.S.O., 1927.

702. MINTO, J. *A History of the Public Library Movement in Great Britain and Ireland.* Pp. 366. Allen and Unwin, 1932.

703. NEWCOMBE, L. *Library Co-operation in the British Isles.* Pp. 184. Allen and Unwin, 1937.
See further VOLLANS, R. F., *Library Co-operation in Great Britain*, pp. 149, National Central Library, 1952; and also Annual Reports of the National Central Library (originally Central Library for Students) from 1916.

704. McCOLVIN, L. R. *The Public Library System of Great Britain: a Report on its Present Condition with Proposals for Post-War Reorganisation* [the McColvin Report]. Pp. 228. Library Association, 1942.
The starting-point of much subsequent discussion, and the basis of the Library Association's proposals: *The Public Library Service, its Post-War Reorganisation and Development*, pp. 16, 1943.

705. OSBORNE, E., and SHARR, F. A. *County Library Practice: a Manual for Students.* Pp. 144. Library Association, 1950.

706. MUNFORD, W. A. *Penny Rate—Aspects of British Public Library History, 1850-1950.* Pp. 160. Library Association, 1951.

707. SCOTTISH EDUCATION DEPARTMENT—ADVISORY COUNCIL ON EDUCATION IN SCOTLAND. *Report on Libraries, Museums and Art Galleries.* Pp. 146. H.M.S.O. Edinburgh, 1951.
Full report on the current situation, with recommendations for future development.

708. MINISTRY OF EDUCATION. *The Structure of the Public Library Service in England and Wales* [the Roberts Report]. Pp. 62. H.M.S.O., 1959.
Includes important recommendations on future organisation.

709. Lives of library pioneers:
GREENWOOD, T. *Edward Edwards, the Chief Pioneer of Municipal Public Libraries.* Pp. 258. Scott Greenwood, 1902.
CARLTON, G. *Spade-Work: the Biography of Thomas Greenwood.* Pp. 176. Hutchinson [1949].
MUNFORD, W. A. *William Ewart, M.P., 1798-1869: Portrait of a Radical.* Pp. 208. Grafton, 1960.

710. Library periodicals:
The Library Assistant. Monthly, Vols. I-LV, 1898-1961 (current). Association of Assistant Librarians.
The Library World. Monthly, Vols. I-LXIII, 1898-1961 (current).
The Library Association Record. Monthly (quarterly 1923-30), Vols. I-LXII, 1899-1961 (current). From 1946 contains periodical notes by PRITCHARD, E. P., on libraries and adult education.
The Librarian and Book World. Monthly, Vols. I-L, 1910-1961 (current).
Library Science Extracts. Quarterly, Vols. I-XII, 1950-61. Library Association.
For journals before 1898 see **702**, pp. 168-70.

Libraries and Adult Education

711. BRITISH INSTITUTE OF ADULT EDUCATION AND LIBRARY ASSOCIATION. *The Public Libraries and Adult Education.* Pp. 14. 1923.

712. McCOLVIN, L. R. *Library Extension Work and Publicity.* Pp. 242. Grafton, 1927.

713. PEERS, R. *The Supply of Books to Adult Classes,* in *L.A.R.*, 3rd Ser., Vol. III, 1933, pp. 137-47.
One of numerous articles on this subject. See, for example, GREEN, E., *Adult Education and the Public Library,* in *L.A.R.*, Vol. XLI, 1939, pp. 320-31.

714. CENTRAL JOINT ADVISORY COMMITTEE ON TUTORIAL CLASSES—SUB-COMMITTEE ON SUPPLY OF BOOKS. *Report,* in *L.A.R.*, 4th Ser., Vol. IV, 1937, pp. 431-4.
Cf. NATIONAL CENTRAL LIBRARY, *Report on an Enquiry into the Provision of Books to Adult Classes,* in *L.A.R.*, Vol. LVIII, 1956, pp. 471-4 (printed also in a number of adult education journals) and commentary by PRITCHARD, E. P., *Books and the Adult Class,* in *T.B.*, Nos. 103-5, 1956, pp. 11-14.

715. LEYLAND, E. *The Wider Public Library.* Pp. 205. Grafton, 1938.

716. THOMSEN, C., SYDNEY, E., and TOMPKINS, M. D. *Adult Education Activities for Public Libraries.* Pp. 112. UNESCO, Paris, 1950.
Essays on Denmark, the United Kingdom, and the U.S.A. For an interesting comparative study of work in the U.S.A. see *Library Trends*, Vol. VIII, No. 1, July 1959: *Current Trends in Adult Education,* ed. STONE, C. W. (Illinois Univ. Graduate School of Library Science).

717. HOULE, C. O. *Libraries in Adult and Fundamental Education: the Report of the Malmö Seminar.* Pp. 187. UNESCO, Paris, 1951.

For library history and organisation see also **1, 4, 23, 32, 260, 342, 349, 366, 397**; and for adult education aspects **509, 562, 614, 622.**

(xxv) Museums and Art Galleries

History

718. GREENWOOD, T. *Museums and Art Galleries.* Pp. 448. 1888.
A general description.

719. MURRAY, D. *Museums, their History and Use.* 3v. MacLehose, Glasgow, 1904.

720. [MIERS, H. A.]. *A Report on the Public Museums of the British Isles (other than the National Museums).* Pp. 222. Carnegie U.K. Trust, Edinburgh, 1928.

721. ROYAL COMMISSION ON NATIONAL MUSEUMS AND GALLERIES. *Interim and Final Reports.* 3v. H.M.S.O., 1928-30.

722. STANDING COMMISSION ON MUSEUMS AND GALLERIES. *Reports.* H.M.S.O., 1933, 1938, 1948, 1954, 1959.

723. [MARKHAM, S. F.]. *The Museums and Art Galleries of the British Isles (other than the National Museums).* Pp. 180. Carnegie U.K. Trust, Edinburgh, 1938.

724. MUSEUMS ASSOCIATION. *Museums and Art Galleries: a National Service.* Pp. 16. 1945.
An official statement on post-war development.

725. WITTLIN, A. S. *The Museum: its History and Tasks in Education.* Pp. 313. Routledge and Kegan Paul, 1949.
A survey on an international scale.

726. *The Science Museum* [London]: *the First Hundred Years.* Pp. 93. H.M.S.O., 1957.

727. Periodical: *Museums Journal.* Quarterly, Vols. I-LXII, 1901-61 (current). Museums Association.

Museums and Adult Education

728. MIERS, H. A. *Museums and Art Galleries in Adult Education,* in *J.A.E.,* Vol. VI, 1932-4, pp. 399-404.
Cf. SCHERER, M. R. *A Note on Adult Education in British Museums,* pp. 47, American Association for Adult Education, New York, 1934.

729. ROSE, H. T. *Museums in Education,* in *A.E.,* Vol. XXV, 1952-3, pp. 297-303.
Report of a UNESCO Seminar in New York. Cf. HARRISON, M., *Museums in Education,* pp. 28, in *Education Abstracts* (63), Vol. VIII, 1956.

730. NATIONAL INSTITUTE OF ADULT EDUCATION. *Museums and Adult Education.* Pp. 66. N.I.A.E., 1956.
Valuable report by a special working party: the fullest statement to date.

See also **23, 26, 27, 43, 219, 349, 373, 392.**

(c) SPECIAL ASPECTS

(i) Rural Adult Education

731. BOARD OF EDUCATION—ADULT EDUCATION COMMITTEE. Paper No. 3. *The Development of Adult Education in Rural Areas.* Pp. 55. H.M.S.O., 1922.

732. NOTTINGHAM UNIVERSITY COLLEGE—DEPARTMENT OF ADULT EDUCATION. *The Educational Possibilities of Village Clubs.* Pp. 38. Nottingham, 1923.
Report on adult educational provision in villages in the Nottingham extra-mural area.

733. WARRILOW, H. *Rural Adult Education*, in *J.A.E.*, Vol. III, 1928-9, pp. 126-33. Other articles of interest are THOMAS, F. G. and D. I., *Fresh Woods and Pastures New* [Devon], in *J.A.E.*, Vol. V, 1930-2, pp. 164-74, 259-81; RITCHIE, W. D., *Adult Education in Rural Areas* [Scotland], in *A.E.*, Vol. X, 1937-8, pp. 324-35; SALT, W. E., *Adult Education in the West of England, ibid.*, pp. 39-45; SPRINGALL, M., *Adult Education in Norfolk Villages*, in *W.A.B.*, 2nd Ser., No. XXVIII, Feb. 1942, pp. 1-5; ARMSTRONG, J. R., *Liberal Adult Education in Rural Areas*, in *A.E.*, Vol. XXV, 1952-3, pp. 56-62.

734. ASHBY, A. W. *The Sociological Background of Adult Education in Rural Districts*. Pp. 27. B.I.A.E., 1935.

735. POOLE, H. E. *Perspectives for Countrymen*. Pp. 43. Allen and Unwin, 1942. A valuable study of rural adult education with special reference to East Anglia, and a plea for the establishment of a residential People's College.

736. LEWIS, D. H. *The Rural Tutors' Conference*, in *T.B.*, No. 87, July 1952, pp. 13-21. Report of a conference convened by the Tutors' Association, 1952.

737. DYKE, E. T. *Evening Centres in Rural Communities*, in *A.E.*, Vol. XXXII, 1959-60, pp. 18-22. Describes an experimental scheme of local authority aid to voluntary committees as an alternative to direct provision in evening institutes.

See also Subject Index.

(ii) Adult Education and Technical Training

738. FERGUSON, R. W. *Education in the Factory*. Pp. 79. Cadbury Bros., Birmingham, 1927. An account of the educational scheme in operation at Cadbury Bros. in 1927 which included provision for non-vocational and liberal studies. See also FERGUSON, R. W. *The Functions of a Works Education Department*, in *J.A.E.*, Vol. VI, 1932-4, pp. 284-91; CADBURY BROS. LTD., *Education in Industry*, pp. 86, Bournville [1938].

739. NUFFIELD COLLEGE. *Industry and Education*. Pp. 38. 1943. Discusses the place of adult education in the general provision of education for workers in industry.

740. HUBBACK, E. M. *Education Through Work*, in *F.E.*, Vol. II, 1948-9, pp. 319-24. Suggests that there is scope for liberal adult education in courses related to people's everyday work. Later articles on this theme are VENABLES, P. F. R., *Liberal Studies in Education for Industry—What is Possible?* in *BACIE Journal*, Vol. VII, 1953, pp. 86-91 (and other articles by the same author in *A.E.*, Vol. XXV, 1952-3, pp. 30-7, and *J.E.*, Vol. LXXXV, 1953, pp. 108-12, 164-6); JONES, J. C., *Liberal Education in a Technical Age*, in *S.A.E.*, No. 15, Dec. 1955, pp. 13-19; MADGWICK, P., *Liberal Studies in a College of Technology*, in *A.E.*, Vol. XXXII, 1959-60, pp. 198-203.

741. NATIONAL INSTITUTE OF ADULT EDUCATION. *Liberal Education in a Technical Age*. Pp. 128. Parrish, 1955. Report of a committee of enquiry on the relationship of vocational and non-vocational education. The subject is pursued in NATIONAL INSTITUTE OF ADULT EDUCATION, *Adult Education and Working Life*, pp. 28, 1955, which includes Conference addresses on liberal studies in technical education.

742. YORKSHIRE COUNCIL FOR FURTHER EDUCATION. *The Liberal Aspect of Technical Education*. Pp. 24. Leeds, 1956.

743. *Dunblane Conference, 1957: "Adult Education and Industry,"* in *S.A.E.*, No. 21, Dec. 1957, pp. 3-23. Report of the 1957 Conference of the Scottish Institute of Adult Education.

744. GOLDWIN, R. A. *Toward the Liberally Educated Executive*, Pp. 125. Fund for Adult Education, White Plains, N.Y., 1957.
A stimulating American view. See also SIEGLE, P., *New Directions in Liberal Education for Executives*, pp. 80, C.S.L.E.A., Chicago, 1958.

745. MINISTRY OF EDUCATION. Circular 323. *Liberal Education in Technical Colleges*. Pp. 7. H.M.S.O., 1957.
Suggests ways of introducing a liberal element into technical education.

746. MINKES, A. L. AND PRITCHARD, E. P. *An Experiment in the Study of Economics and Politics*, in *A.E.*, Vol., XXX, 1957-8, pp. 230-7.
A description of two advanced seminars for industrial executives conducted by the Birmingham Extra-Mural Department. Cf. KIDD, J. R., *Liberal Education for Business Leadership*, ibid., pp. 100-9.

747. INTERNATIONAL FEDERATION OF WORKERS' EDUCATIONAL ASSOCIATIONS. *The Relationship between Vocational and Non-Vocational Adult Education*. Pp. 26. 1959.
Report of a seminar at Geneva in co-operation with I.L.O. and UNESCO.

See also **1023, 1095.**

(iii) Adult Education for Women

748. BOARD OF EDUCATION—ADULT EDUCATION COMMITTEE. Paper No. 4. *The Development of Adult Education for Women*. Pp. 50. H.M.S.O., 1922.
A valuable review of existing provision.

749. SENTURIA, J. J. *Sex and Subject Selection*, in *J.A.E.*, Vol. IV, 1929-30, pp. 166-73.
An analysis of W.E.A. classes 1913-28.

750. HINDER, E. R. *Women's Interests in Adult Education*, in *J.A.E.*, Vol. V, 1930-2, pp. 418-22.
On the need for more classes in domestic science and allied subjects. Cf. *Education for Women*, in *A.E.*, Vol. X, 1937-8, pp. 227-36; BUTCHER, L., *Education in Home-Making*, in *A.E.*, Vol. XXVII, 1954-5, pp. 252-6.

751. TAIT, M. *The Education of Women for Citizenship: Some Practical Suggestions*. Pp. 106. UNESCO, Paris, 1954.
Account of current practice in Britain.

752. SCRIMGEOUR, C. A. *Women and Adult Classes in North Staffordshire*, in *R.H.P.*, Vol. III, VI, 1957-8, pp. 43-8.
Description of special developments since 1954.

753. TIMM, H. *Citizenship Education for Girls*, pp. 26, in *Education Abstracts*, Vol. XI, 1959.
Concerned as much with women as with girls. Full bibliography.

See also Section III (b) (xx), and Subject Index *s.v.* Women.

(iv) Adult Education for the Unemployed

754. WATTS, J. *The Facts of the Cotton Famine*. Pp. 484. 1866.
Includes a description of the extensive provision made for adult education among unemployed cotton operatives during the American Civil War.

755. BLIZZARD, G. P. *Helping the Unemployed to Help Themselves*, in *J.A.E.*, Vol. VI, 1932-4, pp. 60-80.
Description and discussion of various projects, with emphasis on practical work and handicrafts. For other accounts of work in this field see BRITISH INSTITUTE OF ADULT EDUCATION, *Educational Facilities for the Unemployed*, pp. 55, 1933; PARRY, E. A., and KING, H., *New Leisure and Old Learning*, pp. 32, Liverpool U.P., 1934; MESS, H. A., *Unemployment and Adult Education*, pp. 14, Selly Oak Colleges, Birmingham, 1935; WATKINS, Sir P. E., *Adult Education among the Unemployed in South Wales*, in *Year Book of Education*, 1935 (35), pp. 654-83; STEVENS, G., *The Unemployed Centre*, in *A.E.*, Vol. IX, 1936-7, pp. 15-21; and ROBERTS, H., *Women's Clubs*, in *A.E.*, Vol. X, 1937-8, pp. 285-93.

See also **366.**

(v) Adult Education for Retirement

756. DONAHUE, W. T. (ed.). *Education for Later Maturity: a Handbook*. Pp. 352. Whiteside and Morrow, New York, 1955.

757. NATIONAL COUNCIL OF SOCIAL SERVICE. *Preparation for Retirement or Adjustment to Ageing*. Pp. 18. 1959.
Report by the National Old People's Welfare Council. A preliminary consideration of what the content of education for retirement might be and of what action might be taken to secure it.

758. *Adult Leadership*, Vol. IX, No. 1, May 1960. Special issue on Problems of Education for the Aged and Aging.

759. GROOMBRIDGE, B. *Education and Retirement*. Pp. 160. N.I.A.E., 1960.

760. TAMS, E., and WALDEN, A. B., *The Oldsters come to W.E.A. Classes*, in *R.H.P.*, Vol. III, IX, 1960-1, pp. 48-61.
On experimental courses for retired people.

761. HERON, A. *Preparation for Retirement: Solving New Problems*. Pp. 27. N.C.S.S., 1961.
Gives an account of pioneering ventures in education for retirement.

(vi) Religious Adult Education

762. CONFERENCE ON CHRISTIAN POLITICS, ECONOMICS, AND CITIZENSHIP. *Commission Reports, Vol. II: Education*. Pp. 249. Longmans, 1924.
A survey of religious education at all levels, including adult education.

763. YEAXLEE, B. A. *Spiritual Values in Adult Education*. 2v. Oxford U.P., 1925.
A valuable comprehensive survey. Vol. I is concerned with general analysis and the historical development of religious adult education; Vol. II examines current problems and provision.

764. POVAH, J. W. (ed.). *Students and the Faith: The Call of Church Tutorial Classes*. Pp. 143. Longmans, 1927.
A symposium dealing with aims, history and methods.

765. FLEMING, H. *The Lighted Mind: the Challenge of Adult Education to Quakerism*. Pp. 90. Friends' Book Centre, 1929.

766. NATIONAL SOCIETY. *The Church and Adult Education*. Pp. 56. 1944.
Report of a Committee under the chairmanship of Sir Richard Livingstone.

767. *Unto a Perfect Man.* Pp. 103. Liverpool Diocesan Board of Education, Liverpool, 1948.
A report on religious education, including adult education.

768. CHURCH OF ENGLAND COUNCIL FOR EDUCATION—ADULT EDUCATION COUNCIL. *The Tutorial Class in Adult Religious Education.* Pp. 16. Church Information Board, 1951.

769. DALE, A. T. *Adult Education, with special reference to Methodist Organisation.* Pp. 19. Epworth P., 1951.

770. *The Training of God's People.* Pp. 52. Church Information Board, 1953.
Includes in an appendix a statement on Adult Education presented to the Church Assembly by the Church of England Adult Education Council. Discussed by VYSE, J. W. M., *The Church of England and Adult Education*, in *A.E.*, Vol. XXVII, 1954-5, pp. 57-63.

771. BURTON, J. C. G. *Adult Religious Education in Bristol, 1947-53*, in *A.E.*, Vol. XXVI, 1953-4, pp. 101-9.
Describes experiments under the auspices of the Bristol Extra-Mural Department.

772. STANFORD, E. C. D. *The Churches Educate Adults*, in *A.E.*, Vol. XXXIV, 1961-2, pp. 54-7.
A useful short survey of activities.

See also Sections III(b)(i), III(b)(ii), and IV(d)(xv), and Subject Index *s.v.* Religious Adult Education.

(vii) Adult Education and the Mass Media

773. MARTIN, K. *The Press and Adult Education*, in *J.A.E.*, Vol. II, 1927-8, pp. 125-30.
On the need for adult education to counteract the development of the cheap sensationalist press.

774. BRITISH BROADCASTING CORPORATION. *New Ventures in Broadcasting: a Study in Adult Education.* Pp. 131. 1928.
A review of adult educational possibilities, with suggestions for encouraging group listening.

775. COMMISSION ON EDUCATIONAL AND CULTURAL FILMS. *The Film in National Life.* Pp. 216. Allen and Unwin, 1932.
An inquiry into the service that films may render to education and social progress.

776. BOARD OF EDUCATION. Pamphlet No. 92. *Adult Education: Wireless Listening Groups.* Pp. 46. H.M.S.O., 1933.

777. BRITISH INSTITUTE OF ADULT EDUCATION. *Group Listening.* Pp. 32. Chicago U.P., 1933.
A report on British and European experience prepared for the National Advisory Council on Radio in Education.

778. LEAVIS, F. R., and THOMPSON. D. *Culture and Environment: the Training of Critical Awareness.* Pp. 158. Chatto and Windus, 1933.

779. MATHESON, H. *Broadcasting.* Pp. 256. Thornton Butterworth, 1933.
An early discussion of the social implications of broadcasting. For later studies see ROBINSON, E. H., *Broadcasting and a Changing Civilisation*, pp. 166, Lane, 1935; JENNINGS, H., and GILL, W., *Broadcasting in Everyday Life*, pp. 40, B.B.C., 1939; SIEPMANN, C. A., *Radio, Television and Society*, pp. 417, Oxford U.P., New York, 1950.

780. HILL, F. E., and WILLIAMS, W. E. *Radio's Listening Groups: the United States and Great Britain.* Pp. 280. New York, 1941.
Part II, Great Britain, by W. E. Williams, gives a detailed critical review of the Listening Group movement. On this subject see also THOMAS, F. G., *Regional Broadcasting and Adult Education in a Rural Area*, in *A.E.*, Vol. VIII, 1935-6, pp. 240-9; and articles by GIBSON, G. W., in *A.E.*, Vol. XI, 1938-9, pp. 273-80, and *W.A.B.*, 2nd Ser., No. XIX, Nov. 1939, pp. 22-8.

781. ARTS ENQUIRY. *The Factual Film.* Pp. 260. Political and Economic Planning, 1947.
A survey of documentary, news and record films with a chapter on their use in education.

782. TRENAMAN, J. *Understanding Radio Talks: a B.B.C. Experiment*, in *A.E.*, Vol. XXIII, 1950-1, pp. 176-81.
Cf. VERNON, P. E., *The Intelligibility of Broadcast Talks*, in *B.B.C. Quarterly*, Vol. V, 1950-1, pp. 206-12.

783. *Television: a Challenge and a Chance for Education.* UNESCO *Courier*, Vol. VI, No. 3, Mar. 1953.
A series of articles reviewing the educational problems presented by television.

784. HENRY, N. B. (ed.). *Mass Media and Education.* 53rd Yearbook of the National Society for the Study of Education. Pp. 300. Chicago U.P., 1954.
Cf. *Year Book of Education*, 1960 (**35**), ed. BEREDAY, G. Z. F., and LAUWERYS, J. A., *Communication Media and the School.*

785. UNESCO. Reports and Papers on Mass Communications. No. 23. *Cultural Radio Broadcasts: Some Experiences.* Pp. 60. Paris, 1956.

786. HOGGART, R. *The Uses of Literacy.* Pp. 319. Chatto and Windus, 1957.
A study of "aspects of working-class life, with special reference to publications and entertainments." Cf. BRIGGS, A., *Adult Education and Mass Culture*, pp. 24, Fircroft College, Birmingham, 1958, and HOGGART, R., *On the Nature and Quality of Mass-Communications*, pp. 24, Fircroft College, Birmingham, 1959, both of which are concerned with the rôle of adult education in the new social context. LITTLEWOOD, J. C. F., *Mass Civilisation and Adult Education*, in *Univs. Q.*, Vol. XV, 1960-1, pp. 361-72, and Vol. XVI, 1961-2, pp. 67-81, is a critical commentary on Briggs.

787. BRITISH BROADCASTING CORPORATION. *The B.B.C. Looks Ahead.* Pp. 16. 1958.
Extracts from addresses, including one by Sir Ian Jacob on The B.B.C. and Education. Other B.B.C. pamphlets of interest are: *Education in Broadcasting*, pp. 16, 1961; GREENE, H. C., *The B.B.C. and Adult Education*, pp. 15, 1961 (address to N.I.A.E. Conference).

788. BELSON, W. A. *Effects of Television on the Interests and Initiative of Adult Viewers in Greater London*, in *B.J.P.*, Vol. L, 1959, pp. 145-8.

789. CENTRAL COMMITTEE FOR TELEVISION VIEWING. *Television: Responsibility and Response.* Pp. 32. N.I.A.E. [1960].
Three conference addresses.

790. SCHRAMM, W. (ed.). *The Impact of Educational Television.* Pp. 255. Illinois U.P., Urbana, 1960.
Interesting for comparative study. See also U.S. HOUSE OF REPRESENTATIVES—COMMITTEE ON INTERSTATE AND FOREIGN COMMERCE, *Educational Television*, pp. 440, Washington, 1961.

791. GROOMBRIDGE, B. (ed.). *Popular Culture and Personal Responsibility: a Study Outline.* Pp. 56. National Union of Teachers, 1961.
Extracts from proceedings of an N.U.T. Conference about the character and effects of the mass media. Valuable as presenting a variety of views, and has useful bibliography. The N.U.T. also published a duplicated verbatim report under the same title, pp. 356. 1960.

792. INDEPENDENT TELEVISION AUTHORITY. *Educational Television.* Pp. 32. 1961.
A plea for a fourth television service devoted to educational purposes.

See also **85, 382, 1080, 1082, 1088, 1176,** and for history and organisation of the mass media Section II (c).

(viii) Full-time Studies

793. BOARD OF EDUCATION—ADULT EDUCATION COMMITTEE. Paper No. 7. *Full-Time Studies: a Report on the Opportunities given to Adult Students to pursue their Studies on a Full-time Basis at Universities and other Institutions.* Pp. 75. H.M.S.O. 1927.

794. CARTWRIGHT E. S. *The Extra-Mural Student at the University,* in *J.A.E.,* Vol. III, 1928-9, pp. 60-70.
Historical account and discussion of problems based largely on Oxford experience.

795. YOUNG, T. *The Selection of Adult University Students,* in *J.A.E.,* Vol. V, 1930-2, pp. 294-311.
Proposals for reform, by an adult scholar.

796. DATALLER, R. *A Pitman Looks at Oxford.* Pp. 219. Dent, 1933.
Impressions of an adult student.

797. LUNN, W. J. *Adult Scholars at Oxford since the war,* in *R.H.P.,* Vol. III, II, 1953, pp. 66-9.
A comparison of post-war and pre-war experience of adult students. Cf. JACKSON, M., *A Mature Student,* in *A.E.,* Vol. XXVII, 1954-5, pp. 246-51.

798. CHARLTON, D. G. *University Entry for Adult Students,* in *Univs. Q.,* Vol. VIII, 1954, pp. 359-68.
Discussion of methods of selection and the difficulties involved.

(d) ADMINISTRATION
(i) Government Regulations

England and Wales

799. EDUCATION DEPARTMENT. *Code of Regulations for Evening Continuation Schools.* Annually, 1893-1900.

800. BOARD OF EDUCATION. *Regulations for Evening Schools and Classes.* 1901.

801. —— *Regulations for Evening Schools.* 1902.

802. —— *Regulations for Evening Schools, Technical Institutions, and Schools of Art and Art Classes.* Annually, 1903-05.

803. —— *Regulations for Technical Schools, Schools of Art and other Schools and Classes for Further Education.* 1906. Reissued, with some modification of title, annually 1907-10, and also 1913, 1914, 1915, 1918; modifying or amending regulations 1912, 1914, 1917, 1919, 1920, 1920.

804. —— *Regulations for University Tutorial Classes in England and Wales.* 1913. From 1914 embodied with *Regulations for Technical Schools*, etc.

805. —— Grant Regulations No. 33. *Adult Education Regulations*, 1924. S.R.O. No. 24, 1925. With Amending Regulations No. 1, S.R.O. No. 605, 1931; No. 2, Provisional R.O., 1931.

806. —— *Regulations for Further Education*, 1926. S.R.O. No. 919, 1926.

807. —— Grant Regulations No. 14. *Adult Education Regulations*, 1932. S.R.O. No. 75, 1932. With Amending Regulations No. 1, S.R.O. No. 671, 1934; No. 2, S.R.O. No. 661, 1935.

808. —— *Regulations for Further Education*, 1934. S.R.O. No. 303, 1934.

809. —— *Adult Education Regulations*, 1938. S.R.O. No. 597, 1938. With Amending Regulations No. 1, 1939; No. 2, 1941; No. 3, 1941; No. 4, 1942; No. 5, 1943; No. 6, 1944; No. 7, 1944.

810. MINISTRY OF EDUCATION. *Further Education Grant Regulations, No. 6, 1946.* S.R.O. No. 352, 1946. With Amending Regulations No. 1, S.R.O. No. 1067, 1946; No. 2, S.I. No. 847, 1948; No. 3, S.I. No. 142, 1950; No. 4, S.I. No. 1137, 1955.

811. —— *State Scholarships (Mature Students) Regulations, 1947.* S.R.O. No. 1472, 1947. With Amending Regulations No. 1, S.I. No. 1737, 1948; No. 2, S.I. No. 1365, 1949; No. 3, S.I. No. 625, 1950.

812. —— *State Scholarships Regulations, 1951.* S.I. No. 1214, 1951. With Amending Regulations No. 1, S.I. No. 1372, 1952; No. 2, S.I. No. 685, 1953.

813. —— *State Scholarships Regulations, 1954.* S.I. No. 957, 1954. With Amending Regulations No. 1, S.I. No. 933, 1955; No. 2, S.I. No. 1303, 1957; No. 3, S.I. No. 1143, 1958; No. 4, S.I. No. 1621, 1961.

814. —— *Further Education (Local Education Authorities) Regulations, 1959.* S.I. Nos. 393-4, 1959. With Amending Regulations No. 1, S.I. No. 1582, 1961.

Scotland

815. SCOTTISH (originally SCOTCH) EDUCATION DEPARTMENT. *Scotch Evening Continuation School Code.* Edinburgh, annually 1893-1900.

816. —— *Code of Regulations for Continuation Classes in Scotland.* Edinburgh, annually 1901-15.
The 1915 Code continued in operation till 1926, and for classes conducted by voluntary managers till 1936.

817. —— *Code of Regulations for Continuation Classes in Scotland, 1926.* S.R.O. No. 1366, 1925.

818. —— *Adult Education (Scotland) Regulations, 1934 (a).* S.R.O. No. 1343, 1934. With Amending Regulations 1940, No. 742, S.29.

819. —— *Code of Regulations for Continuation Classes in Scotland, 1936.* S.R.O. No. 791, 1936.

820. —— *Adult Education (Scotland) (Residential Institutions) Regulations, 1936.* S.R.O. No. 1292, 1936.

821. —— *Adult Education (Scotland) (Residential Institutions) Regulations Minute, 1938.* S.R.O. No. 811, 1938.

822. —— *Continuation Classes (Scotland) Consolidation Order, 1943.* S.R.O. No. 1170, 1943.

823. —— *Education (Scotland) Social and Physical Training Grant Regulations, 1946.* S.R.O. No. 864, 1946.

824. —— *Adult Education (Scotland) (Residential Institutions) Grant Regulations, 1951.* S.I. No. 740, 1951.

825. —— *Further Education (Scotland) Code, 1952.* S.I. No. 2201, 1952.

826. —— *Further Education (Voluntary Associations) (Scotland) Grant Regulations, 1952.* S.I. No. 2202, 1952.

827. —— *Further Education (Scotland) Regulations, 1959.* S.I. No. 477, S.21, 1959.

(ii) Administrative Relations

828. BOARD OF EDUCATION—ADULT EDUCATION COMMITTEE. Paper No. 1. *Report on Local Co-operation between Universities, Local Education Authorities, and Voluntary Bodies.* Pp. 26. 1922.

829. DEAN, A. E. *Administrative Problems in Rural Areas,* in *J.A.E.,* Vol. I, 1926-7, pp. 100-8.
With special reference to Kent.

830. ADVISORY COUNCIL FOR TECHNICAL EDUCATION, SOUTH WALES AND MONMOUTHSHIRE. *Part-time Education.* Pp. 72. Cardiff, 1939.
A valuable review of provision by the various statutory and voluntary bodies, and of the effects of multiple provision.

831. SCOTTISH EDUCATION DEPARTMENT—ADVISORY COUNCIL ON EDUCATION IN SCOTLAND. *Adult Education Grants.* Pp. 20. H.M.S.O., Edinburgh, 1944.
A report, with recommendations, on the organisation and finance of adult education.

832. *Foundation Papers,* Nos. 1-4, June 1947—Mar. 1948.
These issues include accounts of arrangements for co-operation and consultation, in various parts of the country, between local authorities and other bodies engaged in adult education.

833. MILLIGAN, F. S. *Community Associations and Local Authorities.* Pp. 30. 1948.
On the principles of relationship. First part was also printed in *F.P.,* No. 5, June 1948. For arrangements in Manchester and Surrey see *F.P.,* No. 1, June 1947, pp. 6-9.

834. HUTCHINSON, E. M. *The Economics of Adult Education,* in *A.E.,* Vol. XXIV, 1951-2, pp. 269-76.
An estimate of expenditure on adult education. See also articles by the same author in *A.E.,* Vol. XXXI, 1958-9, pp. 243-7, and Vol. XXXII, 1959-60, pp. 7-13.

835. RAYBOULD, S. G. *Voluntary Responsible Bodies in English Adult Education,* in *B.J.E.S.,* Vol. I, 1952-3, pp. 143-53.

836. MINISTRY OF EDUCATION. *The Organisation and Finance of Adult Education in England and Wales* [the Ashby Report]. Pp. 72. H.M.S.O., 1954.
Reviews the operation of the system then current and makes important recommendations.

837. NATIONAL ASSOCIATION OF PUBLIC SCHOOL ADULT EDUCATORS. *Public School Adult Education: a guide for administrators and teachers.* Pp. 156. Washington, 1956.
Useful for comparative study. Cf. PARKYN, G. W. (ed.), *The Administration of Education in New Zealand*, pp. 121, New Zealand Institute of Public Administration, Wellington, 1954, on the rôle of the New Zealand Council of Adult Education.

838. LAWRENCE, B. E. *The Work and Spirit of a Local Education Authority*, in *A.E.*, Vol. XXXI, 1958-9, pp. 87-99.
Survey of existing administrative machinery and its work.

(iii) Accommodation

839. THE NATIONAL COUNCIL OF SOCIAL SERVICE. *Village Halls and Social Centres in the Countryside.* Pp. 85. 1930, 5th ed. 1945.

840. YORKSHIRE COUNCIL FOR FURTHER EDUCATION. *The Situation, Construction, Furniture and Equipment desirable for Day Schools in which Technical, Commercial, Art, and/or Adult Classes will be held in the Evening.* Pp. 12. Leeds, 1930.

841. DUDLEY, J. *The Housing and Material Equipment of Adult Education*, in *A.E.*, Vol. XVII, 1944-5, pp. 101-19.
Report submitted by the British Institute of Adult Education to the Ministry of Education.

842. ARTS COUNCIL OF GREAT BRITAIN. *Plans for an Arts Centre.* Pp. 40. 1945.
Detailed plans for an educational centre devoted to the arts.

843. SCOTTISH EDUCATION DEPARTMENT. *Planning for Community Centres, Village Halls, and Playing Fields.* Pp. 39. H.M.S.O., Edinburgh, 1947.

844. NATIONAL FOUNDATION FOR ADULT EDUCATION. *Accommodation for Adult Education: some Examples and Suggestions.* Pp. 32. 1948.

845. HOGAN, J. M. *Buildings for Further Education*, in *F.E.*, Vol. II, 1948-9, pp. 291-306.
A factual survey with special reference to Birmingham and Somerset.

846. NATIONAL FEDERATION OF COMMUNITY ASSOCIATIONS. *Community Centres: Building Possibilities and Achievements.* Pp. 32. N.C.S.S., 1949.

847. MINISTRY OF EDUCATION. *Building Bulletin No. 5. New Colleges of Further Education.* Pp. 79. H.M.S.O., 1951, 3rd edn. 1959.

848. ADULT EDUCATION ASSOCIATION OF THE U.S.A.—COMMISSION ON ARCHITECTURE. *Architecture for Adult Education: a graphic guide for those who are planning physical facilities for adult education.* Pp. 74. 1957.
Cf. HUNSAKER, H. C., and PIERCE, R. (eds.), *Creating a Climate for Adult Learning*, pp. 116, Adult Education Association of the U.S.A., Commission on Architecture, and Purdue University, Division of Adult Education, 1959.

849. NATIONAL COUNCIL OF SOCIAL SERVICE. *Design of New School Halls for Music and Drama.* Pp. 12. 1960.

850. HUTCHINSON, E. M. *Accommodation: a few figures*, in *A.E.*, Vol. XXXIII, 1960–1, pp. 335–6.
Brief particulars of costs and impact on student numbers of specially provided accommodation in five areas.

851. *On Accommodation, the Report of a Study Group arising from a London University Extension Course on Adult Education*, in *A.E.*, Vol. XXXIII, 1960–1, pp. 295–309. Also printed separately.

(iv) National and International Co-ordinating and Consultative Bodies

852. WORLD ASSOCIATION FOR ADULT EDUCATION. *Annual Reports*, 1920–45.

853. BRITISH INSTITUTE OF ADULT EDUCATION. *Annual Reports*, 1921–47.
For the origins see also *The British Institute of Adult Education*, in *W.A.B.*, 1st Ser., No. IX, Aug. 1921, pp. 1–17; and Ch. ix of HALDANE, R. B. (Lord), *Richard Burdon Haldane: an Autobiography*, pp. 376, Hodder and Stoughton, 1929.

854. NATIONAL FOUNDATION FOR ADULT EDUCATION. *Annual Report and Summary of Conference Proceedings*. 1949. Report for 1947/8 is in **571.**

855. NATIONAL INSTITUTE OF ADULT EDUCATION. *Report and Financial Statement*. Annually from 1950 (from 1961 incroporated in *Year Book* (**40**)).
For Universities Extra-Mural Consultative Committee and Universities Council for Adult Education, see **499, 500**; for Central Joint Advisory Committee on Tutorial Classes see **535.**

IV. THEORY AND METHOD

(a) GENERAL SOCIAL AND EDUCATIONAL THEORY

A selection of works particularly relevant to adult education.

856. SADLER, M. E., and CLARKE, F. *The Philosophy Underlying the System of Education in England*, in *Columbia Educational Year Book*, 1929 (**30**), pp. 1-129.
Cf. CAVENAGH, F. A., *The Development of Educational Thought in the United Kingdom, 1920-35*, in *Year Book of Education*, 1936 (**35**), pp. 270-92.

857. THOMSON, G. H. *A Modern Philosophy of Education*. Pp. 283. Allen and Unwin, 1929.

858. WHITEHEAD, A. N. *The Aims of Education*. Pp. 256. Williams and Norgate, 1929, latest edn. Benn, 1959.

859. JACKS, L. P. *The Education of the Whole Man*. Pp. 255. Univ. of London P., 1931.
Stresses the importance of educating body as well as mind. Last chapter is an address to the British Institute of Adult Education 1929.

860. RUSSELL, B. *Education and the Social Order*. Pp. 254. Allen and Unwin, 1932, new edn. 1947.

861. WHEELER, O. A. *Creative Education and the Future*. Pp. 373. Univ. of London P., 1936.
Surveys educational practice, from a psychological point of view, from birth to maturity, with numerous references to adult education.

862. HOGBEN, L. (ed.) *Political Arithmetic: a Symposium of Population Studies*. Pp. 531. Allen and Unwin, 1938.
See especially Chs. viii-x on ability in relation to educational opportunity.

863. BIAGGINI, E. G. *Education and Society*. Pp. 250. Hutchinson, 1939.

864. COHEN, J. L., and TRAVERS, R. W. M. (eds.). *Educating for Democracy*. Pp. 488. Macmillan, 1939.
See especially Ch. vii by GREEN, E., Educating Men and Women.

865. CLARKE, F. *Education and Social Change*. Pp. 78. Sheldon P., 1940.
See also the same author's *Freedom in the Educative Society*, pp. 104, Univ. of London P., 1948, and for other studies on this theme ALLAWAY, A. J., *Social and Educational Change since 1900*, in *Sociological Review*, Vol. XLIII, 1951, pp. 143-57; DOBINSON, C. H. (ed.), *Education in a Changing World*, pp. 153, Clarendon P., Oxford, 1951; FINER, S. E., *Then and Now: Fifty Years of Social Change*, in *A.E.*, Vol. XXVI, 1953-4, pp. 179-89; HODGKIN, R. A., *Education and Change*, pp. 150, Oxford U.P., 1957.

866. MANNHEIM, K. *Man in Society*. Pp. 494. Kegan Paul, 1940.
Studies in social structure. See also MANNHEIM's *Freedom, Power, and Democratic Planning*, pp. 403, Routledge and Kegan Paul, 1951; and *Essays in the Sociology of Culture*, pp. 262, Routledge and Kegan Paul, 1956—both particularly relevant to adult education.

867. LIVINGSTONE, R. W. *The Future in Education*. Pp. 137. Cambridge, U.P., 1941.
An influential book which urged extended provision for adult education, especially residential adult education. See also by the same author: *Education for a World Adrift*, pp. 174, Cambridge U.P., 1943; *Some Tasks for Education*, pp. 106, Oxford U.P., 1946.

868. Cole, M. *Education for Democracy.* Pp. 70. Allen and Unwin, 1942.
Argues that education should be planned in relation to its final stages, i.e. university, technical and adult education.

869. Green, E. *Education for a New Society.* Pp. 192. Routledge and Kegan Paul, 1942, 2nd edn. 1947.
A review of the educational system by the then General Secretary of the W.E.A.

870. Stead, H. G. *The Education of a Community.* Pp. 165. Univ. of London P., 1942.
A study of social values revealed by the educational system.

871. Shepherd, T. B. *Living Education.* Pp. 206. Epworth P., 1944.

872. Harvard University. *General Education in a Free Society.* Pp. 281. Cambridge U.P., 1945.
An important statement by a special committee appointed by the President of the University.

873. Joad, C. E. M. *About Education.* Pp. 172. Faber, 1945.
The author was a tutor of adult classes in the London area for many years.

874. Moore, R. W. (ed.). *Education Today and Tomorrow.* Pp. 214. Joseph, 1945.
Includes addresses by Yeaxlee, B. A., on army education, and by Livingstone, R. W., on adult education.

875. Jacks, M. L. *Total Education.* Pp. 168. Routledge and Kegan Paul, 1946.
Ch. ix is concerned with university and adult education.

876. Eliot, T. S. *Notes towards a Definition of Culture.* Pp. 128. Faber, 1948.

877. Folsom, J. K. *The Family and Democratic Society.* Pp. 766. Routledge and Kegan Paul, 1948.
A comprehensive survey which discusses among other things the educational needs of young married women.

878. Mumford, L. *The Culture of Cities.* Pp. 600. Secker and Warburg, 1948.
A noted and influential historical survey: see especially Ch. vii, Social Basis of the New Urban Order.

879. Shearman, H. C. *Education—the New Horizon.* Pp. 128. Nicholson and Watson, 1948.
Ch. vii shows the relationship of adult and further education to the educational system established by the 1944 Act.

880. Chase, S. *The Proper Study of Mankind.* Pp. 288. Phoenix, 1950.
A stimulating introduction to the study of human relations.

881. Jacks, M. L. *Modern Trends in Education.* Pp. 208. Melrose, 1950.

882. Jeffreys, M. V. C. *Glaucon: an Inquiry into the Aims of Education.* Pp. 183. Pitman, 1950.

883. Riesman, D. *The Lonely Crowd.* Pp. 395. Yale U.P., 1950.
An American study of social change, with much that is relevant to contemporary Britain.

884. Valentine, C. W. *Psychology and its Bearing on Education.* Pp. 674. Methuen, 1950.

885. Huxley, J. (ed.). *Freedom and Culture.* Pp. 270. Wingate, 1951.
Compiled by UNESCO: includes chapters on Culture—a Human Right, The Right to Education, Freedom of Information, and Freedom of Science.

886. OTTAWAY, A. K. C. *Education and Society*. Pp. 192. Routledge and Kegan Paul, 1953.
A study of education as a function of society with reference to recent work in sociology, anthropology and psychology.

887. *Scottish Adult Education*, No. 9, Dec. 1953. *Conference Number*.
Contains addresses by HETHERINGTON, Sir H., on Objectives in Education; HUNTER, G., on education and Culture; and CALDER, R., on We andThey—Education for a Changing World.

888. CAUTER, T., and DOWNHAM, J. S. *The Communication of Ideas. A Study of Contemporary Influences on Urban Life*. Pp. 342. Chatto and Windus, 1954.
Based on a survey of leisure-time interests and activities in Derby.

889. GLASS, D. V. (ed.). *Social Mobility in Britain*. Pp. 420. Routledge and Kegan Paul, 1954.
Analysis of such concepts as class and status, and studies in the extent of social mobility.

890. JACKS, M. L. *The Education of Good Men*. Pp. 192. Gollancz, 1955.
Concerned particularly with aims and principles.

891. JUDGES, A. V. (ed.). *Looking Forward in Education*. Pp. 174. Faber, 1955.
Includes address by KING, E. J., on The Prospect for Adult Education.

892. THORNDIKE, R. L. and HAGEN, E. *Measurement and Evaluation in Psychology and Education*. Pp. 575. Wiley, New York, and Chapman and Hall, 1955.

893. FLOUD, J. E. (ed.), HALSEY, A. H., and MARTIN, F. M. *Social Class and Educational Opportunity*. Pp. 172. Heinemann, 1956.

894. MOGEY, J. *Family and Neighbourhood*. Pp. 198. Oxford U.P., 1956.
Studies made in Oxford revealing the emergence of new working-class attitudes. Cf. WILLMOT, P., and YOUNG, M., *Family and Kinship in East London*, pp. 252, 1957, and *Family and Class in a London Church*, pp. 202, 1960 (both Routledge and Kegan Paul).

895. O'CONNOR, D. J. *An Introduction to the Philosophy of Education*. Pp. 156. Routledge and Kegan Paul, 1957.
A brief and astringent survey.

896. GALBRAITH, J. K. *The Affluent Society*. Pp. 288. Hamish Hamilton, 1958.
Important on education in relation to affluence. See also by the same author *The Liberal Hour*, pp. 192, Hamish Hamilton, 1960.

897. SPROTT, W. J. H. *Human Groups*. Pp. 219. Penguin, 1958.

898. WILLIAMS, R. *Culture and Society, 1780–1950*. Pp. 383. Chatto and Windus, 1958.
"An account and an interpretation of our responses in thought and feeling to changes in English society since the late eighteenth century". *The Long Revolution*, by the same author, pp. 384, Chatto and Windus, 1961, is a sequel, and includes a review of some major cultural developments, e.g., education, the growth of the reading public, and the growth of the popular press.

899. YOUNG, M. *The Rise of the Meritocracy*. Pp. 160. Thames and Hudson, 1958.
Satirical but penetrating on the possible long-term effects of recent developments. Cf. DRUCKER, P., *The Landmarks of To-morrow*, pp. 215, Heinemann, 1959.

900. COLLIER, K. G. *The Social Purposes of Education*. Pp. 252. Routledge and Kegan Paul, 1959.

901. PRESSLEY, S. L., ROBINSON, F. P., and HORROCKS, J. E. *Psychology in Education*. Pp. 658. Harper, New York, 1959.
A revised edition of a work originally published as PRESSLEY, S. L., *Psychology and the New Education*, 1933. A general review of the principles of learning,

902. ABERCROMBIE, M. L. *The Anatomy of Judgment.* Pp. 168. Hutchinson, 1960.

903. DUCRET, B., and RAFE-UZ-ZAMAN (eds.). *The University Today: its Rôle and Place in Society. An International Study.* World University Service, Geneva [1960].

904. PEEL, E. A. *The Pupil's Thinking.* Pp. 200. Oldbourne, 1960.
The process of thinking studied genetically from early childhood to adolescence. Relevant to adult learning since childhood patterns influence thinking in later life.

905. ANDERSON, N. *Work and Leisure.* Pp. 296. Routledge and Kegan Paul, 1961.
The latest examination of this problem. Other are: BURNS, C. D., *Leisure in the Modern World*, pp. 216, Allen and Unwin, 1932; MISSEN, L. R., *The Employment of Leisure*, pp. 184, Wheaton, 1935; BOYD, W. (ed.), *The Challenge of Leisure*, pp. 245, New Education Fellowship, 1936; DURANT, H. W., *The Problem of Leisure*, pp. 286, Routledge, 1938.

(b) THEORY OF ADULT EDUCATION

(i) General

906. BRITISH INSTITUTE OF ADULT EDUCATION. Reports of Annual Conferences, especially:
Report of Proceedings at the First Conference. Pp. 25. Oxford, 1922.
The Groundwork of Adult Education. Pp. 135. 1926.
Adult Education in the Life of the Nation. Pp. 126. 1926.
Next Steps in Adult Education. Pp. 87. 1928.
Adult Education and the Changing World. Pp. 101. 1933.
Report of the Thirteenth Annual Conference, in *A.E.*, Vol. VII, 1934-5, pp. 125-47.
Report of the Sixteenth Annual Conference, in *A.E.*, Vol. X, 1937-8, pp. 129-83.
Adult Education: its Place in Post-War Society, in *A.E.*, Vol. XVI, 1943-4, pp. 35-91.
New Responsibilities for Adult Education, in *A.E.*, Vol. XVIII, 1945-6, pp. 47-98.
Cultural Forces in British Life Today. Pp. 48. 1947.
The Individual in Contemporary Society. Pp. 88. 1947.
These reports contain papers on a great variety of aspects of adult education—meaning and purpose, methods and organisation, and relation to contemporary society. Other Conference reports are listed at **562, 1097, 1165**.

907. NEWMAN, Sir G. *Some Notes on Adult Education in England.* Pp. 31. N.A.S.U., 1930.
Also published in *J.A.E.*, Vol. V, 1930-32.

908. WORLD ASSOCIATION FOR ADULT EDUCATION. *World Conference on Adult Education, Cambridge, 1929.* Pp. 580. 1930.
A valuable conspectus of activities and discussion of problems.

909. BRYSON, L. *Adult Education.* Pp. 213. American Book Co., New York, 1936.
An attempt to systematise the theory and practice of adult education.

910. MANSBRIDGE, A. (ed. CLARKE, L.). *The Kingdom of the Mind.* Pp. 220. Dent, 1944.
Essays and addresses 1903-37, mostly on adult education, by the founder of the W.E.A.

911. BRITISH INSTITUTE OF ADULT EDUCATION. *Adult Education after the War.* Pp. 76. Oxford U.P., 1945.
One of several studies undertaken at this time. Cf. ASSOCIATION OF TUTORS IN ADULT EDUCATION, *The Future of Adult Education*, pp. 36, Leeds, 1944.

912. *The Dunblane Conference,* in *A.E.,* Vol. XX, 1947-8, pp. 60-74.
Account of the annual conference of the British Institute of Adult Education (Scottish branch), dealing with the place of adult education in plans for further education.

913. CLARKE, F. *Adult Education, What Now?* Pp. 24. N.A.S.U., 1949.

914. UNESCO. *Summary Report of the International Conference on Adult Education.* Pp. 40. Paris, 1949.
Report of a conference at Elsinore, 1949, on the purposes, content and organisation of adult education. Some of the addresses are printed in *Adult Education: Current Trends and Practices,* pp. 148, Paris, 1949.

915. PEERS, R. *The Future of Adult Education,* in *A.E.,* Vol. XXV, 1952-3, pp. 87-95.
The substance of an address to the Annual Meeting of the Tutors' Association.

916. *Challenge and Response in Adult Education,* in *A.E.,* Vol. XXVII, 1954-5, pp. 166-96.
Papers by ALEXANDER, W. P., WALLER, R. D., HUNTER, G., and TYLECOTE, M.

917. ASHBY, E. *The Pathology of Adult Education.* Pp. 24. Boyd, Belfast, 1955.
Analyses some of the symptoms of adult education to-day and suggests remedies.

918. KEMPFER, H. *Adult Education.* Pp. 442. McGraw Hill, New York, 1955.
Comprehensive treatment from an American viewpoint. Other American surveys which contain much theoretical material are ESSERT, P. L., *Creative Leadership of Adult Education,* pp. 347, Prentice-Hall, New York, 1951; and SHEATS, P. H., JAYNE, C. D., and SPENCE, R. B., *Adult Education: the Community Approach,* pp. 544, Dryden P., New York, 1953.

919. WEST RIDING OF YORKSHIRE COUNTY COUNCIL. *Bingley Vacation Course on Further Education, 1954. A Selection of Main Addresses.* Pp. 52. 1955.
Includes addresses by HUNTER, G., on Adult Education, by RAYBOULD, S. G., on The Present Economic and Industrial Background, and by CLEGG, A. B., on The Social Background of Further Education.

920. BLAKELEY, R. J. (ed. KIDD, J. R.). *Adult Education in a Free Society.* Pp. 192. Guardian Bird P., Toronto, 1958.
A collection of addresses on various aspects of adult education.

921. LENGRAND, P. *Adult Education,* in *F.A.E.,* Vol. X, 1958, pp. 91-100.
Review from an international viewpoint of the nature of adult education, the types of institutions which provide it, and the methods employed.

922. BRUNNER, E. DE S., WILDER, D. S., KIRCHNER, C., and NEWBERRY, J. S. *An Overview of Adult Education Research.* Pp. 287. Adult Education Association of the U.S.A., Chicago, 1959.

923. TYLECOTE, M. *The Future of Adult Education.* Pp. 32. Fabian Society, 1960.
See also **350, 352, 356, 361,** and Sections III (c) and IV (a).

(ii) Philosophy of Adult Education

924. STANLEY, O. (ed.). *The Way Out.* Pp. 121. Oxford U.P., 1923.
Valuable collection of essays on meaning and purpose of adult education.

925. HEATH, A. E. *A Philosophy of Adult Education,* in *W.A.B.,* 1st Ser., No. XXVIII, May 1926, pp. 20-32.

926. LINDEMAN, E. C. *The Meaning of Adult Education.* Pp. 242. New Republic, New York, 1926, repr. Harvest House Ltd., Montreal, 1961.
Expounds the principle that "the whole of life is learning".

927. HERMES, G. *Die geistigen Grundlagen der englischen Erwachsenenbildung.* Pp. 143. Rohland und Berthold, Crimmitschau, 1927.
Discusses the Christian, "neutral", and Marxist approaches to adult education, with emphasis on the last.

928. *The Highway and the Strait Gate,* in *W.A.B.,* 1st Ser., No. XL, May 1929, pp. 3-14.
An interesting attempt to arrive at a realistic philosophy of adult education.

929. BROWN, A. B. *The Meaning of Bias in Adult Education,* in *J.A.E.,* Vol. VI, 1932-4, pp. 310-16.
See also brief comments on this subject by ADAMS, W. S., in *Hwy.,* Vol. XXXIX, 1947-8, pp. 76-8, and EVANS, R., in *T.B.,* Winter 1950-51, pp. 13-14.

930. CLARKE, F. *Re-interpretation.* Pp. 16. N.F.A.E., 1948.
An address at the National Foundation's First Annual Conference, mainly on the nature and function of adult education.

931. WOOD, H. G. *Ideals and Realities in Adult Education.* Pp. 16. Fircroft College, 1949.

932. GRANT, G. *Philosophy and Adult Education,* in *A.E.,* Vol. XXVI, 1953-4, pp. 247-53.
Discussion of the place and purpose of adult education to-day.

933. McLEISH, J. *The Philosophical Basis of Adult Education,* in UNIVERSITY OF LEEDS INSTITUTE OF EDUCATION, *Researches and Studies,* No. 11, Jan. 1955, pp. 65-74, and No. 12, May 1955, pp. 27-37.

934. HUTCHINSON, E. M. *The Nature and Rôle of Adult Education,* in *F.A.E.,* Vol. X, 1958, pp. 100-5.

935. WILTSHIRE, H. C. *Adult Education: Way and Purpose—A Review,* in *S.A.E.,* No. 24, Dec. 1958, pp. 5-9.
Discusses the meaning and objectives of adult education in the mid-twentieth century.

936. BELTH, M., and SCHUELER, H. *Liberal Education for Adults Re-examined.* Pp. 7. C.S.L.E.A., Chicago, 1959.

937. SIMONS, H. *Higher Adult Education: its Place and Function.* Pp. 20. C.S.L.E.A., Chicago, 1959.

938. VERNER, C. *A Conceptual Scheme for the Identification and Classification of Processes for Adult Education.* Pp. 55 (duplicated). Florida State University, School of Education, Tallahassee, 1959.

See also **966,** and Sections IV(a), IV(b)(i).

(iii) Psychology of Adult Education

939. PEERS, R. *Some Applications of Educational Theory to Adult Education,* in *J.A.E.,* Vol. I, 1926-7, pp. 36-49.
See also SPEARMAN, C., *What is Really Wrong with Adults?* in *J.A.E.,* Vol. II, 1927-8, pp. 12-19, which challenges Peers's views and attempts an assessment of adult learning abilities; and PEERS, R., *This Adult Business, ibid.,* pp. 158-62.

940. THORNDIKE, E. L. and Others. *Adult Learning.* Pp. 335. Macmillan, New York, 1928.
A valuable and comprehensive survey of American experimental studies in various aspects of adult learning. See also the same authors' informative and suggestive study, *Adult Interests,* pp. 265, Macmillan, New York, 1935. More recent studies are OVERSTREET, H. A., *The Mature Mind,* pp. 295, Gollancz, 1950 (a general survey taking account of Thorndike's ideas); KIDD, J. R., *How Adults Learn,* Association P., New York, 1959.

941. ROSENSTOCK, E. *The Social Function of Adult Education,* in *W.A.B.,* 1st Ser., No. XLIV, May 1930, pp. 10-16.
An early study of the working of the group in adult education. For more recent investigations see below (**953**).

942. RUCH, F. L., *Adult Learning,* in *Psychological Bulletin,* Vol. XXX, 1933, pp. 387-414.
A review of studies in learning ability as related to age. For more recent investigations in this field see below (**956, 957**).

943. WEISENBURG, T., ROE, A., and McBRIDE, K. E. *Adult Intelligence: A Psychological Study of Test Performances.* Pp. 169. Commonwealth Fund, New York, 1936.
Based on a sample of hospital patients.

944. GLOVER, E. *Psychological Obstacles to Learning—I,* in *A.E.,* Vol. IX, 1936-7, pp. 110-18.
Deals with emotional difficulties in the way of learning and suggests applications to the teaching of adults.

945. BUSWELL, G. T. *How Adults Read.* Pp. 171. Chicago U.P., 1937.
See also GRAY, W. S., and ROGERS, B., *Maturity in Reading: its Nature and Appraisal,* pp. 285, Chicago U.P., 1956; NELSON, H. B., *Adult Reading* (National Society for the Study of Education, 55th Yearbook, Part II), pp. 299, Chicago U.P., 1956; VERNON, M. D., *The Improvement of Reading,* in *B.J.E.P.,* Vol. XXVI, 1956, pp. 85-93.

946. WECHSLER, D. *The Measurement and Appraisal of Adult Intelligence.* Pp. 307. Williams and Wilkins, Baltimore, 1939, 4th edn. 1958.
See also MAXWELL, A. E., *An Adult Test of General Mental Attainment,* pp. 11 (duplicated), Univ. of Leeds Institute of Education, 1953; HEIM, A. W., *The Appraisal of Intelligence,* pp. 180, Methuen, 1954.

947. BURT, C. *The Education of Illiterate Adults,* in *B.J.E.P.,* Vol. XV, Part I, Feb. 1945 pp. 20-7.
Another valuable study, based on army experience, is WALL, W. D., *The Backward Adult,* in *Army Education,* Vols. XXII, 1948, pp. 145-56, and XXIII, 1949, pp. 30-6, 75-82. LEWIS, M. M., *The Importance of Illiteracy,* pp. 187, Harrap, 1953, discusses extent, causes and possible remedies.

948. COATES, T. H. *The Measurement of Adult Interests.* Unpublished Ph.D. thesis, London Univ., 1950.
A methodological study aimed at establishing a suitable method of inquiry, especially among students in adult classes.

949. FROEHLICH, C. P. and DARLEY, J. G. *Studying Students.* Pp. 429. Science Research Associates, Chicago, 1952.
A useful review of methods of study, most of them applicable to adult students.

950. RAVEN, J. C. *Human Nature: its Development, Variations, and Assessment.* Pp. 226. Bell, 1952.

951. McLEISH, J. *Maturity,* in *A.E.,* Vol. XXVII, 1954-5, pp. 86-96.
Discussion of the meaning of "maturity" in the context of adult education.

952. MURPHY, G., and KUHLEN, R. G. *Psychological Needs of Adults: a Symposium.* Pp. 27. C.S.L.E.A., Chicago, 1955.

953. KLEIN, J. *The Study of Groups.* Pp. 210. Routledge and Kegan Paul, 1956.
A survey of the results of inquiries into the development of relationships in small groups. See also SCHACHTER, S., *The Psychology of Affiliation: Experimental Studies in the Sources of Gregariousness*, pp. 151, Stanford U.P., 1959; THIBAUT, J. W., and KELLEY, H. H., *The Social Psychology of Groups*, pp. 326, Chapman and Hall, 1959. MANN, R. D., *A Review of the Relationship between Personality and Performance in Small Groups*, in *Psychological Bulletin*, Vol. LVI, 1959, pp. 241-70, summarises studies in this field 1900-57. For the adult educational significance of groups see two duplicated papers by STYLER, W. E., *Group Psychology and the W.E.A. Class*, pp. 20, and *W.E.A. Tutors and their Groups*, pp. 21 (both Manchester Univ. Extra-Mural Dept., 1958); PEERS, R., *Aims and Methods of Adult Education*, in *F.A.E.*, Vol. VI, 1954, pp. 127-31; and articles by LIPPETT, R., and BRADFORD, L. P., in *F.A.E.*, Vol. VIII, 1956, pp. 157-67.

954. MILES, H. B. *Some Determinants of Academic Performance amongst Adult Students.* Unpublished M.Sc. thesis, Univ. of Wales (Cardiff), 1956.
A suggestive study of candidates (men and women) for the London Sister Tutor's Diploma.

955. FRIEDMANN, S. *The Role of Attitudes in Comprehension*, in *B.J.P.*, Vol. XLIX, 1958, pp. 222-9.

956. WELFORD, A. T. *Ageing and Human Skill.* Pp. 310. Oxford U.P., 1958.
A report centred on work by the Nuffield Unit for Research into Problems of Ageing. See next entry.

957. BIRREN, J. E. (ed.) *Handbook of Aging and the Individual.* Pp. 951. Chicago U.P., 1959.
Part IV deals with psychological aspects of the subject, and offers "an authoritative technical summary of the scientific and professional literature". This book and Welford's are the most substantial recent works in this field, but there are numerous articles, e.g. McLEISH, J., *The Age Factor in Adult Education*, in UNIVERSITY OF LEEDS, INSTITUTE OF EDUCATION, *Researches and Studies*, No. 6, May 1952, pp. 26-45; VINCENT, D. F., *The Linear Relationship between Age and Score of Adults in Intelligence Tests*, in *Occupational Psychology*, Vol. XXVI, 1952, pp. 243-9; CLAY, H. M., *Changes of Performance with Age on Similar Tasks of Varying Complexity*, in *B.J.P.*, Vol. XLV, 1954, pp. 7-13; BROMLEY, D. B., *Some Experimental Tests of the Effects of Age on Creative Intellectual Output*, in *Journal of Gerontology*, Vol. XI, 1956, pp. 74-82; WALLACE, J. G., *Some Studies of Perception in Relation to Age*, in *B.J.P.*, Vol. XLVII, 1956, pp. 283-97.
   The *Journal of Gerontology*, published quarterly since 1946 by the Gerontological Society, St. Louis, Missouri, has in each issue a section dealing with psychological and social aspects of ageing. HAND, S. E., *Adult Education: a Review of Physiological and Psychological Changes in Aging and their Implications for Teachers of Adults*, pp. 33 (duplicated) State Dept. of Education, Tallahassee, Florida, 3rd edn. 1957, is a handy guide to American inquiries.

958. CHOWN, S. M. *Rigidity—a Flexible Concept*, in *Psychological Bulletin*, Vol. LVI, 1959, pp. 195-223.
Rigidity, whether in personality organisation, or in the response to particular circumstances, is an important topic in adult learning.

959. MAVES, P. B. *Understanding Ourselves as Adults.* Pp. 217. Abingdon P., New York, 1959.
A Christian approach to the study of adults, in an American context.

960. ABELSON, H. I. *Persuasion: How Opinions and Attitudes are Changed.* Pp. 127. Crosby Lockwood, 1960.
Based on American work, but concise review of main findings and bibliography are useful.

961. ADER, J. (ed.). *Processus du perfectionnement des connaissances et de la formation personnelle chez l'adulte.* Pp. 79. Unesco Institute for Education, Hamburg, 1961.
Report of a conference at Hamburg in 1960 dealing with the relation between educational needs and the personal development of the adult. Includes reports on researches in eight European countries.

See also **861, 884, 886, 892, 901, 904.**

(iv) Social Aspects

962. PAUL, E. and C. *Proletcult.* Pp. 159. Parsons, 1921.
Argues the case for independent working-class education as preparation for a social revolution. The same point of view is put by HORRABIN, J. F., *Independent Working-Class Education,* in *J.A.E.,* Vol. I, 1926-7, pp. 80-6, and in publications of the National Council of Labour Colleges (**547**). For the opposing view see COLE, G, D. H., *Labour in the Commonwealth,* pp. 223, Heatley [1918] (Chs. vii-ix); and *The Place of the W.E.A. in Working Class Education,* pp. 14, W.E.A., 1924.

963. KOTINSKY, R. *Adult Education and the Social Scene.* Pp. 230. Appleton-Century, New York, 1933.
Valuable study of the function of adult education in a democratic society.

964. LAMBERT, R. S. *The Dynamics of Adult Education,* in *Year Book of Education,* 1934 (**35**), pp. 657-67.
Considers the problem of adjustment to changing circumstances.

965. AMERICAN ASSOCIATION FOR ADULT EDUCATION. *Adult Education and Democracy.* Pp. 85. New York, 1936.
Addresses by BEARD, C. A., ADAMS, W. G. S., MARTIN, E. D., and others.

966. HEWITT, D., and MATHER, K. F. *Adult Education: a Dynamic for Democracy.* Pp. 200. Appleton-Century, New York, 1937.
Covers such topics as philosophy of adult education, adult interests, teaching techniques. Bibliography.

967. PEERS, R. *Adult Education and the Needs of Democracy,* in *A.E.,* Vol. X, 1937-8, pp. 208-18.
On the inadequacy of current adult educational provision.

968. SHEARMAN, H. C. *Adult Education for Democracy.* Pp. 95. W.E.A., 1944.
A valuable study by the then Education Officer of the W.E.A.

969. REAVELEY, C., and WINNINGTON, J. *Democracy and Industry.* Pp. 175. Chatto and Windus, 1947.
Considers the effects of modern industrial organisation on the worker, and urges a new approach to adult education in the spirit of the Danish Folk High Schools. Cf. BROWN, A. B., *The Machine and the Worker,* pp. 218, Nicholson and Watson, 1934.

970. JEFFREYS, M. V. C. *Education, Freedom and Community.* Pp. 24. N.A.S.U., 1948.
Stresses particularly the need for a Christian education.

971. ALLAWAY, A. J. *Adult Education in a Changing Society.* Pp. 30. University College, Leicester, 1951.
Reviews the history of adult education and analyses the purposes which it should now seek to fulfil.

972. CADBURY, G. *Adult Education in an Industrial Society.* Pp. 18. Fircroft College [1952].

973. JESSUP, F. W. (ed.). *Adult Education towards Social and Political Responsibility.* Pp. 144. Unesco Institute for Education, Hamburg, 1953.
Report of addresses and other contributions made at an international conference in Hamburg in 1952; concerned for the most part with Western Europe.

974. VERNER, C. *Adult Education for Tomorrow's World,* in *A.E.,* Vol. XXVI, 1953-4, pp. 32-41.
American criticism of the aims, methods and organisation of adult education today.

975. MILLS, C. W. *Mass Society and Liberal Education.* Pp. 17. C.S.L.E.A., New York, 1954.
Urges that adult education should aim at creating a public living in accordance with adequate definitions of reality.

976. KING, E. J. *The Relationship between Adult Education and Social Attitudes in English Industrial Society.* Unpublished Ph.D. thesis, London Univ., 1955.
Argues that industrialisation has "disrupted the immemorial patterns of social education", and that conventional adult education must rethink its philosophy.

977. STYLER, W. E. *Adult Education and Social Planning,* in *B.J.E.S.,* Vol. V, 1956-7, pp. 37-46.
Suggests experiments to create "active" adult education linked directly to plans for social development.

978. GROOMBRIDGE, B. *New Objectives for Adult Education,* in *A.E.,* Vol. XXX, 1957-8, pp. 197-215.
Expounds the view that adult education will advance by relating itself directly to contemporary problems and social change.

979. JESSUP, F. W. *Trends and Resources,* in *A.E.,* Vol. XXX, 1957-8, pp. 167-80.
Reviews the changes since 1919 and the functions and importance of adult education.

980. MACK, J. *Adult Education and the Dynamics of Community,* in *S.A.E.,* No. 24, Dec. 1958, pp. 10-19.
Analyses contemporary patterns of social cohesion and their significance for adult education.

981. *Leisure in a Technical Age,* in *A.E.,* Vol. XXXII, 1959-60, pp. 137-65.
Conference addresses by various speakers on the challenge of social change to adult education. Cf. ADAMS, J. W. L., *Challenge and Opportunity,* in *S.A.E.,* No. 33, Dec. 1961, pp. 6-12, and succeeding addresses in the same issue.

982. WORKERS' EDUCATIONAL ASSOCIATION. *Aspects of Adult Education.* Pp. 83. 1960.
Report of a working party with special reference to the W.E.A. and social change.

See also **906, 919-20,** and Section IV (a).

(c) METHODS OF TEACHING AND STUDY

(i) General

983. COLE, G. D. H. (ed.). *The Tutor's Manual.* Pp. 40. Association of Tutorial Class Tutors, Letchworth, n.d.

984. RATCLIFF, A. J. J. *The Adult Class.* Pp. 172. Nelson, 1938.
Designed to provide guidance for teachers of adults and adolescents.

985. YORKSHIRE COUNCIL FOR FURTHER EDUCATION. *Handbook for Part-time Teachers.* Pp. 45. Leeds, 1944.

986. BREW, J. M. *Informal Education.* Pp. 383. Faber, 1946.
Though primarily concerned with youth education, has considerable relevance to adult education.

987. SPENCER, F. H., and INGRAM, B. *The Art of the Part-Time Teacher.* Pp. 80. Pitman, 1947.

988. WISEMAN, D. *Informal Education,* in *Year Book of Education,* 1948 (**35**), pp. 109-20.
Discusses informal methods of adult education used during the Second World War.

989. KNOWLES, M. S. *Informal Adult Education.* Pp. 288. Associated P., New York, 1950, new edn. 1955.

990. NORTHERN ADVISORY COUNCIL FOR FURTHER EDUCATION. *Suggestions for Part-time Teachers of Women's Subjects.* Pp. 34. Newcastle, 1950.

991. HIGHET, G. *The Art of Teaching.* Pp. 282. Methuen, 1951.
Stimulating book with much that is directly relevant to work in adult classes.

992. HOPKINSON, D. M. *Residential Short Courses—Planning and Method,* in *A.E.,* Vol. XXIV, 1951-2, pp. 294-300.

993. KELLAWAY, F. W. *Part-time Teaching.* Pp. 124. Bell, 1952.
Designed particularly for technical and further education.

994. MILLS, H. R. *Techniques of Technical Training.* Pp. 196. Cleaver-Hume P., 1953.
Contains much advice of general application.

995. ADULT EDUCATION ASSOCIATION OF THE U.S.A. *How to Teach Adults.* Pp. 48. Chicago, 1955.
Elementary but useful.

996. UNIVERSITY OF SYDNEY—DEPARTMENT OF TUTORIAL CLASSES. *Some Papers in Adult Education.* Pp. 112. Sydney [1956?].
Mainly concerned with teaching methods, e.g. in literature, psychology, trade union studies, music, world affairs, philosophy.

997. CLARKE, G. K. *The Art of Lecturing.* Pp. 24. Heffer, Cambridge, 1957.

998. MILLER, M. U. (ed.). *On Teaching Adults: an Anthology.* Pp. 108. C.S.L.E.A., Chicago, 1960.

999. MORGAN, B., HOLMES, G. E., and BUNDY, C. E. *Methods in Adult Education.* Pp. 188. Interstate Printers, Danville, Ill., 1960.

1000. STATON, T. F. *How to Instruct Successfully: Modern Teaching Methods in Adult Education.* Pp. 298. McGraw Hill, New York, 1960.
Includes chapters on the lecture-method, the demonstration-performance, the group-discussion, and the rôle-playing method.

1001. McFARLAND, H. S. N. *University Lectures,* in *Univs. Rev.,* Vol. XXXIV, 1961-2, pp. 5-11.
A stimulating analysis by no means irrelevant to extra-mural teaching.

See also **322, 966.**

(ii) Student Personnel, Motives and Attitudes

1002. HOY, J. D. *An Enquiry as to Interests and Motives for Study among Adult Evening Students*, in *B.J.E.P.*, Vol. III, 1933, pp. 13-26.
Reviews results of a questionnaire to students in evening institutes.

1003. WILLIAMS, W. E., and HEATH, A. E., *Learn and Live—the Consumers' View of Adult Education*. Pp. 279. Methuen, 1936.
Valuable analysis of the reactions of over 500 members of adult classes of various types.

1004. BIRKINSHAW, M. *The Leisure of the Adult Student—a Sample Investigation in London*, in *A.E.*, Vol. IX, 1936-7, pp. 203-16. Also published separately by London District W.E.A.
Report of an investigation by a Southall tutorial class.

1005. FLOOD, W. E., and CROSSLAND, R. W. *The Origin of Interest and Motives for Study of Natural Sciences and Psychology among Adult Students in Voluntary Courses*, in *B.J.E.P.*, Vol. XVIII, 1948, pp. 105-17.
Cf. CROSSLAND, R. W., *Interests in Natural History among Adults*, unpublished M.Ed. thesis, Manchester Univ., 1955, based on samples of adult students and Y.H.A. members.

1006. LEEDS UNIVERSITY DEPARTMENT OF EXTRA-MURAL STUDIES—JOINT TUTORIAL CLASSES COMMITTEE. *Tutorial Class Students: Report of an Enquiry carried out in the Session 1946-47*. Pp. 99 (duplicated). 1949.

1007. STYLER, W. E. *Who Were the Students?* Pp. 28. N.I.A.E., 1950.
Report on inquiries into the student personnel of tutorial and sessional classes in the Manchester University area, 1947-49. Other aspects of this subject are explored in articles by ABRAHART, B. W., DEES, N., LEWIS, G. I., STYLER, W. E., and WALLER, R. D., in *A.E.*, Vols. XXIII-XXV, 1950-3, *passim*; and articles by Styler in *Brit. Journ. of Sociology*, Vol. V, 1953, pp. 79-83, and by NICOL, B. de B., in *S.A.E.*, No. 7, Apr. 1953, pp. 10-13.

1008. LEES, J. P. *The Social Mobility of a Group of Eldest-born and Intermediate Adult Males*, in *B.J.P.*, Vol. XLIII, 1952, pp. 210-21.
A study of a group of Nottingham extra-mural students who attended day-release courses 1924-29 under the Miners' Welfare Scholarship Scheme.

1009. GREEN, E. *Adult Education: Why this apathy?* Pp. 146. Allen and Unwin, 1953.
Based on enquiry into the views of students in adult classes.

1010. MAYLOR, W. D. *University Extension Students in London, 1950-51: a Survey and Report*. Pp. 24. London Univ. Extra-Mural Dept., 1954.
Valuable survey of types of student, motives and interests.

1011. TRENAMAN, J. *Education in the Adult Population—Part I*, in *A.E.*, Vol. XXX, 1957-8, pp. 216-24 (reprinted Vol. XXXIV, 1961-2, pp. 303-11).
Summary of a valuable unpublished study (typescript copy at N.I.A.E.) dealing with "attitudes to opportunities for further education in relation to educational environment in samples of the adult population".

1012. WEST RIDING OF YORKSHIRE COUNTY COUNCIL. *Vacation Course on Further Education, 1957: Authority and Changing Values*. Pp. 108. 1958.
Addresses on the social and educational background of further education students.

1013. GOULD, J. D. *The Recruitment of Adult Students*. Pp. 63. Vaughan College Papers, No. 5. Leicester Univ., 1959.
Report of an enquiry into the sociological factors influencing recruitment in University and W.E.A. classes.

1014. HOULE, C. O. *The Inquiring Mind: a Study of the Adult who Continues to Learn.* Pp. 101. Wisconsin U.P., Madison, 1961.
Reflections by an experienced American adult educationist based on interviews with adult students.

See also **749-50, 940, 966, 1170.**

(iii) Aims and Approaches

1015. WOOTTON, B. *A Plea for Constructive Teaching*, in *A.E.*, Vol. X, 1937-8, pp. 91-105.
On the dangers of encouraging a purely critical outlook in adult students.

1016. MEARNS, H. *The Creative Adult.* Pp. 308. Doubleday Doran, New York, 1940.
Urges a new approach to the teaching of adults "to rescue their creative spirit from the annihilating imprisonment of conformity".

1017. RAYBOULD, S. G. *The Approach to W.E.A. Teaching.* Pp. 28. W.E.A., 1947.
Discusses the relationship of the tutor to the W.E.A. as well as the details of teaching method. Cf. COLE, G. D. H., *The Tutor and the Working Class Movement*, in *T.B.*, 2nd Ser., No. 22, Apr. 1939, pp. 1-10.

1018. HOGGART, R. *Some Notes on Aim and Method in University Tutorial Classes*, in *A.E.*, Vol. XX, 1947-8, pp. 187-94.
See comment by WILLIAMS, R., in *A.E.*, Vol. XXI, 1948-9, pp. 96-8.

1019. PURSER, A. O. *Methods and Aims in Teaching Adults*, in *A.E.*, Vol. XXII, 1949-50, pp. 96-103.
Comments on several problems by a former tutor of Hillcroft.

1020. DAVIES, L. *The General Approach to Adult Teaching*, in *A.E.*, Vol. XXIII, 1950-1, pp. 182-90.
Mainly concerned with evening institute work.

1021. HODGKIN, T. *Objectivity, Ideologies and the Present Political Situation*, in *Hwy.*, Vol. XLII, 1950-1, pp. 79-81.
See also replies and comments by various writers later in the same volume.

1022. HUNTER, G. *Vocation and Culture—A Suggestion*, in *A.E.*, Vol. XXV, 1952-3, pp. 7-19.
Mainly on the need for an approach through vocational interests. Cf. the same author's paper to the N.I.A.E. Conference 1954 (**916**).

1023. ASHBY, E. *Growing Points in Adult Education: Strategy and Tactics*, in *S.A.E.*, No. 15, Dec. 1955, pp. 5-12.
Address advocating "technological humanism" as one desirable growing point. See also discussion in next issue, and the author's paper on *Technological Humanism* in *Journal of the Institute of Metals*, Vol. LXXXV, 1956-7, pp. 461-7.

1024. ELSDON, K. T. *Standards and Methods in Adult Education*, in *A.E.*, Vol. XXXI, 1958-9, pp. 25-37.
Suggests the need for a new approach and new methods in adult classes, with stress on orientation towards people and communities.

1025. WALLER, R. D. *Teaching Aims in Adult Education*, in *A.E.*, Vol. XXXI, 1958-9, pp. 251-2.
Report of an enquiry into the teaching aims of part-time tutors taking Joint Committee classes in the Manchester region.

(iv) Special Methods

1026. FISHER, N. G. *The Brains Trust as a Method of Adult Education*, in *A.E.*, Vol. XVIII, 1944-5, pp. 46-57.

1027. DODD, W. *Project Work in General Education*, in *A.E.*, Vol. XXIII, 1950-1, pp. 91-6.

1028. KING, E. J. *Projects and Research Methods with Adult Students*, in *A.E.*, Vol. XXIII, 1950-1, pp. 250-7.

1029. PRESLAND, J. M. *T.G. Reconnaissance*, in *A.E.*, Vol. XXV, 1952-3, pp. 228-33.
Describes a method of study which has been used by many Townswomen's Guilds.

(v) Students' Reading and Written Work

1030. CROWTHER, D. *Written Work in Adult Education (I) Values and Types*, in *A.E.*, Vol. XV, 1942-3, pp. 189-94.

1031. STYLER, W. E. *Written Work*, in *T.B.*, Autumn 1950, pp. 3-7.

1032. JONES, R. H. *Reading in the Adult Class*, in *A.E.*, Vol. XXV, 1952-3, pp. 197-204.
On methods of achieving satisfactory reading by adult students.

1033. SAUNDERS, J. W. *In Order to Understand: the Necessity for Writing in Extra-Mural Classes*, in *A.E.*, Vol. XXVIII, 1955-6, pp. 279-93.
Analysis of objections to written work and reasons for it. Suggests ways of approach and gives a specimen syllabus of written work in a three-year Literature course.

(vi) Discussion Method

1034. McBURNEY, J. H., and HANCE, K. G. *Discussion in Human Affairs*. Pp. 443. Harper, New York, 1939, rev. edn. 1950. Originally published as *The Principles and Methods of Discussion*.
Deals at length with the philosophy, techniques, and organisation of discussion.

1035. EWBANK, H. L., and AUER, J. J. *Discussion and Debate*. Pp. 526. Crofts, New York, 1941.
An exhaustive analysis, containing incidentally much sound advice.

1036. HUBBACK, E. M. *How to Lead Discussion Groups*. Pp. 24. Association for Education in Citizenship, 1942.

1037. LLOYD, W. E. *How to Run Discussion Groups*. Pp. 28. W.E.A. n.d.
Valuable. Also appeared in a somewhat different form, *Discussion Groups and their Leadership*, pp. 20, W.E.A. n.d.

1038. HEITLAND, B. *How to Conduct a Discussion Group*. Pp. 87. Allen and Unwin, 1949.
Directed mainly to the needs of youth organisations.

1039. BUREAU OF CURRENT AFFAIRS. *Discussion Method: the Purpose, Nature, and Application of Group Discussion*. Pp. 100. 1950.
Thorough and practical. In effect an enlarged version of the B.C.A.s *Discussion Method: Background Handbook*, No. 1, pp. 32.

1040. STYLER, W. E. *Questions and Discussion*. Pp. 30. W.E.A., 1952.

1041. BURTON, J. (ed.). *Group Discussion in Educational, Social and Working Life.* Pp. 92. Central Council for Health Education, 1954, 2nd edn. 1956.
Articles on group discussion method and its use in a variety of situations. Full bibliography.

(vii) Teaching Aids

1042. BRITISH INSTITUTE OF ADULT EDUCATION. *The Educational Uses of the Gramophone.* Pp. 30. 1937.

1043. KELLY, T. *Sources of Visual Aid Material for Use in the Adult Teaching of History and Contemporary Affairs.* Pp. 16. N.F.A.E. [1948].
A handlist of maps, charts, films and film-strips. Still the only list drawn up specifically for adult teaching. Up to date information must be sought in the various visual education year-books and periodicals (**58, 61, 64, 69**), and in the Catalogues issued since 1949 by the Educational Foundation for Visual Aids. These contain assessments of new material and apparatus, and occasionally have short articles on the use of visual aids in adult education—a number of these are listed in the 1952 edn. of this bibliography, No. 775.

1044. HILL, C. A. *Film-Strip Projection.* Pp. 96. Fountain P., 1949.

1045. UNESCO. *Films on Art.* Pp. 80. Paris, 1949, 3rd edn. 1953.
A valuable international catalogue.

1046. BUCHANAN, A. *The Film in Education.* Pp. 256. Phoenix, 1952.

1047. *Health Education Journal* (**672**), Vol. XIII, No. 1, 1955.
Special edition on visual education compiled in co-operation with UNESCO, and including chapters on evaluation, the use of still pictures, film-strips and films, and the work of audio-visual aids centres in Puerto Rico, Ceylon and London. Bibliography.

1048. SHAWE-TAYLOR, D. *The British Institute of Recorded Sound,* in *A.E.,* Vol. XXVIII, 1955-6, pp. 189-94.
A description of the work of the Institute.

1049. UNESCO. Reports and Papers on Mass Communications. No. 25. *Adult Educational Groups and Audio-Visual Techniques.* Pp. 36. Paris, 1958. No. 26. *The Kinescope and Adult Education.* Pp. 40. Paris, 1958. (On French experiments in the use of telerecordings.)

1050. —— Manuals on Adult and Youth Education. No. 1. *Filmstrips: Use, Evaluation and Production.* Pp. 54. Paris, 1959.

1051. POWELL, L. S. *A Guide to the Use of Visual Aids.* Pp. 41. British Association for Commercial and Industrial Education, 1961.

See also **37, 44, 58, 61, 64, 69, 85, 1082.**

(viii) Students' Manuals

1052. HENDERSON, B. L. K., and FREEMAN, A. *Manual of Essay Writing for Students in W.E.A. and Tutorial Classes.* Pp. 173. 1914, reprinted by W.E.A., *c.* 1921.

1053. ADAMS, Sir J. *The Student's Guide.* Pp. 254. Univ. of London P., 1916, 5th edn. Eng. Univs. P., 1938.

1054. STYLER, W. E. *How to Study.* Pp. 31. W.E.A., 1950, 2nd edn. 1955.

1055. CHAPMAN, R. *How shall I write it?* Pp. 32. W.E.A., 1957.
Pamphlet produced for trade union students.

1056. CORFIELD, A. J. *How to be a Student.* Pp. 38. W.E.A., 1957.
Includes advice on how to use libraries and books, how to make notes, how to write an essay and how to select a course of study.

(ix) Standards and Evaluation

1057. WOOTTON, B. *The Need for Differentiation*, in *J.A.E.*, Vol. II, 1927-8, pp. 55-67.
On the grading of students in adult education.

1058. WORKERS' EDUCATIONAL ASSOCIATION. *Aims and Standards in W.E.A. Classes.* Pp. 48. [1938].

1059. RAYBOULD, S. G. *University Standards in W.E.A. Work.* Pp. 34. W.E.A., 1948.

1060. BROOK, F. G. *The Problem of Comparing Standards in the Tutorial Class*, in *A.E.*, Vol. XXI, 1948-9, pp. 23-7.

1061. LEE, C. *University Standards in Extra-Mural Work*, in *A.E.*, Vol. XXII, 1949-50, pp. 31-8.

1062. MILLER, K. M. *Evaluation in Adult Education*, in *International Social Science Bulletin*, Vol. VII, 1955, pp. 430-42.
Surveys the difficulties of evaluation and discusses the criteria and methods.

1063. STYLER, W. E. *The W.E.A.'s Best*, in *A.E.*, Vol. XXXII, 1959-60, pp. 192-6.
A survey of reports from tutors taking some of the best classes in the Manchester area in recent years.

1064. MILLER, H. L., and McGUIRE, C. H. *Evaluating Liberal Adult Education.* Pp. 194. C.S.L.E.A., Chicago, 1961.
Report on an attempt to define objectives and to discover satisfactory methods of measuring achievement.

(x) Tutors and Tutor-training

1065. BOARD OF EDUCATION—ADULT EDUCATION COMMITTEE. *Paper No. 2. Report on the Recruitment, Training and Remuneration of Tutors.* Pp. 26. H.M.S.O., 1922.

1066. BRITISH INSTITUTE OF ADULT EDUCATION AND TUTORS' ASSOCIATION. *The Tutor in Adult Education: an Enquiry into the Problems of Supply and Training.* Pp. 251. Carnegie U.K. Trust, Dunfermline, 1928.

1067. ASSOCIATION OF TUTORS IN ADULT EDUCATION. *Report on the Duties of Organising Tutors.* Pp. 7. 1938.

1068. MINISTRY OF EDUCATION—COMMITTEE ON RECRUITMENT, TRAINING AND CONDITIONS OF SERVICE OF YOUTH LEADERS AND COMMUNITY CENTRE WARDENS. *Report.* Pp. 20. H.M.S.O., 1949.
See further MINISTRY OF EDUCATION—NATIONAL ADVISORY COUNCIL ON THE TRAINING AND SUPPLY OF TEACHERS, *Second Report: The Recruitment and Training of Youth Leaders and Community Centre Wardens*, pp. 14, H.M.S.O., 1951.

1069. ABRAHART, B. W. *The Training of Tutors in Adult Education*, in *Journal of the Institute of Education of Durham University*, Vol. V, 1953, pp. 19-22.
Description of some of the problems of training, with an account of courses. Cf. COLE, G. D. H., *The Tutor*, in *Hwy.*, Vol. XLIV, 1952-3, pp. 280-5; BURMEISTER, W., *The Tutor's Qualities*, in *A.E.*, Vol. XXVI, 1953-4, pp. 10-15; STYLER, W. E. (ed.), *The Good Tutor: a Student View*, pp. 22, N.W. District W.E.A., Manchester 1956.

1070. STYLER, W. E., and WALLER, R. D. *Tutors and their Training*. Pp. 31 (duplicated). U.C.A.E., 1954.
Memorandum prepared for the Universities' Council for Adult Education.

See also **521, 570, 1084, 1117, 1153.**

(d) PARTICULAR SUBJECTS
(i) Classics

1071. LIVINGSTONE, R. W. *The Place of Classics in Adult Education*. Pp. 8. B.I.A.E., 1922.
Cf. the same author's *Education for a World Adrift* (**867**), which stresses the need for adult education based on history and literature, especially classical literature.

1072. CAREY, R. M. *Greece and the Factory Worker*, in *Greece and Rome*, Vol. XV, 1946, pp. 61-3.
On residential courses for factory workers.

1073. PYM, D. *Outlines for Teaching Greek Reading*. Pp. 16. Murray, 1946.
Based on experience with adult students at Bristol.

1074. HOWIE, G. *An Experiment in Greek Studies*, in *A.E.*, Vol. XXVI, 1953-4, pp. 71-5.
Description of the first year's work in an experimental class in Greek language at Swarthmore Educational Centre, Leeds.

(ii) Drama

1075. WOOD, J. *Drama in Adult Education*, in *A.E.*, Vol. IX, 1936-7, pp. 194-9.
A useful survey. See also NEWTON, R. G., *Drama in Villages and Clubs, ibid.*, pp. 271-6.

1076. RATCLIFF, N. *Rude Mechanicals: a Short Review of Village Drama*. Pp. 163. Nelson, 1938.

1077. TAYLOR, G. *Drama as Literature in the One-Year Class*, in *T.B.*, No. 84, Oct. 1951, pp. 12-16.
Cf. WILLIAMS, J. R., *Interpreting Drama*, in *A.E.*, Vol. XXXIII, 1960-1, pp. 254-60.

1078. JAMES, D. G. *Amateur Drama and the Community*, in *A.E.*, Vol. XXIV, 1951-2, pp. 170-9.

1079. JAMES, D. G. (ed.). *The Universities and the Theatre*. Pp. 123. Allen and Unwin, 1952 (*Colston Papers* Vol. IV).
A symposium including a number of papers which have a bearing on university extra-mural teaching in this field.

1080. HAINSWORTH, J. D. *Television Drama and the Adult Class*, in *A.E.*, Vol. XXXIV, 1961-2, pp. 126-9.

See also **314, 352, 562, 635, 659, 666, 679, 1136.**

(iii) Economics

1081. COLE, G. D. H. *The Teaching of Economic History and Theory*, in *J.A.E.*, Vol. I, 1926-7, pp. 227-35.

Other articles of interest are: FORD, P., *Some Problems in the Teaching of Economics*, in *A.E.*, Vol. VIII, 1935-6, pp. 30-7; SILBERMAN, L., *Economics on the Job*, in *F.E.*, Vol. III, No. 4, 1950, pp. 232-6 (on the teaching of theory in relation to a particular industry); GLOVER, F. J., *The Adult Student and Economics*, in *Hwy.*, Vol. XLIII, 1951-2, pp. 50-3 (a comment from the student's angle); WAY, J. J., *Some Teaching Suggestions*, in *Economics*, Vol. II, 1956, pp. 96-9.

1082. WORKERS' EDUCATIONAL ASSOCIATION. *The Film in Economics Classes*. Pp. 15. [1942].

Report on the use of a diagrammatic film on "Unemployment and Money". See also RAYBOULD, S. G., in *A.E.*, Vol. XV, 1942-3, pp. 195-8.

1083. JOHNSON, A. *Some Problems Associated with the Teaching of Economics*. Pp. 24. C.J.A.C., 1950.

1084. OXFORD UNIVERSITY—TUTORIAL CLASSES COMMITTEE. *Tutor-training: Teaching Methods in Adult Education with special reference to Trade Union Education*. Pp. 9. 1960.

The Committee issued at the same time a considerable amount of documentary material for use with trade union classes, e.g. case studies relating to passenger transport disputes.

1085. ECONOMICS ASSOCIATION. *The Teaching of Economics*. Pp. 52. [1961].

Designed for "pre-University and Final Professional level", but has much that is relevant to adult education.

(iv) Fine Arts (except Music)

1086. CONSTABLE, W. G. *Art and Adult Education*, in *A.E.*, Vol. VII, 1934-5, pp. 8-17.

Mainly on practical work in the visual arts. THOMAS, D. R. O., *An Experiment in Teaching the Appreciation of Art*, in *C.R.*, No. 40, July 1936, pp. 17-20, and LOEWENTHAL, H., *Education through Art for All*, in *A.E.*, Vol. XX, 1947-8, pp. 172-7, both suggest a combination of creative work with art history. ROSENAU, H., *The Approach to Art in Adult Education*, in *A.E.*, Vol. XIV, 1941-2, pp. 35-44, suggests a closer link with social studies. See also BAILLIE, M., *Some Remarks on Art Education and the Use of Colour Slides*, in *S.A.E.*, No. 14, Aug. 1955, pp. 19-22.

1087. BODKIN, T. *Adult Education in the Fine Arts*. Pp. 16. Selly Oak Colleges, Birmingham [1937].

1088. MANVELL, R. *Film Appreciation in Adult Education*, in *A.E.*, Vol. XVIII, 1945-6, pp. 16-21.

Cf. WILLIAMS, R., *Film as a Tutorial Subject*, in *R.H.P.*, Vol. III, II, 1953, pp. 27-37; HUNTLEY, J., *Film Appreciation: a Lecturer's Notebook*, in *A.E.*, Vol. XXIX, 1956-7, pp. 270-9.

1089. JESSUP, F. W. *The Arts and Adult Education*, in *A.E.*, Vol. XXI, 1948-9, pp. 117-27.

See also **37, 44, 364, 372-3, 376, 384, 660, 664, 668, 775, 781, 1045-6.**

(v) English Language

1090. EDWARDS, W. A. *English in the Tutorial Class*, in *J.A.E.*, Vol. VI, 1932-4, pp. 328-41.

1091. GROVE, V. *Adult Education and the English Language*, in *A.E.*, Vol. XXIV, 1951-2, pp. 7-14.

1092. LEVITT, J. *Language in Adult Education*, in *A.E.*, Vol. XXIX, 1956-7, pp. 24-32.
Description of a W.E.A. one-year course on language in general.

1093. BARCLAY, J. B. *Effective Reading*, in *University of Edinburgh Gazette*, No. 17, June 1957.
Report of an extra-mural course to improve reading speed and comprehension.

1094. DAVIES, C. W. *Clear Expression in Writing: a Teaching Experiment*, in *A.E.*, Vol. XXXI, 1958-9, pp. 42-6.
Account of content and methods in a one-week residential course.

1095. NEWMARK, P. *English in Technical Colleges*, in *A.E.*, Vol. XXXI 1958-9 pp. 100-6.

1096. WILLIAMS, S. H. *English for Foreigners*, in *A.E.*, Vol. XXXI, 1958-9, pp. 116-24.

(vi) Handicrafts

1097. BRITISH INSTITUTE OF ADULT EDUCATION. Report of Tenth Annual Conference. *Mind and Hand in Adult Education*. Pp. 101. 1931.
Addresses mainly concerned with the place of arts and crafts in adult education and with the education of the unemployed.

1098. TWEEDY, R. *Hardly Education? On Practical Work in Evening Institutes*, in *J.A.E.*, Vol. VI, 1932-4, pp. 415-24.
Cf. STEVENS, G. A., *Art and Craft in the Community Centre*, in *F.P.*, No. 3, Dec. 1947, pp. 6-10.

1099. SPALDING, Lucile. *Craft Standards for Townswomen's Guilds and Others*. Pp. 48. N.U.T.G. and N.I.A.E. [1956].
Discusses the problems of establishing a national craft standard and ways in which judging and teaching may be improved. See also by the same author *Craft Judging for Townswomen's Guilds and Others*, pp. 38, N.U.T.G. and N.I.A.E. [1959].

See also **750.**

(vii) History

1100. LYLE, E. A. *History: the Key Subject in Adult Education*, in *A.E.*, Vol. XVI, 1943-4, pp. 7-15.

1101. HOLLEY, N. M. *History for the Adult Student*, in *A.E.*, Vol. XX, 1947-8, pp. 87-94.
Deals particularly with history textbooks.

1102. MINISTRY OF EDUCATION. *Teaching History*. Pp. 92. H.M.S.O., 1952.
See Ch. viii on the formal teaching of history in adult classes.

1103. WRIGHT, E. *Agony and Re-appraisal: a Tutor's Reflections*, in *S.A.E.*, No. 14, Aug. 1955, pp. 13-16.
Critical comments on the teaching of international affairs and history to W.E.A. classes.

Archaeology

1104. WEBSTER, G. *Archaeology in Adult Education*, in *A.E.*, Vol. XXXII, 1959-60, pp. 166-78.
On the development of archaeological research groups in the West Midlands by the Birmingham Extra-Mural Department.

1105. WARRINER, F. *Local History and Adult Education*, in *A.E.*, Vol. IX, 1936-7, pp. 21-8.
A plea for the study of the subject, and suggestions for undertaking it. SPRINGALL, M., *History in a Rural Area*, in *A.E.*, Vol. XVIII, 1945-6, pp. 136-9, is similar in scope.

1106. ALLAWAY, A. J. *Everyone his own Historian: Local History as a Subject for Adult Students*, in *Social Service*, Vol. XXII, 1948-9, pp. 165-9.
An account of work done in Vaughan College on local history.

1107. DOW, L. *History on Your Doorstep*, in *F.E.*, Vol. IV, 1950-1, pp. 228-35.
On the need for the study of local history, and the work of the Standing Conference for Local History. Cf. **679.**

1108. BESTALL, J. M. *Local History in Adult Education*, in *A.E.*, Vol. XXVIII, 1955-6, pp. 181-8.
Surveys the position of the subject and teaching problems.

(viii) International Relations

1109. KEETON, G. W. *"International Relations" in Adult Classes*, in *A.E.*, Vol. VII, 1934-5, pp. 25-33.
A sound and stimulating essay.

1110. HARRISON, J. F. C. *Towards an Interpretation of International Relations*, in *A.E.*, Vol. XXI, 1948-9, pp. 75-81.

1111. *International Relations: Some Study Material*, in *A.E.*, Vol. XXIV, 1951-2, pp. 82-5.
Summary of the material available from embassies, legations, etc.

1112. PEAR, R. H. *Lecturing on American Affairs* in *A.E.*, Vol. XXIV, 1951-2, pp. 284-93.

1113. MONKHOUSE, E. *The Teaching of International Relations*, in *T.B.*, No. 95/96, June-Sept. 1954, pp. 12-15.
See also by the same author *Ici on parle français*, in *T.B.*, No. 103/5, pp. 21-4, June-Dec. 1956 (description of experimental class on French life and institutions).

1114. HOULE, C. O., and NELSON, C. A. *The University, the Citizen and World Affairs*. Pp. 195. American Council on Education, Washington, 1956.
A valuable commentary, by no means irrelevant to English conditions, on the ways in which universities may provide adult education in world affairs.

See also **360, 1103.**

(ix) Literature

1115. BOARD OF EDUCATION—DEPARTMENTAL COMMITTEE. *The Teaching of English in England*. Pp. 394. H.M.S.O., 1933.
Ch. viii is on literature and adult education.

1116. POOLE, H. E. *The Teaching of Literature in the W.E.A.* Pp. 52. B.I.A.E., 1938.
The best general study. WILLIAMS, R., *Some Experiments in Literature Teaching*, in *R.H.P.*, Vol. II, x, 1948-9, pp. 9-15, is a valuable adjunct. See also the same author's *Reading and Criticism*, pp. 152, Muller 1950, and comments by THOMAS, T. W., *Practical Criticism and the Literature Class*, in *A.E.*, Vol. XXIV, 1951-2, pp. 20-9. HEWITT. D., *The Literary Critic and the Historian*, in *T.B.*, No. 88, Oct. 1952, pp. 10-14, points out some of the inadequacies of the practical criticism method.

1117. WILLIAMS R. *Literature in Relation to History, 1850-75*, in *R.H.P.*, Vol. III, 1, 1949-50, pp. 36-44.
A discussion of the correlation of subjects, based on an Oxford course for tutors.

1118. BLAND, D. S. *Literature and Adult Education*, in *Cambridge Journal*, Vol. IV, 1950, pp. 172-80.
Claims for literature a central position in adult education.

1119. CHARLTON, D. G. *French Literature for English Extra-Mural Students*, in *A.E.*, Vol. XXV, 1952-3, pp. 280-5.
Critical review of types of courses.

1120. HOGGART, R. *Poetry and the Adult Group*, in *A.E.*, Vol. XXV, 1952-3, pp. 180-8.
A discussion of aims and methods. Cf. the same author's *Notes on Aim and Method* (**1018**), and *Some Notes on Extra-Mural Teaching*, in *A.E.*, Vol. XXXIII, 1960-1, pp. 105-9, 178-82.

1121. BUTTS, D. *The Development of Literature Teaching in the Oxford Tutorial Classes*, in *R.H.P.*, Vol. III, VII, 1958-9, pp. 13-19.
An examination of trends in literature classes organised by the Oxford Delegacy for Extra-Mural Studies since 1917.

(x) Modern Languages

1122. BRERETON, C. S. H. *Modern Language Teaching in Day and Evening Schools.* Pp. 295. Univ. of London P., 1930.
Valuable practical suggestions and comments.

1123. HAGBOLDT, P. H. *Language Learning.* Pp. 175. Chicago U.P., 1935.
One of a number of works which, though not concerned specifically with the teaching of languages to adults, are of considerable value. Others are: STOTT, D. H., *Language Teaching* in the New *Education*, pp. 100, Univ. of London P., 1946; DUFF, C., *How to Learn a Language*, pp. 148, Blackwell, Oxford, 1947; INCORPORATED ASSOCIATION OF ASSISTANT MASTERS, *The Teaching of Modern Languages*, pp. 359, 1949; HODGSON, F. M., *Learning Modern Languages*, pp. 100, Routledge and Kegan Paul, 1955; THIMANN, I. C., *Teaching Languages*, pp. 151, Harrap, 1955; MINISTRY OF EDUCATION, Pamphlet No. 29, *Modern Languages*, pp. 119, H.M.S.O., 1956.

1124. HICKS, W. C. R. *Language Learning for Adults*, in *A.E.*, Vol. XVI, 1943-4, pp. 172-84.
A plea for language study, especially in connection with the study of foreign cultures. Cf. GATENBY, E. V., *Language-Learning for Adults*, in *A.E.*, Vol. XIX, 1946-7, pp. 105-14; AUSTIN, A. E., *Adult Students and Foreign Languages*, in *F.E.*, Vol. II, 1948-9, pp. 56-62; NEWMARK, P., *An Approach to Modern Language Teaching*, in *A.E.*, Vol. XXIII, 1950-1, pp. 44-55; NEWMARK, P., *Speaking Foreign Languages*, in *Technical Education*, Vol. II, 1960, No. 7, pp. 29-31, No. 8, pp. 18-19; HARGREAVES, P. H., *Modern Language Classes*, in *A.E.*, Vol. XXXIV, 1961-2, pp. 23-7.

1125. STACK, E. M. *The Language Laboratory and Modern Language Teaching.* Pp. 149. Oxford U.P., New York, 1960.

1126. NEWMARK, P., LOCKWOOD, E., and RUDDOCK, R. *Three Studies in Problems of Language*, in *A.E.*, Vol. XXIV, 1951-2, pp. 193-206.
Discussion of the difficulties of foreign languages to English students, and English to foreigners.

1127. HARVARD, J. *Teaching Adults to Speak a Foreign Language.* Pp. 64. Univ. of London P., 1961.

1128. *Adult Education*, Vol. XXXIV, No. 5, Jan. 1962. Special issue devoted to *Modern Languages in Adult Education.*
Articles by NEWMARK, P., and others, pp. 238-66.
See also **1113.**

(xi) Music

1129. WALTERS, P. M. *Music and the Adult Student*, in *A.E.*, Vol. V, 1930-2, pp. 423-9.

1130. THOMAS, G. *Music in Wales*, in *A.E.*, Vol. XI, 1938-9, pp. 199-212.
A survey by a music tutor at Coleg Harlech. See also the chapter by the same author on *The Appreciation Movement in Musical Education*, in *Harlech Studies* (**365**).

1131. MELLERS, W. H. *Musical Culture To-day*, in *Tempo*, No. 7, June 1944, pp. 2-5.
On the purpose of adult education in music today. Continued in *New Audiences for Old*, in *Tempo*, No. 12, Sept. 1945, pp. 5-8.

1132. SHAW, H. W. (ed.). *Musical Education.* Pp. 259. Hinrichsen, 1946.
A symposium of which several sections are relevant to adult education.

1133. BARFORD, P. T. *The Place of Formal Analysis in Adult Musical Education*, in *Monthly Musical Record*, Vol. VIII, 1951, pp. 120-5.
See comments by JACOBS, R. L., in *T.B.*, No. 84, Oct. 1951, pp. 17-19.

1134. PYBUS, E. *The Teaching of Musical Appreciation.* Pp. 28. C.J.A.C., 1953.
A valuable and suggestive survey of practical teaching problems.

1135. BUSH, G. *Musical Creation and the Listener.* Pp. 121. Muller, 1954.
Designed mainly to help the ordinary listener but is relevant to teaching problems in adult classes.

1136. JONES, H. A. *Music and Drama in Adult Education: Some Experiments in Partnership*, in *A.E.*, Vol. XXVII, 1954-5, pp. 273-9.
Describes joint enterprises, combining appreciation and practical work, by University, L.E.A., and Community Council.

1137. HAVERGAL, H. *Music as a Form of Adult Education*, in *S.A.E.*, No. 18, Dec. 1956, pp. 14-18.
Discusses the principles upon which musical education for adults should be based. Other short but useful recent articles are ELSDON, K. T., *Music Appreciation: an Experiment*, in *A.E.*, Vol. XXX, 1957-8, pp. 127-34; ROOPER, J., *Fresh Thoughts on the Music Class*, in *R.H.P.*, Vol. III, VII, 1958-9, pp. 30-3; WILSON, T. B., *Music in Adult Education*, in *S.A.E.*, No. 25, Apr. 1959, pp. 16-19.
For other works, mainly historical and descriptive, see Subject Index s.v. Music.

(xii) Philosophy

1138. CARRÉ, M. H. *Philosophy in Adult Education*, in *A.E.*, Vol. X, 1937-8, pp. 105-10.
On some of the difficulties and how they may be surmounted; argues for a historical approach.

1139. CROWTHER, D. *The Science and Art of Thought*, in *W.A.B.*, 2nd Ser., No. XXXIII, May 1943, pp. 9-14.
A plea for courses in clear thinking, with detailed suggestions.

1140. CAMERON, J. M. *The Teaching of Philosophy to Adult Students.* Pp. 20. C.J.A.C. [1951].
See also comments by RICKMAN, P., and MELLING, J., in *T.B.*, No. 86, Apr. 1952, pp. 17-22.

1141. RICKMAN, H. P., and LEWIS, G. I. *Experimental Approaches: I—Philosophy; II—Politics*, in *A.E.*, Vol. XXXI, 1958-9, pp. 51-60, 215-18.

(xiii) Physical Education

1142. JACKS M. L. *Physical Education.* Pp. 134. Nelson 1938.
Deals with the effect of physical education on the development of personality. See especially Ch. vi.

1143. BIBBY, C. *Health Education for Adults*, in *W.A.B.*, 2nd Ser., No. XXXIX, Nov. 1944, pp. 12-20.

1144. BUCHER, C. A. *Foundations of Physical Education.* Pp. 456. Kimpton, 1952, 2nd edn. 1956.

1145. RANDALL, M. W. *Modern Ideas on Physical Education.* Pp. 128. Bell, 1952, rev. edn. 1960.

1146. TIBBLE, J. W. *Physical Education and the Educative Process.* University of London Institute of Education, Studies in Education, No. 5. Pp. 23. 1953.

1147. BRAILSFORD, D. W. *Physical Education and Social Psychology*, in *Physical Education*, Vol. XLVIII, 1956, pp. 48-52.

1148. MCINTOSH, P. C. (ed.). *Landmarks in the History of Physical Education.* Pp. 232. Routledge and Kegan Paul, 1957.

1149. BRITISH EMPIRE AND COMMONWEALTH CONFERENCE ON PHYSICAL EDUCATION. *Report on the Second Conference . . . 1958.* Pp. 80. Committee for International Conferences on Physical Education, 1959.

1150. CENTRAL COUNCIL OF PHYSICAL RECREATION. *Sport and the Community.* Pp. 135. 1960.
Report of the Wolfenden Committee.

NOTE.—The Reports of The Central Council of Physical Recreation, available at the Head Office of the organisation, contain lists of organisations concerned with physical recreation, many of which also undertake some activity of a directly educational kind.

See also **36, 45, 672, 683, 1047, 1188.**

(xiv) Psychology

1151. WORKERS' EDUCATIONAL ASSOCIATION, ASSOCIATION OF TUTORS IN ADULT EDUCATION, AND CENTRAL JOINT ADVISORY COMMITTEE FOR TUTORIAL CLASSES. *Psychology and the Adult Student.* Pp. 35. 1937.
Report of a conference of adult educationists, embodying the views of a number of distinguished psychologists.

1152. HEMMING, J. *Humanity is Various*, in *Hwy.*, Vol. XL, 1948-9, pp. 184-6.
A suggestive survey of an approach to one-year classes in psychology.

1153. RUDDOCK, R. *The Psychology of Psychologists*, in *Hwy.*, Vol. XLIII, 1951-2, pp. 135-7.
Short discussion of types of psychology tutors and their approach to W.E.A. classes.

(xv) Religion

1154. WOODARD, A. L. (ed.). *The Teaching Church*. Pp. 221. S.P.C.K., 1928.
A survey by various hands of the method and content of religious adult education.

1155. PARSONS, R. E. *Re-educating Adults: an Essay on Religious Adult Education*. Pp. 32. Churches' Committee for Supplementing Religious Education among Men in H.M. Forces, 1945.
On the basis of Services experience outlines a policy for adult religious education.

1156. JESSOP, T. E. *Education and Evangelism*. Pp. 139. S.C.M., 1947.
Discusses the attitude of young soldiers to religion, and the educational approach most likely to be effective.

1157. —— *Christianity for Adults*. Pp. 16. Epworth P., 1950.
On content and method.

1158. LINDHORST, F. A. *Teaching Adults*. Pp. 160. Abingdon P., New York, 1951.
A study of content and method in religious adult education.

1159. OLDHAM, J. H. *Approach to Christian Adult Education*, in *A.E.*, Vol. XXV, 1952-3, pp. 38-46.
A plea for a new approach and new experiments.

See also Section III(c)(vi).

(xvi) Science

General Works on Science

1160. HUMBY, S. R., and JAMES, E. J. F. *Science and Education*. Pp. 153. Cambridge U.P., 1942.
Includes chapters on science and society and the teaching of scientific method.

1161. CALDIN, E. F. *Science in Society*, in *Endeavour*, Vol. V, 1946, pp. 70-3; *The Values of Science*, *ibid.*, pp. 160-3.
Essays on the relationship of science and technology to society.

1162. NOKES, M. S. *Science in Education*. Pp. 166. Macdonald, 1949.
Discusses many points of interest to the adult educationist. Useful bibliography.

1163. BRONOWSKI, J. *Science and Values*, in *A.E.*, Vol. XXV, 1952-3, pp. 96-100.
A personal statement. See further the same author's articles on *Science and Human Values*, in *Univs. Q.*, Vol. X, 1955-6, pp. 247-59, 324-38, and Vol. XI, 1956-7, pp. 26-42.

Science in Adult Education

1164. BOARD OF EDUCATION—ADULT EDUCATION COMMITTEE. Paper No. 8. *Natural Science in Adult Education*. Pp. 60. H.M.S.O., 1927
On the part that various branches of science can play in adult education. Still important.

1165. BRITISH INSTITUTE OF ADULT EDUCATION. Report of Sixth Annual Conference. *Science and Adult Education*. Pp. 111. 1927.

1166. BRITISH ASSOCIATION FOR THE ADVANCEMENT OF SCIENCE. *Science Teaching in Adult Education*, in *Annual Report*, 1933, pp. 330-57. Also issued separately (Reprint No. 32).
See also *Annual Report*, 1937, pp. 305-32, and *Science in Adult Education*, in *The Advancement of Science*, Vol. VI, No. 22, July 1949 (reprinted by Brit. Ass. and N.I.A.E., pp. 15, 1949).

1167. FORD, A. C. *Towards a Wider Appreciation of Science*, in *A.E.*, Vol. VIII, 1935-6, pp. 23-30.
On the desirability of a marriage between the humanities and the sciences in adult education. Cf. LAYTON, D., *A Hope for Science*, in *A.E.*, Vol. XXV, 1952-3, pp. 112-18.

1168. CLIFFORD, M. H. *Taking Science to the Adult*, in *Discovery*, Vol. VII, 1946, pp. 279-81, 306-10.
An account of field experience in the Cambridge extra-mural area. CROSSLAND, R. W., *Science in Adult Educaton*, in *F.E.*, Vol. II, 1948-9, pp. 232-42, describes courses under the Birmingham Extra-Mural Department, and an inquiry into student motives. For the Sheffield area see TURNER, H. D., *Developments in Science Teaching*, in *A.E.*, Vol. XXVII, 1954-5, pp. 35-50.

1169. ——— *The Place of Science in Adult Education*, in *A.E.*, Vol. XIX, 1946-7, pp. 134-45.
A review of the position of science in adult education, its value, purpose, methods of approach and difficulties. Cf. the same author's article in *Nature*, Vol. CLIX, 1947, pp. 560-5.

1170. FLOOD, W. E. *People's Particular Interests in Science*, in *A.E.*, Vol. XXI, 1948-9, pp. 67-74.
On the relative appeal of the various branches of science. Cf. DIXON, C., *Science in Adult Education, ibid.*, pp. 123-7, and FLOOD, W. E., *Viewpoints and Approaches in Popular Science*, in *A.E.*, Vol. XXII, 1949-50, pp. 113-21.

1171. OXFORD UNIVERSITY—DELEGACY FOR EXTRA-MURAL STUDIES. *The Teaching of Science in Adult Education*. Pp. 48 (duplicated). 1951.
Summary report of a conference dealing with a variety of teaching problems.

1172. CROSSLAND, R. W. *The Reading of Adult Students attending Science Courses: an Investigation of Reading Difficulties*, in *A.E.*, Vol. XXV, 1952-3, pp. 205-18.
Detailed discussion of the supply and use of books.

1173. PEERS, R. *Science in the Extra-Mural Work of Universities*. Pp. 20. U.C.A.E., 1954.
Discussion of the place of science in adult education, with details of extra-mural courses in science 1950-3. See comment by PICKVANCE, T. J., in *A.E.*, Vol. XXVII, 1954-5, pp. 205-13. STYLER, W. E., *Science and the Lay Public*, in *A.E.*, Vol. XXX, 1957-8, pp. 288-92, analyses science provision by the universities and the W.E.A. during the previous decade.

1174. PICKVANCE, T. J. *University Vacation Schools for Graduates*, in *A.E.*, Vol. XXVIII, 1955-6, pp. 135-41.
On vacation courses arranged for science graduates by Birmingham Extra-Mural Department.

1175. CLARKE, J. *Science in Adult Education*. Unpublished M.A. (Ed.) thesis, London Univ., 1957.

1176. SIMONS, J. R. *Science and the Third Programme*, in *Discovery*, Vol. XVIII, 1957, pp. 258-9.
Describes the policy of the B.B.C. in science broadcasts for adults.

See also the chapter on Science and Adult Education by OWEN, M. D., in *Harlech Studies* (**365**).

Biological Sciences

1177. LEE, G. F. *Teaching About Living Things*, in *F.E.*, Vol. III, 1949-50, pp. 236-42.
A plea for a broader and less conventional approach to biology. Cf. CROSSLAND, R. W., *The Teacher of Biology in Adult Education*, in *A.E.*, Vol. XXIX, 1956-7, pp. 45-53, which surveys the kind of topics suitable for different groups; and WHITEHEAD, F. H., *A Suggestion for Botanical Work in Adult Education Classes*, in *R.H.P.*, Vol. III, IV, 1955-6, pp. 24-7.

1178. PATTISON, G. *Anthropology for Adults*, in *T.B.*, Spring 1951, pp. 10-12.
A plea for anthropology as a subject in adult education.

1179. BRAMBELL, F. W. R. *The Educational Value of Zoology*, in *Univs. Q.*, Vol. VIII, 1953-4, pp. 62-7.
Puts the case for the study of zoology as part of a liberal education.

1180. NICHOLSON, E. M. *The Modern Naturalist*, in *Discovery*, Vol. XIX, 1958, pp. 456-9.
Deals with the amateur naturalist, and the organisations attempting to help and train him.

Physical Sciences

1181. COCHRANE, C. *Physics and the Adult Class*, in *J.A.E.*, Vol. V, 1930-2, pp. 186-92.
An account of work at Glasgow 1927-31. See further *A Tutorial Class in Physics*, by the same writer, *J.A.E.*, Vol. VI, 1932-4, pp. 146-63. See also MENDELSSOHN, K. A. G., *The Teaching of Physics in Adult Education*, in *R.H.P.*, Vol. II, X, 1948-9, pp. 16-21; and articles describing extra-mural courses in atomic and nuclear physics by MATSUKAWA, E., and RUSSELL, P. C., in *A.E.*, Vols. XXX, 1957-8, pp. 59-63, and XXXI, 1958-9, pp. 143-5.

1182. MACDONALD, T. L. *Astronomy for Adult Classes*, in *J.A.E.*, Vol. V, 1930-2, pp. 317-26.
An account of a Glasgow experiment.

See also **328, 330, 331, 345, 365,** and Subject Index s.v. Societies, Scientific.

(xvii) Other Subjects

1183. HUBBACK, E. M., and Others. *Training for Citizenship and Adult Education*, in *A.E.*, Vol. X, 1937-8, pp. 17-29.
On the aims, content and methods of education for citizenship. See also comments in following issue, pp. 120-9; and earlier articles by various writers in *A.E.*, Vol. VII.

1184. ASSOCIATION FOR EDUCATION IN CITIZENSHIP. *Roads to Citizenship: Suggestions for Various Methods of Informal Education in Citizenship.* Pp. 62. Oxford U.P., 1940.

1185. COLE, G. D. H. *Technology and the Social Studies*, in *R.H.P.*, Vol. III, I, 1949-50, pp. 25-35. Reprinted as pamphlet, C.J.A.C., 1950.
Paper read at a conference on the Teaching of Science in Adult Education.

1186. BRENNAN, T. *A Research Experiment in Social Studies*, in *A.E.*, Vol. XXIV, 1951-2, pp. 33-43.
Report of an experimental study of various sociological aspects of S.W. Wales by seven groups of adult students (see **169**).

1187. KAIM-CAUDLE, R. R. *Statistics and the Adult Student.* Pp. 20. C.J.A.C., 1952.
Discusses the ways in which the study of statistics may be included in adult classes.

1188. BURTON, J. *Methods and Media in Health Education*, in *F.A.E.*, Vol. VI, 1954, pp. 151-8.
Discusses a variety of techniques which, though here related to health education campaigns, have a general reference.

1189. ARMSTRONG, J. R., and HOPKINS, P. G. H. *Local Studies*. Pp. 78. W.E.A., 1955.
Suggestions concerning the content and methods of local studies, together with booklists, syllabuses, descriptions of practical work and visual aids.

1190. WEDDELL, M. *Training in Home Management*. Pp. 204. Routledge and Kegan Paul, 1955.
Chs. x-xi describe the work of the Women's Institutes and other voluntary organisations.

1191. JEPSON, N. A. *Adult Education and the Police*, in *A.E.*, Vol. XXIX, 1956-7, pp. 205-15.
An account of three-year courses in criminology arranged by Leeds University.

1192. FORDHAM, P. *Extra-Mural Geography in Disguise*, in *A.E.*, Vol. XXXI, 1958-9, pp. 302-7.
On the approach to geography through current problems.

1193. WILMOT, G. F. A. *A Way to Teach Geography*, in *A.E.*, Vol. XXXI, 1958-9, pp. 14-20.
Describes London extra-mural courses in railway and transport geography.

1194. STERN, H. H. *Learning the Parental Rôle—a Study of 71 Families*, in UNIVERSITY OF HULL—INSTITUTE OF EDUCATION, *Studies in Education*, Vol. III, 1959, pp. 167-87.
Cf. **319, 383.**

1195. BRODETSKY, P. *Law as a Liberal Study*, in *A.E.*, Vol. XXXII, 1959-60, pp. 53-61.
The case for law as a suitable subject for adult classes, with comment on types of syllabuses and methods.

AUTHOR INDEX

Except where otherwise indicated, numbers are those of entries, not pages. The titles of the works cited have been abbreviated wherever practicable. Periodicals are listed together under that head, and anonymous works are listed by title.

Abbey, C. J., and Overton, J. H., *English Church in the Eighteenth Century*, 127.

Abbott, A., *Education for Industry and Commerce*, 245.

Abelson, H. I., *Persuasion*, 960.

Abercrombie, M. L., *Anatomy of Judgment*, 902.

Abrahart, B. W., *Training of Tutors*, 1069.

Abram, A., *English Life and Manners in the Later Middle Ages*, 89; *Social England in the Fifteenth Century*, 89.

Acland, A. H. D., and Jones, B., *Working Men Co-operators*, 452.

Acts of Parliament: *Education Acts*, 208; *Public Libraries Acts*, 694.

Adam, Sir R., *Problems in Adult Education*, 380.

Adams, Sir J., *Student's Guide*, 1053.

Adams, J. W. L. *Challenge and Opportunity*, 981.

Adams, W. G. S., *Library Provision and Policy*, 698.

Adamson, J. W., *Education*, 212; *English Education 1789-1902*, 242; *"The Illiterate Anglo-Saxon,"* 220; *Pioneers of Modern Education*, 229; *Short History of Education*, 213.

Ader, J., *Perfectionnement des connaissances et de la formation personnelle chez l'adulte*, 961.

Adult Education Association of the U.S.A., *Architecture for Adult Education*, 848; *How to Teach Adults*, 995.

Adult Education in Wales, 388.

Adult Leadership, *Education for the Aged and Aging*, 758.

Advisory Council for Technical Education, S. Wales and Mon., *Part-time Education*, 830.

Alderton, E., *Bexley Adult Education Centre*, 590.

Alexander, W. P., *Education in England*, 272.

Allaway, A. J., *Adult and Further Education in Leicester and Leicestershire*, 395; *Adult Education in a Changing Society*, 971; *Adult Education in England*, 317; *David James Vaughan*, 479; *Educational Centres Movement*, 589; *Everyone his own Historian*, 1106; *Social and Educational Change since 1900*, 865; *W.E.A. in Leicester*, 532.

—— and Rawson, J., *Rossendale Branch of the W.E.A.*, 532.

Allen, W. O. B., and McClure, E., *History of the S.P.C.K.*, 131.

Altick, R. D., *English Common Reader*, 285.

American Association for Adult Education, *Adult Education and Democracy*, 965.

Anderson, N., Work and Leisure, 905.

Arch, J., *Joseph Arch*, 158.

Archer, R. L., *Secondary Education in the Nineteenth Century*, 241.

Armfelt, R., *Structure of English Education*, 274.

Armstrong, J. R., *Liberal Adult Education in Rural Areas*, 733.

—— and Hopkins, P. G. H., *Local Studies*, 1189.

Armytage, W. H. G., *Civic Universities*, 226.

Arts Council, *Annual Reports*, 662; *Plans for an Arts Centre*, 842.

Arts Enquiry, *The Factual Film*, 781; *Music*, 375; *Visual Arts*, 373.

Ashby, A. W., *Sociological Background of Adult Education*, 734.

—— and Byles, P. G., *Rural Education*, 261.

Ashby, *Growing Points in Adult Education*, 1023; *Pathology of Adult Education*, 917; *Technological Humanism*, 1023.

Ashby, M. K., *Joseph Ashby*, 158.

Ashton, J., *Social Life in the Reign of Queen Anne*, 128.

Ashton, T. S., *Economic History of England*, p. 7.

Aspinall, A., *Lord Brougham*, 157.

Association for Education in Citizenship, *Roads to Citizenship*, 1184.

Association of Tutors in Adult Education, *Duties of Organising Tutors*, 1067; *Future in Adult Education*, 911.

Atkins, E., *Vaughan Working Men's College*, 479.

Austin, A. E., *Adult Students and Foreign Languages*, 1124.

Avoncroft College, *Avoncroft*, 610.

Avoncroft College for Rural Workers, 610.

Axon, W. E. A., *Annals of Manchester*, p. 8.

Bailey, J., *British Co-operative Movement*, 468.

Fielding, J. T., *Evening Institute in Further Education in the E. Midlands*, 574.

Finer, S. E., *Then and Now*, 865.

Firth, A. S., *Adult Education and the Trade Union Movement*, 543.

Fisher, N. G., *Brains Trust as a Method of Adult Education*, 1026.

Fitter, R. S. R., *Field Studies and Further Education*, 674.

Fleming, H., *Beechcroft*, 590; *Educational Settlements Association*, 587; *Lighted Mind*, 765.

Flood, W. E., *People's Interests in Science*, 1170; *Viewpoints and Approaches in Popular Science*, 1170.

—— and Crossland, R. W., *Interest and Motives for Study of Natural Sciences and Psychology*, 1005.

Floud, J. E., Halsey, A. H., and Martin, F. M., *Social Class and Educational Opportunity*, 893.

Flower, F. D., *Adult Education in the Technical College*, 571.

Folsom, J. K. *Family and Democratic Society*, 877.

Ford, A. C., *Towards a Wider Appreciation of Science*, 1167.

Ford, B., *Bureau of Current Affairs*, 670; *Guide to English Literature*, p. 7.

Ford, P., *Teaching of Economics*, 1081.

Fordham, P., *Extra-Mural Geography*, 1192.

Formation Colleges, 620.

Forth, E. M., *Adult Education according to Women*, 574.

Fox, Sir L. W., *English Prison and Borstal Systems*, 636; *Modern English Prison*, 636.

Fraser, G. M., *Aberdeen Mechanics' Institution*, 444.

Freeman, A., *Education through Settlements*, 579.

Friedmann, S., *Attitudes in Comprehension*, 955.

Froehlich, G. P., and Darley, J. G., *Studying Students*, 949.

Frost, T., *Forty Years' Recollections*, 158.

Furniss, H. S. (Lord Sanderson), *Memories of Sixty Years*, 610.

Gairdner, J., *Lollardy and the Reformation*, 88.

Galbraith, J. K., *Affluent Society*, 896; *Liberal Hour*, 896.

Gallie, W. B., *New University*, 514.

Gardiner, A. G., *Geroge Cadbury*, 420.

Gardiner, F. J., *Fiftieth Birthday of a Model Institute*, 486.

Gardiner, R. K., and Judd, H. O., *Development of Social Administration*, 170.

Garratt, R., *Co-operative College*, 610.

Gasquet, F. A., *Parish Life in Medieval England*, 87.

Gatenby, E. V., *Language-Learning*, 1124.

George, M. D., *England in Transition*, 142; *London Life in the XVIIIth Century*, 140.

Gibbon, A. M., *Skipton Mechanics' Institute*, 444.

Gibbs, F. W., *George Wilson*, 330.

Gibson, G. W., on radio listening groups, 780.

Gillman, F. J., on Adult Schools, 415; *Workers and Education*, 584; *York Adult Schools*, 421.

Glass, D. V., *Social Mobility*, 889.

Glass, R., *Social Background of a Plan*, 167.

Glover, E., *Psychological Obstacles to Learning*, 944.

Glover, F. J., *Adult Student and Economics*, 1081.

Godard, J. G., *George Birkbeck*, 441.

Goddard, C., *Institution for Teaching Adults to Read*, 411.

Godfrey, E., *Social Life under the Stuarts*, 107.

Goldman, F., *International Conference on University and Adult Education*, 508.

Goldwin, R. A., *Liberally Educated Executive*, 744.

Gordon, C., *Art for the People*, 364.

Gorell, Lord, *Education and the Army*, 615.

Gorham, M., *Broadcasting and Television*, 302.

Gould, J. D., *Recruitment of Adult Students*, 1013.

Graham, H. G., *Social Life of Scotland in the 18th Century*, 129.

Granada T.V., *Viewership Survey*, 308.

Granger, J., *Nottingham Mechanics' Institution*, 444.

Grant, G., *Philosophy and Adult Education*, 932.

Grant, J., *Newspaper Press*, 288.

Grattan, C. H., *In Quest of Knowledge*, 320.

Gray, A., *Socialist Tradition*, 137.

Gray, W. S., and Rogers, B., *Maturity in Reading*, 945.

Green, E., *Adult Education and the Public Library*, 713; *Adult Education: Why this Apathy?* 1009; *Education for a New Society*, 869.

Green, J. A. H., *Nottingham Mechanics' Institution*, 444.

Greene, H. C., *B.B.C. and Adult Education*, 787.

Greenwood, A., *Education of the Citizen*, 349; *Rochdale Equitable Pioneers Society*, 451.

Greenwood, T., *Edward Edwards*, 709; *Museums and Art Galleries*, 718; *Public Libraries*, 695.

Gregg, P., *Social and Economic History*, 150.

Gregory, W. C. E., *Three Aspects of the W.E.T.U.C.*, 548.

Grier, I., *Achievement in Education*, 511.

Griffin, J., *Adult Education in Scotland*, 394.

Grobel, M. C., *Society for the Diffusion of Useful Knowledge*, 281.

Hogan, J. M., *Buildings for Further Education*, 845.

Hogben, L., *Political Arithmetic*, 862.

Hoggart, R., *Aim and Method in University Tutorial Classes*, 1018; *Extra-Mural Teaching*, 1120; *Nature and Quality of Mass-Communications*, 786; *Poetry and the Adult Group*, 1120; *Uses of Literacy*, 786; *Uses of Television*, 307.

Holbrook, D., *Sweetness and Light for Hodge*, 563.

Hole, J., *Literary, Scientific, and Mechanics' Institutes*, 436.

Hole, R. H., *Adult Education in a Community Centre*, 599.

Holland, R. W., *Adversis Major*, 614.

Holley, N. M., *History for the Adult Student*, 1101.

Holt, A., *Joseph Priestley*, 424.

Holyoake, G. J., *Co-operative Education*, 453; *Sixty Years of an Agitator's Life*, 158.

Hope, R., *Further Education for Merchant Seafarers*, 631; *International Understanding and the Seafarer*, 631; *Spare Time at Sea*, 632.

Hopkinson, D., *Family Inheritance*, 483.

Hopkinson, D. M., *Residential Short Courses*, 992.

Horobin, I. M., *Mansfield House University Settlement*, 583.

Horrabin, J. F., *Independent Working-Class Education*, 962.

—— and W., *Working-Class Education*, 312.

Houle, C. O., *Inquiring Mind*, 1014; *Libraries in Adult and Fundamental Education*, 717.

—— and Nelson, C. A., *University, Citizen and World Affairs*, 1114.

Hovell, M., *Chartist Movement*, 136.

Howard, D. L., *Education as Social Rehabilitation*, 635.

Howarth, E., and Platnauer, H. M., *Directory of Museums and Art Galleries*, 26.

Howie, G., *Experiment in Greek Studies*, 1074.

Hoy, J. D., *Interests and Motives for Study among Adult Evening Students*, 1002.

Hubback, E. M., *Education through Work*, 740; *Discussion Groups*, 1036.

—— and Others, *Training for Citizenship*, 1183.

Hudson, A. K., *Taunton Mechanics' Institute*, 444.

Hudson, D., and Luckhurst, K. W., *Royal Society of Arts*, 253.

Hudson, J. W., *History of Adult Education*, 311.

Hughes, A. M., *Short-Term Adult Residential College*, 612.

Hughes, H. D., *Long Term Residential Colleges*, 608.

Hughes, M. W., *Experiment in Adult Education*, 590.

Hullah, F. R., *John Hullah*, 340.

Hulton Readership Survey, 292.

Humby, S. R., and James, E. J. F., *Science and Education*, 1160.

Hume, A., *Learned Societies and Printing Clubs*, 428.

Hunsaker, H. C., and Pierce, R., *Creating a Climate for Adult Learning*, 848.

Hunter, G., *Residential Colleges*, 611; *Vocation and Culture*, 1022.

Hunter, M., *Village College*, 563.

Huntley, J., *Film Appreciation*, 1088.

Hutchinson, E. M., *Accommodation*, 850; *Economics of Adult Education*, 834; *Nature and Rôle of Adult Education*, 934.

Huxley, G., *Lady Denman*, 643.

Huxley, J., *Freedom and Culture*, 885.

Huxley, L., *T. H. Huxley*, 347.

Ibberson, E. M., *Rural Music Schools*, 665; *L.E.A. and the Rural Music School*, 665.

Incorporated Association of Assistant Masters, *Teaching of Modern Languages*, 1123.

Independent Television Authority, *Educational Television*, 792.

Informational Film Year Book, 37.

Ingram, B., *Education in Prisons*, 635.

International Labour Organisation, *Bibliography on Workers' Education*, 17; *Activities of the I.L.O. in Workers' Education*, and other reports, 555.

International Relations: Some Study Material, 1111.

Iremonger, F. A., *William Temple*, 531.

Irving, J., *Youth and Adult Education*, 523.

Irwin, R., *Origins of the English Library*, 689.

Jacks, M. L., *Education of Good Men*, 890; *Modern Trends in Education*, 881; *Physical Education*, 1142; *Total Education*, 875.

Jacks, L. P., *Education of the Whole Man*, 859.

Jackson, M., *Mature Student*, 797.

Jaeger, M., *Before Victoria*, 153.

James, C., *Adult Education in Rural Lancashire*, 566.

James, D. G., *Amateur Drama*, 1078; *Universities and the Theatre*, 1079.

James, M., *Social Problems and Policy during the Puritan Revolution*, 113.

Jarman, T. L., *Charles Knight*, 286; *Landmarks in the History of Education*, 223; *Society for the Diffusion of Useful Knowledge*, 283.

Jeffreys, M. V. C., *Education, Freedom and Community*, 970; *Glaucon*, 882.

Jenkins, D. E., *Religious Societies*, 102; *Thomas Charles*, 407.

Jenkins, I., *History of the Women's Institute*, 644.

Newcombe, L., *Library Co-operation*, 703.
Newman, Sir G., *Adult Education in England*, 907.
Newmark, P., *Approach to Modern Language Teaching*, 1124; *English in Technical Colleges*, 1095; *Speaking Foreign Languages*, 1124.
—— Lockwood, E., and Ruddock, R., *Three Studies in Problems of Language*, 1126.
Newton, J., *Burton Manor*, 613.
Newton, R. G., *Drama in Villages and Clubs*, 1075.
Nichols, J., *Literary Anecdotes*, 336.
Nicholson, E. M., *Modern Naturalist*, 1180.
Nicholson, F., *Literary and Philosophical Society*, 427.
Nicholson, J. H., *New Communities*, 168; *Why Adult Education?* 537.
Nicol, W. B. de B., *Dumfries and Maxwelltown Mechanics' Institute*, 444.
Nokes, M. S., *Science in Education*, 1162.
Northampton Polytechnic, Jubilee history, 560.
Northern Advisory Council for Further Education, *Suggestions for Part-time Teachers of Women's Subjects*, 990.
Northern Polytechnic, Jubilee history, 560.
Nottingham Mechanics' Institution, *Fifteen Years' Record*, 444.
Nottingham University College, Department of Adult Education, *Educational Possibilities of Village Clubs*, 732.
Nowell-Smith, S., *House of Cassell*, 287.
Nuffield College, *Industry and Education*, 739.

O'Connor, D. J., *Philosophy of Education*, 895.
Official Year-Book of Scientific and Learned Societies, 21.
Ogle, J. J., *Free Library*, 695.
Oldham, J. H., *Approach to Christian Adult Education*, 1159.
Oldman, C. B., Munford, W. A., and Nowell-Smith, S., *English Libraries 1800-1850*, 690.
On Accommodation, 851.
Onions, C. T., *Shakespeare's England*, 109.
Opsinous, *Robin Hood Society*, 335.
Ormerod, H. A., *Liverpool Royal Institution*, 423.
Osborne, E., and Sharr, F. A., *County Library Practice*, 705.
Ottaway, A. K. C., *Education and Society*, 886.
Overstreet, H. A., *Mature Mind*, 940.
Overton, J. H., *Life in the English Church*, 105.
Owen, R., *Life*, 138; *New View of Society*, 138.
Owst, G. R., *Preaching in Medieval England*, 94.
Oxford and Working-Class Education, 534.
Oxford University (Delegacy for Extra-Mural Studies), *Teaching of Science*, 1171.

Oxford University (Tutorial Classes Committee), *Teaching Methods with special reference to Trade Union Education*, 1084.

Pafford, J. H. P., *Books and Army Education*, 622.
Paice, D. R., *Do you Know Hillcroft?* 610.
Palfrey, H. E., *Stourbridge Institute*, 444.
Pantin, W. A., *English Church in the Fourteenth Century*, 101.
Parkyn, G. W., *Education in New Zealand*, 837.
Parry, A. W., *Education in the Middle Ages*, 231.
Parry, E. A., and King, H., *New Leisure and Old Learning*, 755.
Parry, H. Ll., *Royal Albert Memorial College, Exeter*, 514.
Parry, R. St. J., *Cambridge Essays on Adult Education*, 350.
Parsons, R. E., *Re-educating Adults*, 1155.
Paton, J. L., *J. B. Paton*, 344.
Patterson, A. T., *Radical Leicester*, p. 8.
Pattison, G., *Anthropology for Adults*, 1178.
Paul, E. and C., *Proletcult*, 962.
Paulu, B., *British Broadcasting*, 304; *British Broadcasting in Transition*, 304.
Peaples, F. W., *Education Department of the Bolton Co-operative Society*, 459.
Pear, R. H., *Lecturing on American Affairs*, 1112.
Pearse, I. H., and Crocker, L. H., *Peckham Experiment*, 594.
Pearson, A. F. S., *Thomas Cartwright*, 112.
Pearson, H., *Doctor Darwin*, 424.
Peel, E. A., *Pupil's Thinking*, 904.
Peers, R., *Adult Education: a Comparative Study*, 322; *Adult Education and the Needs of Democracy*, 967; *Adult Education in Practice*, 361; *Adult Education in the E. Midlands*, 512; *Aims and Methods*, 953; *Extra-Mural Adult Education in the E. Midlands*, 512; *Future of Adult Education*, 322, 915; *Nottingham Experiment*, 512; *Science in the Extra-Mural Work of Universities*, 1173; *Some Applications of Education Theory*, 939; *Supply of Books to Adult Classes*, 713; *This Adult Business*, 939; *Thomas Cooper*, 158.
Periodicals: *Adult Education*, 74; *Adult Education (U.S.)*, 81; *Adult Leadership*, 83; *Adult School*, 422; *Army Education*, 627; *Australian Journal of Adult Education*, 86. *Bacie Journal*, 60; *Blue Triangle*, 657; *British Friend*, 422; *British Institute and N.C.S.S. Monthly Bulletin*, 680; *British Journal of Educational Psychology*, 57; *British Journal of Educational Studies*, 65; *British Y.M.C.A. Review*, 653; *Bulletin of the World Association*, 71. *Cambridge Bulletin of Extra-Mural Studies*, 515; *Christian Democrat*, 671; *Club and*

Williams, W. M., *Selections from Welsh Piety*, 402.
Willis, Z. F., *Y.M.C.A. and Adult Education*, 656.
Willmot, P., and Young, M., *Family and Class*, 894; *Family and Kinship*, 894.
Wilmot, G. F. A., *Way to Teach Geography*, 1193.
Wilson, J. D., *Schools of England*, 264.
Wilson, N. S., *Education in the Forces*, 624.
Wilson, T. B., *Music in Adult Education*, 1137.
Wiltshire, H. C., *Adult Education: Way and Purpose*, 935; *Great Tradition*, 502; *Impington and Adult Education*, 563.
Winks, J. F., *History of Adult Schools*, 412.
Winstanley, G., *Selections from his Works*, 329.
Winterbottom, A., *T.U.C. Training Courses*, 550.
Wiseman, D., *Informal Education*, 988.
Wittlin, A. S., *Museum: its History and Tasks in Education*, 725.
Wood, A. C., *University College, Nottingham*, 514.
Wood, E. M., *Polytechnic and its Founder*, 560.
Wood, H. G., *Ideals and Realities in Adult Education*, 931.
—— and Ball, A. E., *Tom Bryan*, 610.
Wood, I. M., *Southport University Extension Society*, 513.
Wood, J., *Drama in Adult Education*, 1075.
Woodard, A. L., *Teaching Church*, 1154.
Woods, R. A., *English Social Movements*, 575.
Woodward, H. B., *Geological Society of London*, 428.
Woodward, J., *Rise and Progress of Religious Societies*, 102.
Wootton, B., *Need for Differentiation*, 1057; *Plea for Constructive Teaching*, 1015.
Workers' Educational Association, *Adult Student as Citizen*, 524; *Aims and Standards in W.E.A. Classes*, 1058; *Annual Reports*, 516; *Aspects of Adult Education*, 982; *Education for a Changing Society*, 529; *Education Year Book*, 28; *Film in Economics Classes*, 1082; *Implications of the Ashby Report*, 528; *Jubilee Addresses*, 527; *Memorandum on Matters within the Scope of the [Ashby] Committee*, 528; *Purpose and Organisation*, 522; *Trade Union Education*, 553; *Workers' Education*, 524; *W.E.A. and the Working Class Movement*, 546; *Workers' Educational Association, 1946-52*, 527; *W.E.A. Retrospect*, 527.

Workers' Educational Association, Tutors' Association and Central Joint Advisory Committee, *Psychology and the Adult Student*, 1151.
Workers' Educational Association and Workers' Educational Trade Union Committee, *Statement submitted at the Invitation of the T.U.C.*, 557.
Workers' Educational Trade Union Committee, *Annual Reports*, 544; *Workers' Education and the Trade Union Movement*, 545; *Workers' Educational Trade Union Committee*, 548.
Working Men's Club and Institute Union, *Annual Reports*, 484; *Short History*, 486.
World Association for Adult Education, *Annual Reports*, 852; *International Handbook*, 34; *World Conference, 1929*, 908.
Wormald, F., and Wright, C. E., *English Library before 1700*, 691.
Wort, R. S., *Story of the Y.M.C.A.*, 653.
Wright, B., *Use of the Film*, 298.
Wright, E., *Agony and Re-appraisal*, 1103.
Wright, E. M., *Joseph Wright*, 158.
Wright, L. B., *Middle Class Culture in Elizabethan England*, 327.
Wright, L. C., *Scottish Chartism*, 136.
Wylie, W. H., *Old and New Nottingham*, p. 8.

Year Book of Education, 35.
Yeaxlee, B. A., *Educated Nation*, 349; *Lifelong Education*, 356; *Settlements and their Outlook*, 580; *Spiritual Values in Adult Education*, 763.
Yorkshire Council for Further Education, *Handbook for Part-time Teachers*, 985; *Liberal Aspect of Technical Education*, 742; *Situation, Construction, Furniture and Equipment for Day Schools in which Technical or Adult Classes will be held in the Evening*, 840.
Young, G. M., *Victorian England*, 146; *Portrait of an Age*, 146.
Young, M., *Rise of the Meritocracy*, 899.
Young, T., *Selection of Adult University Students*, 795.
Young Women's Christian Association. *Annual Reports*, 657.

Zweig, *British Worker*, 176; *Life, Labour and Poverty*, 176; *Women's Life and Labour*, 176; *Worker in the Affluent Society*, 176.

SUBJECT INDEX

Numbers are those of entries, not pages. Main entries are shown in bold type.

Accommodation, 839-51.

Administrative relations, 828-38.

Adult education: religious, social and economic background, **87-176**, 349; history and organisation, 221, 223, 234, 240, 250, 252, 263-4, 271, **311-401**; early development in connection with day schools and Sunday schools, 233, 246, **402-9**; regulations, **799-827**. *For particular movements, organisations and aspects of adult education, and also for theory and teaching method, see separate entries.*

Adult education centres, non-residential, 29, 366, **575-604**, 1074. *See also* Evening Institutes, Village Colleges, etc.

Adult education centres, residential. *See* Residential Colleges.

Adult schools, 24, 177-8, 311, 342, 397, 407, **409-22**, 605.

Archaeology, 1104.

Art, 364, 372-3, 375-6, 384, 1045, 1086-7, 1089. *See also* Societies.

Art galleries, 23, 26, 43, 373, **718-25**; and adult education, **728-30**.

Bibliography, 1-20.

Books, **279-87**, 323, 344.

Broadcasting, 14, 41, 44, 85, **300-10**, 382; and adult education, 774, 776-7, 779-80, 782-3, 785, 787-90, 792, 1080, 1176.

Chartism, 136, 158, 447-8.

Citizenship education, 751, 753, 1183-4.

Coffee-houses, 122.

Community centres, 168, 366, **592-604**, 833, 846, 1068, 1098.

Co-operation: history and organisation, 133, 138, 158, 348; education, **449-73**, 610.

Co-ordinating and consultative organisations, 852-5.

Directories, 21-46.

Drama, 314, 352, 562, 635, 659, 666, 679, 849, **1075-80**, 1136.

Economics, 1081-5.

Education: reference works, 2, 9, 11, 15, 25, 28, 30, 35, 49, 51; periodicals, **52-70**; history and organisation, **177-278**; Education Acts, 208, 270; social and educational theory, **856-905**. *See also* Adult Education, Literacy.

Educational settlements and centres, **584-91**, 1074.

Encyclopaedias, 47-51.

Evening schools and institutes, 180, 233, 235, 254, 316, 344, 418-19, **559-74**, 737, **799-827**, 847, 1002, 1122, 1124.

Films, 37, 44, 295-9, 660, 664, 668; and adult education 775, 781, 1082, 1088.

Forces, H.M., 221, 264, 349, 596, **614-27**, 656, 874, 1155-6.

Full-time studies, **793-8**, 811-13, 954.

Geography, 1192-3.

Handicrafts, 750, 1097-9.

Health education, 36, 594, 650, 672, 1047, 1143, 1188.

History, in adult education, 679, **1100-8**.

Home management, 1190.

Hospitals, 633-4.

International affairs, 360, **1109-14**.

Languages: classics, **1071-4**; English, **1090-6**, 1126; foreign, 1113, **1122-8**.

Law, 1195.

Leisure, 888, 905, 1004.

Libraries: reference works, 1, 4, 23, 32; history and organisation, 260, 342, 349, 366, 397, **684-710**; and adult education, 509, 562, 614, 622, **711-17**.

Literacy, 89, 123, 249, 617, 947.

Literary institutes, 565.

Literature, 1115-21.

Local education authorities, 260, 342, 366, 376, 379, 382, **559-74**, **739-42**, 745, 828, 832-3, 1012, 1136. *See also* Evening Institutes.

Local history. *See* History.

Local studies, 1189.